To: Halifax C...
of Commerce

Come From Away With a Camera

Four years of exploring our new home,
One frame at a time

Thanks so much for
the ongoing support!
It means the world!

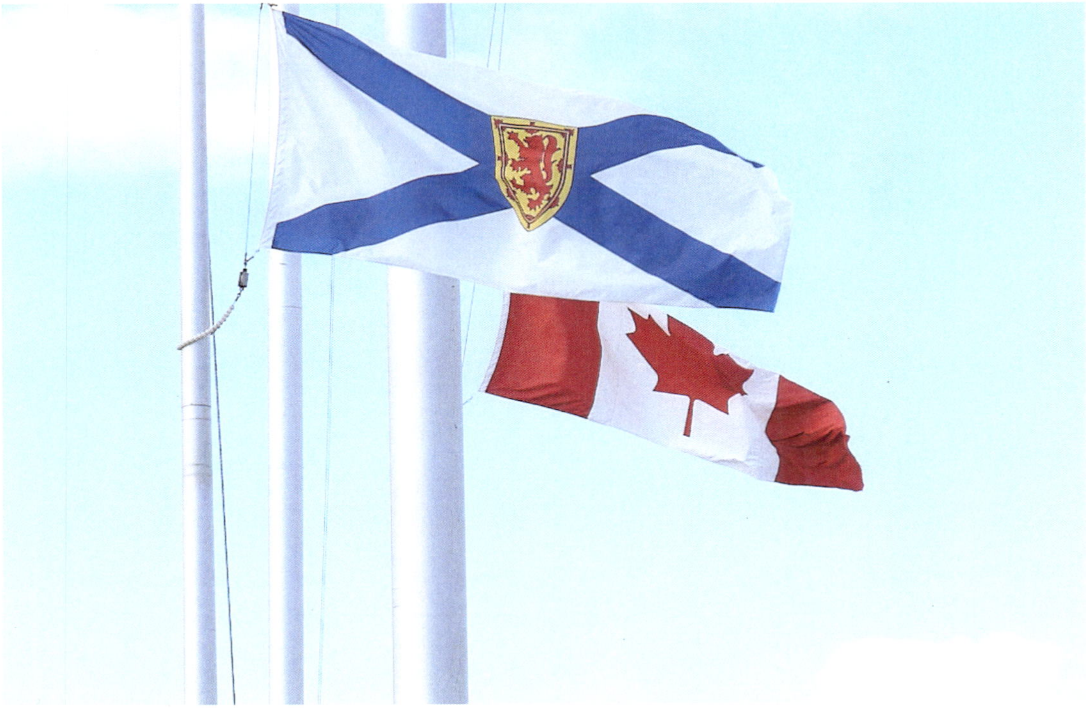

Come From Away With a Camera

Jay Fisher

Jay Fisher
PHOTOGRAPHY

Jay Fisher

Dartmouth, NS, Canada

www.comefromawaywithacamera.ca

Print ISBN: 978-1-0690773-0-1

To our Nova Scotia Family, for welcoming us with open arms
And for Ashley, who put up with all of this, and without whose support none of this would have been possible

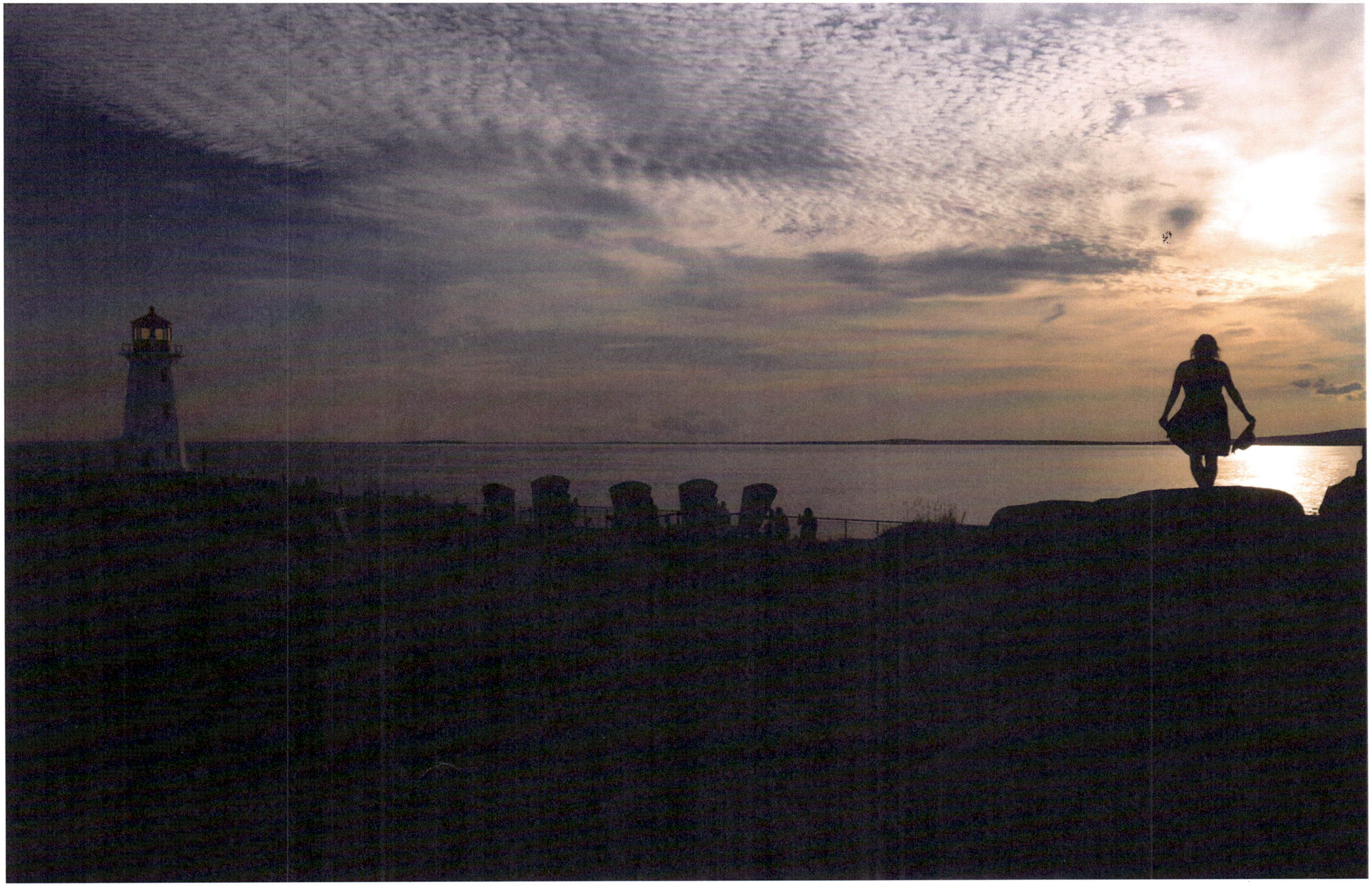

Contents

Come from Away: Someone visiting [Eastern Canada], or someone who lives here now but wasn't born here
(slang/colloquialism from Newfoundland, adopted by the Atlantic Provinces)
Also adopted, lovingly, and with tongue firmly planted in cheek, for this book

Intro:

When The World Shut Down

"Do you want to move to Nova Scotia?"

I mulled it over for about three seconds before looking back up at her and responding "Yes. Yes I do."

And that was that. Within four months we had found a place and packed up our lives to make the big move east. The world was just getting into the thick of a global pandemic, and so much of what had made up our lives in the big city shut down. Work was gone, connections were quickly fading, and it became increasingly difficult to hold on to reasons to stay. We were part of the 'global reset' that was happening, and we were part of the tens of thousands of people who needed a change and made the move.

In the time we've been here, a lot of people have asked why we decided to come to Halifax? We had no family here, no friends, contacts, or jobs waiting - we just needed a change and something here called to us. And to be honest, I'm still amazed at how quickly Nova Scotia felt like home. Sometimes it feels like we've been here forever, and sometimes we can't believe it's already been four years. We've been welcomed into our new home by wonderful people and are building community every day. This province is beautiful, and every part of it is beautiful in a different way, as I quickly found out. The inspiration for this book came organically from my travels around the province, seeing the beauty and meeting the people. Nova Scotia is not without its own problems and issues, but everywhere in this mix of people, cultures, and customs, there is a determination, a pride, and a desire to be better and stronger.

I've travelled the province from one end to the other, always with my camera, and I'm excited to share it with you. This book is in no way the complete picture of Nova Scotia, and that's aside from the several thousand images sitting on a hard drive....somewhere.... (I hope). Think of it as a highlight reel, and hopefully one that invites you to come see the full story for yourself. It's my love letter to my new home.

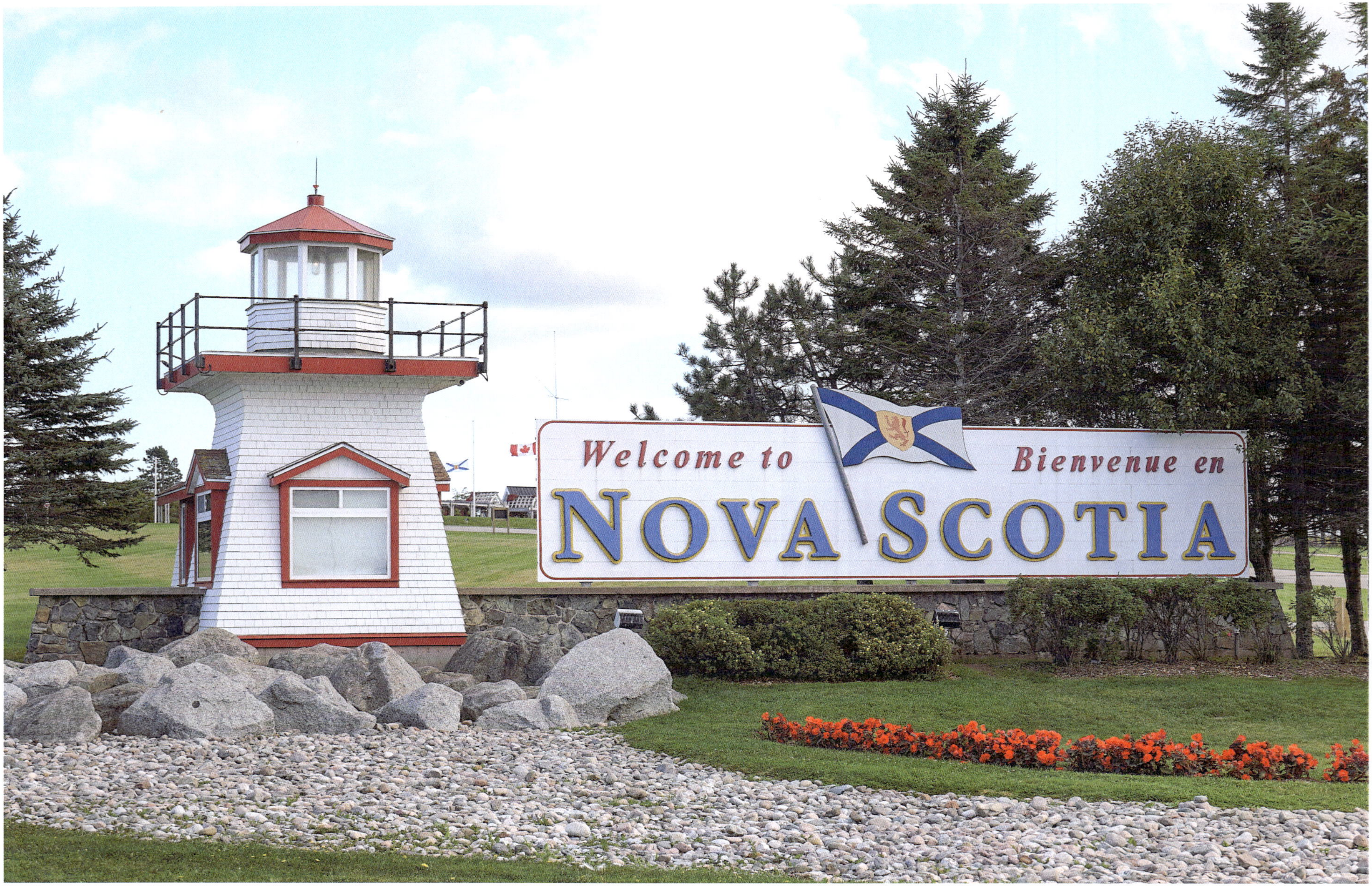

The sign that greeted us as we crossed into Nova Scotia. It continues to greet us every time we come back home.

Chapter 1
We're Home -
Halifax & Dartmouth

Just across the Bedford Basin from Halifax is the City of Dartmouth. With it's 23 lakes, parks, cute downtown, and the best views of Halifax, it's where we call home. Despite initially thinking we'd just hop across the bridge to Halifax 'all the time', we quickly fell in love with the so called 'Dark Side'.

Dartmouth's Lake Banook is a staple in the world rowing community, and Alderney Landing hosts annual summer concerts with some of the biggest names in rock. Shubie Park, along the Shubinacadie canal is a 40 acre urban park that is popular with hikers, cyclists, dog owners, and anyone just looking for an afternoon in nature.

The last 10 years here have seen lots of businesses, shops, and amenities come to Dartmouth, and it's no surprise that families choose to make a life here.

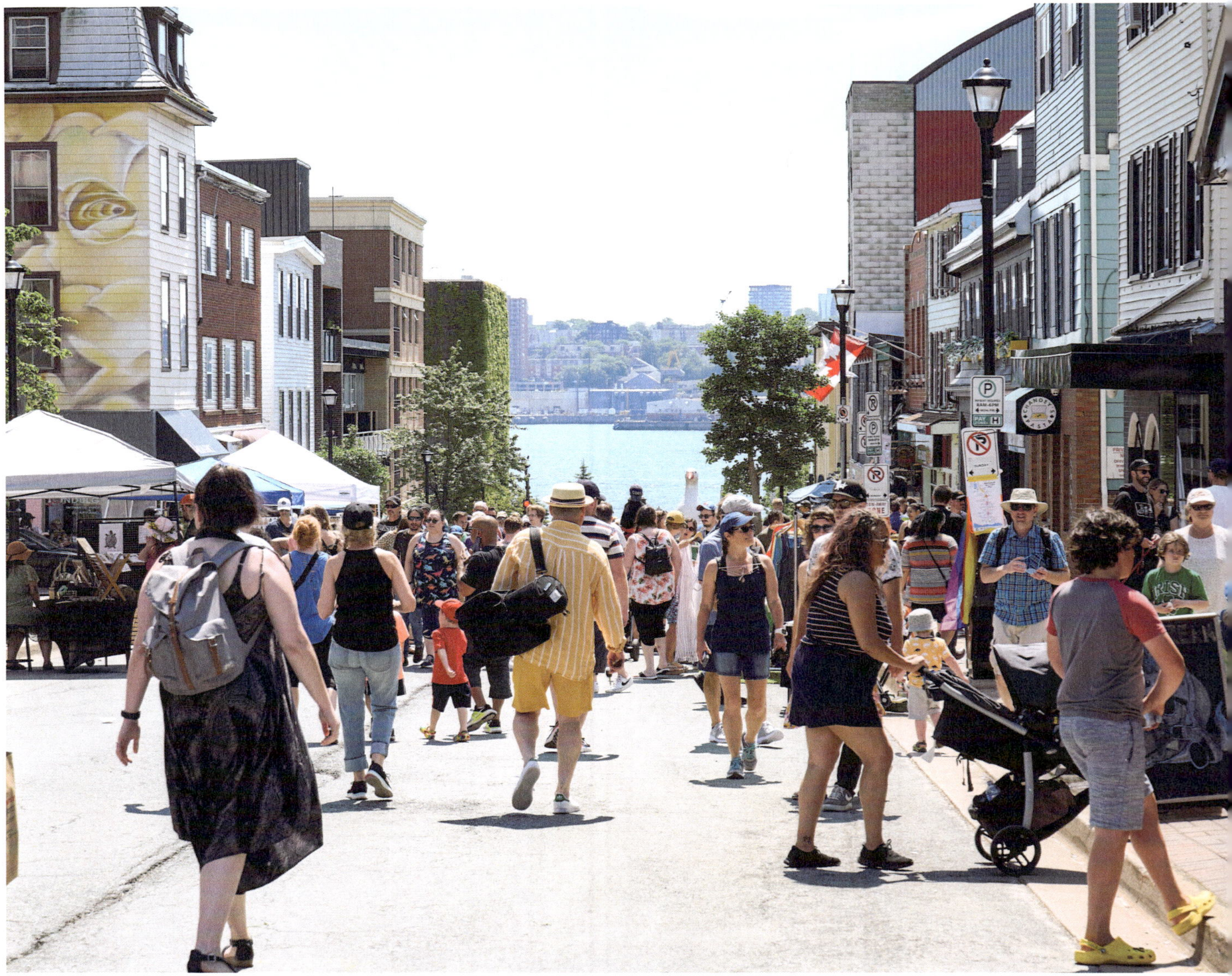

Crowds of people enjoying the annual Downtown Dartmouth Open Street Sund

Opposite page: Downtown Dartmou

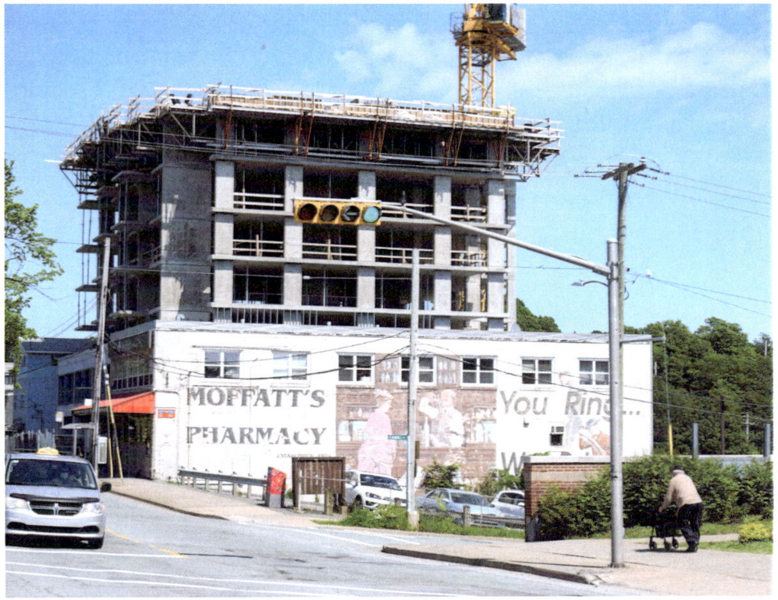
MOFFATT'S
PHARMACY
You Ring...

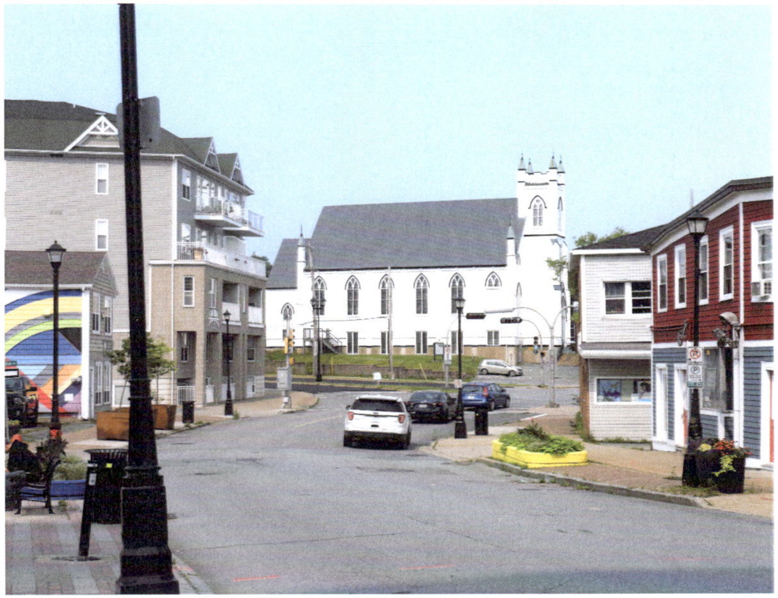

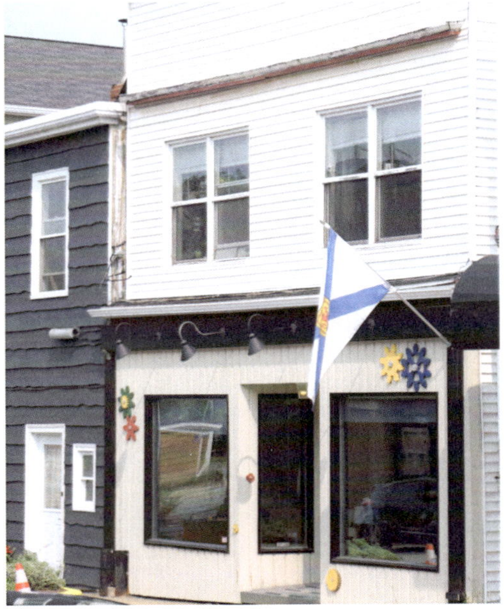

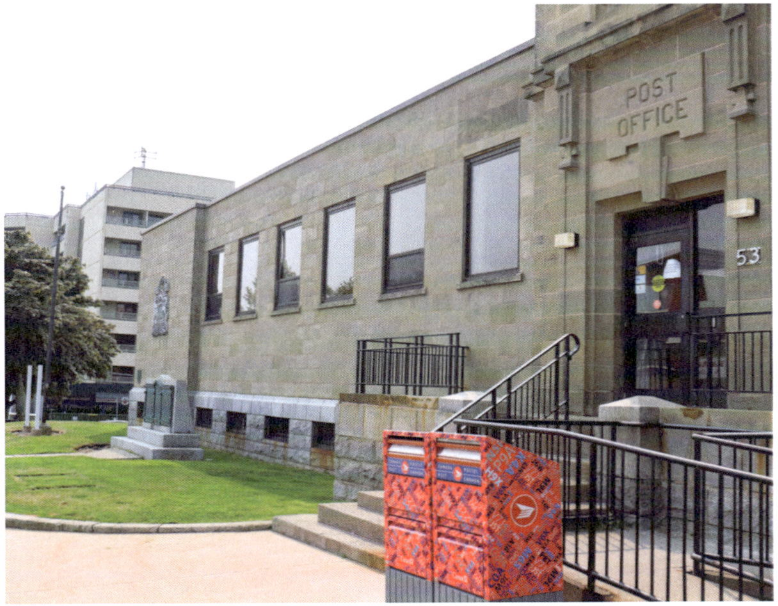
POST
OFFICE
53

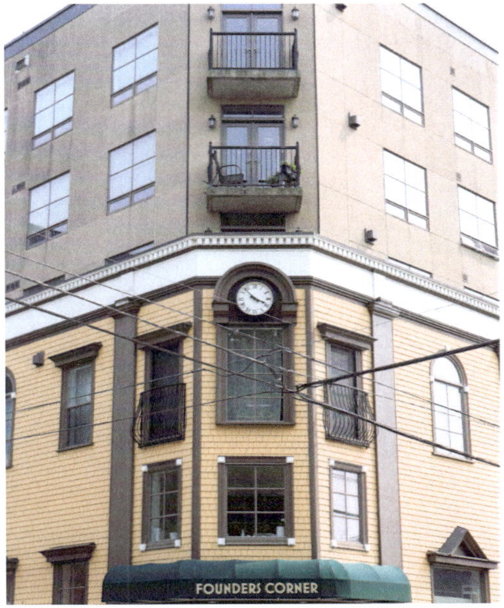
FOUNDERS CORNER

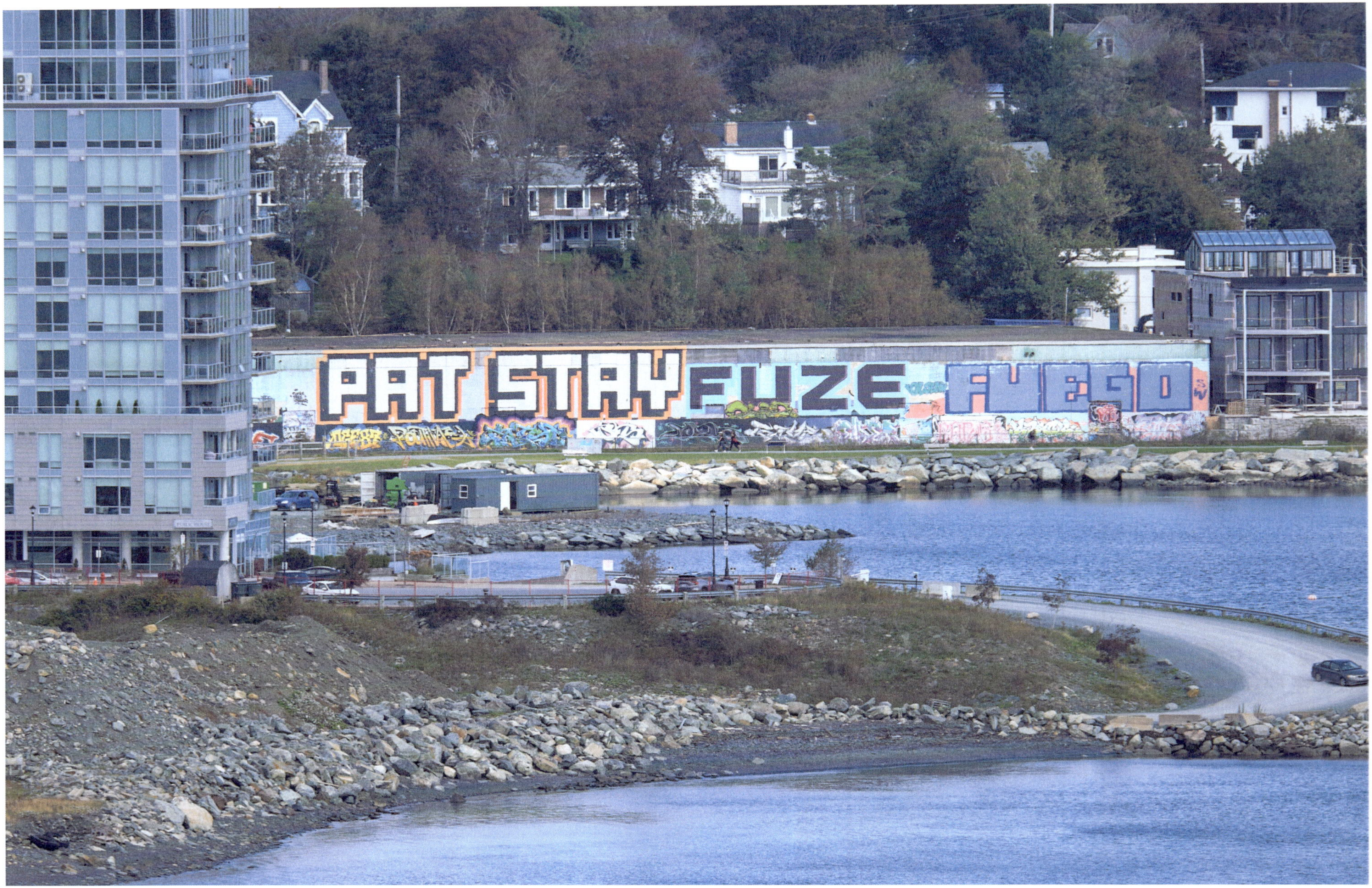

Dartmouth Cove, and fan-painted memorial for musician Pat Stay. In-filling due to development threatens this vital part of the city's waterfront

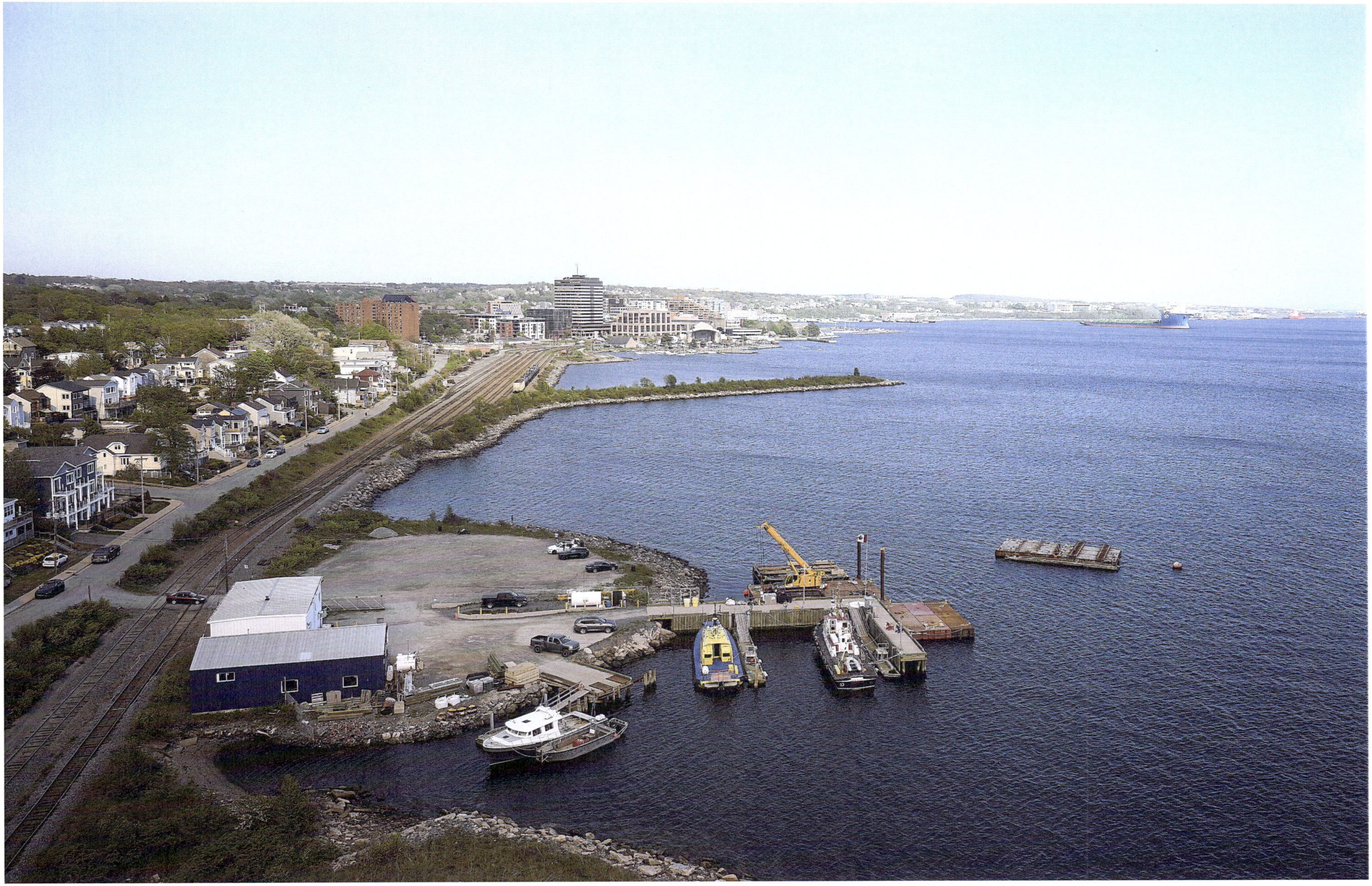

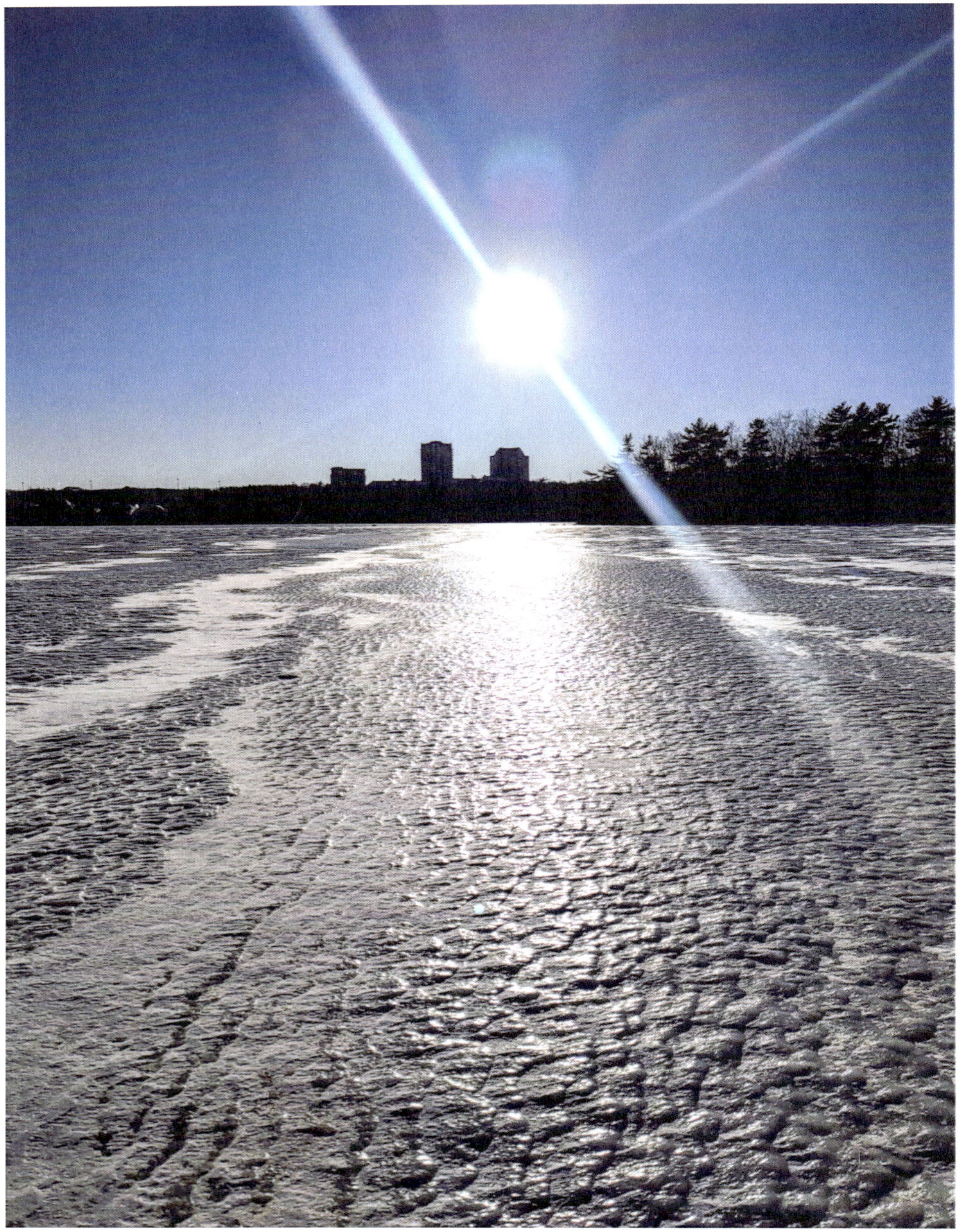

Frozen Lake Micmac, seen from Shubie Park

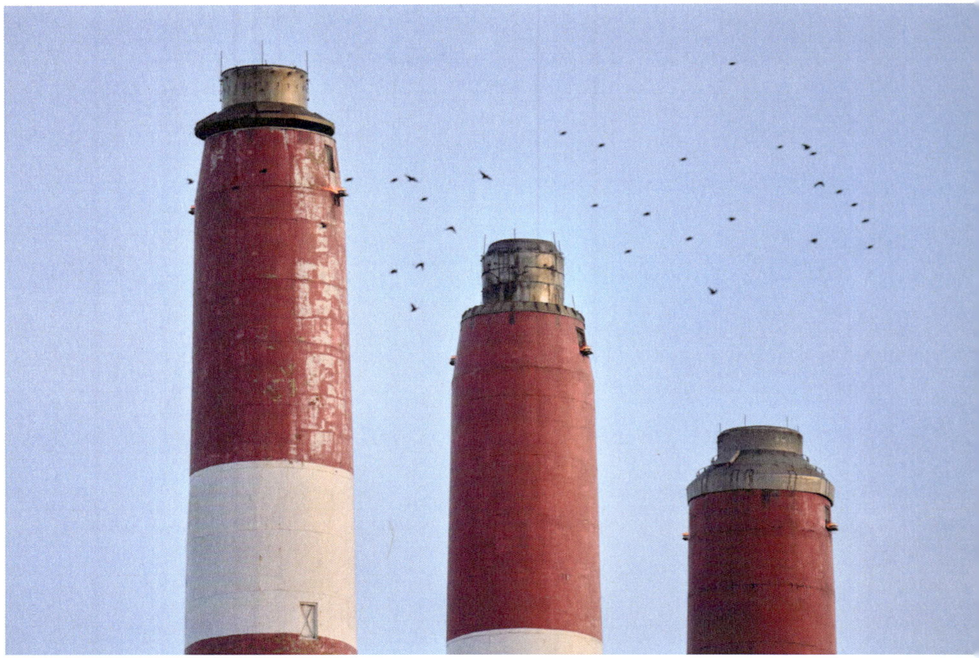

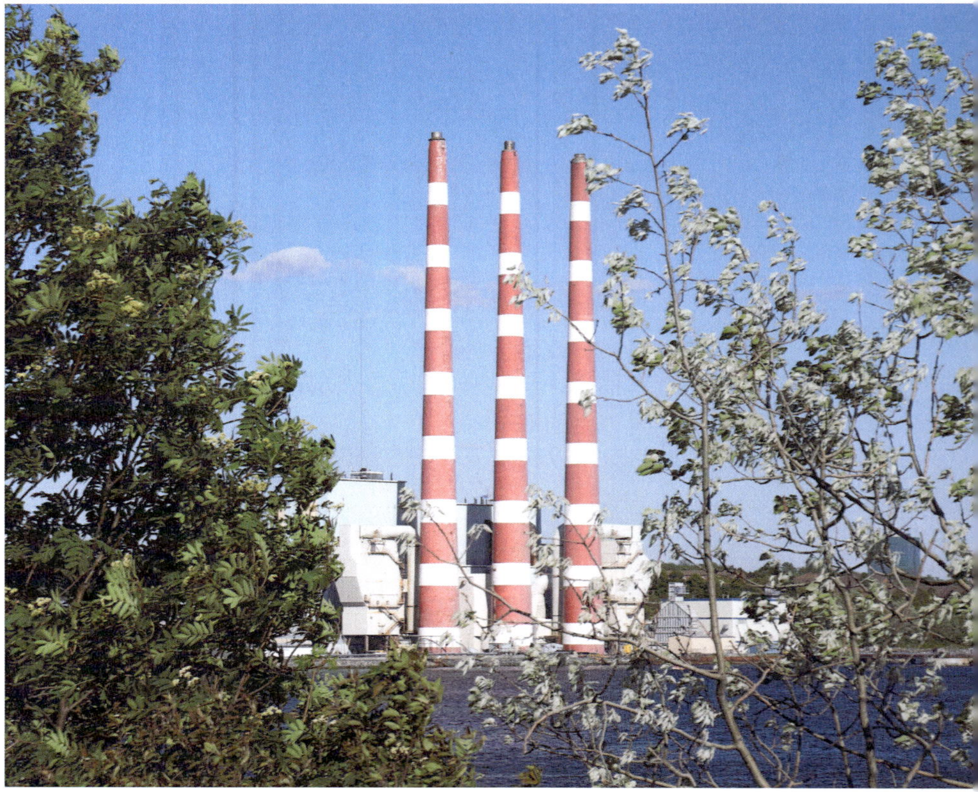

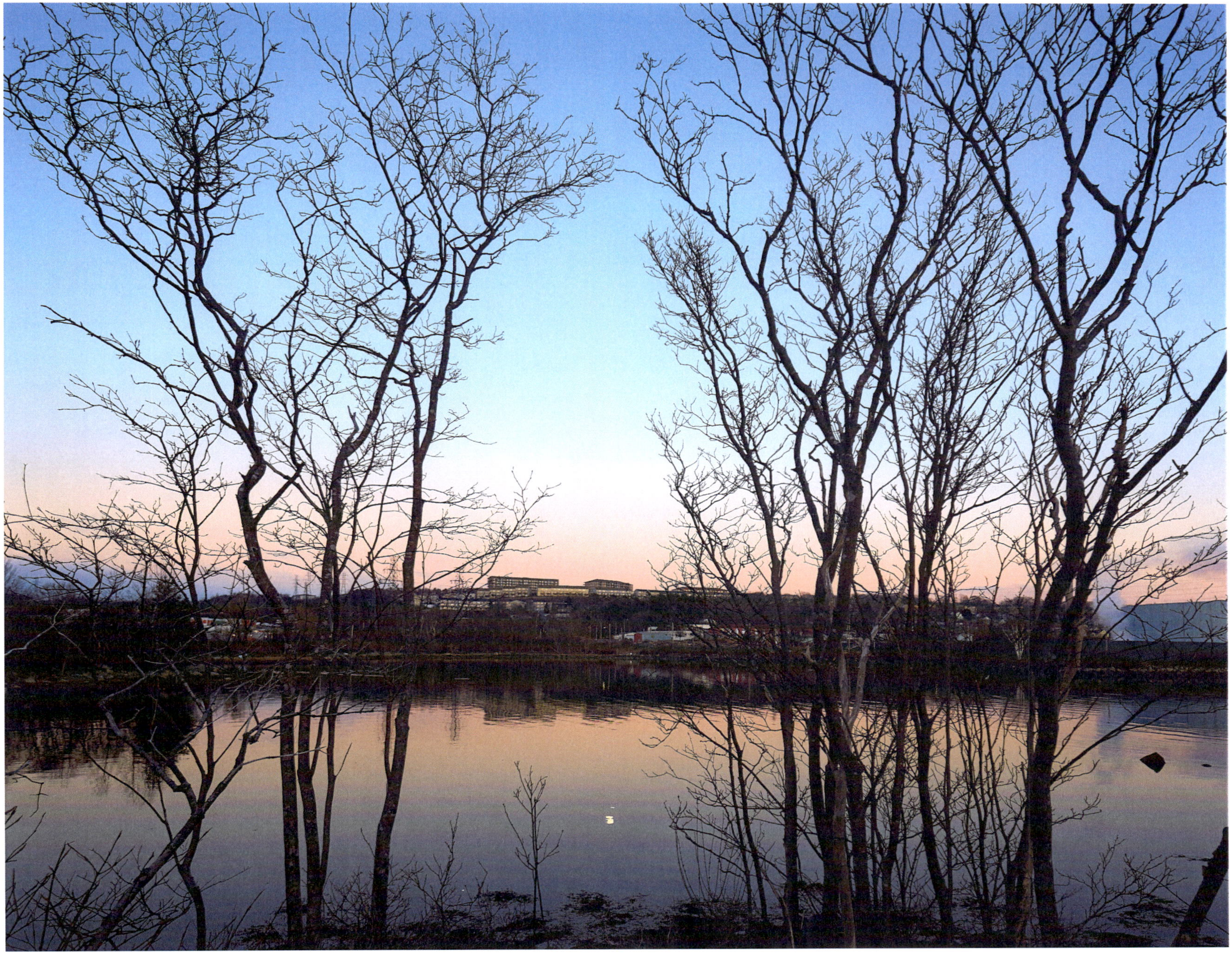

Tufts Cove at sunset
Opposite page: Dartmouth's iconic striped smokestacks at the Tufts Cove Generating Plant

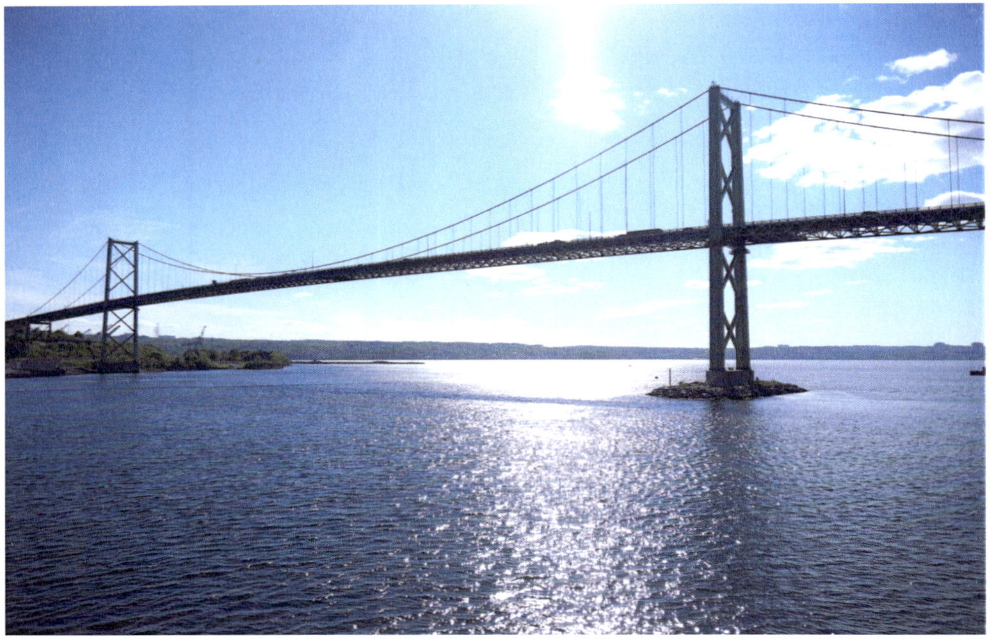

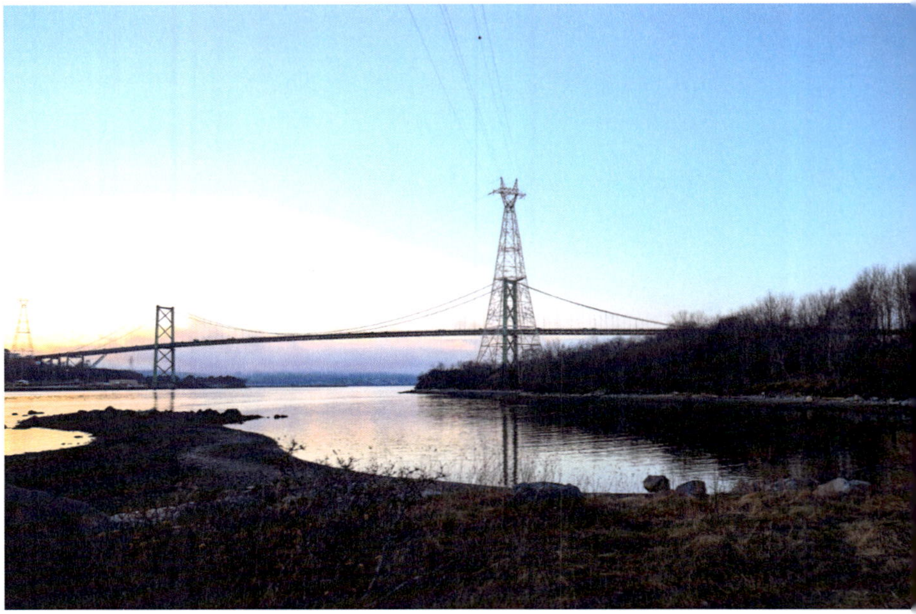

The MacKay Bridge (the "New" bridge) seen from Tufts Cove

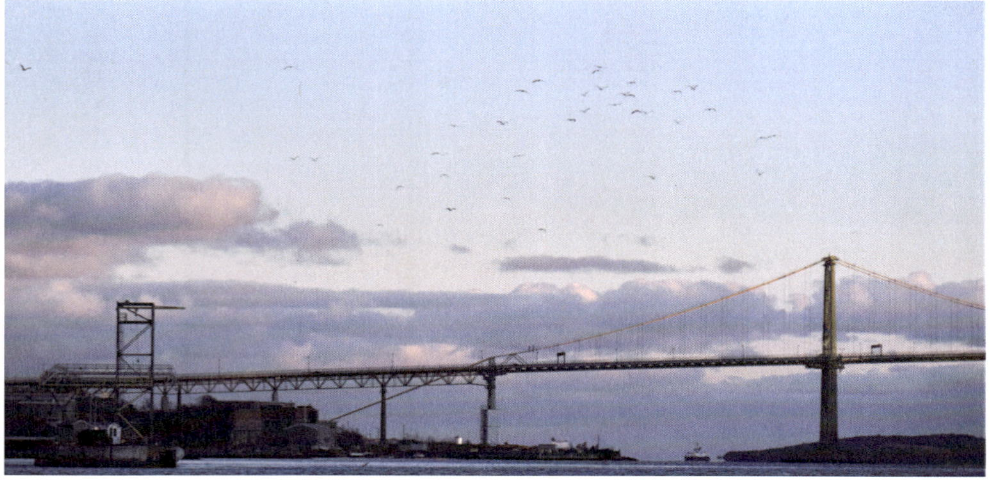

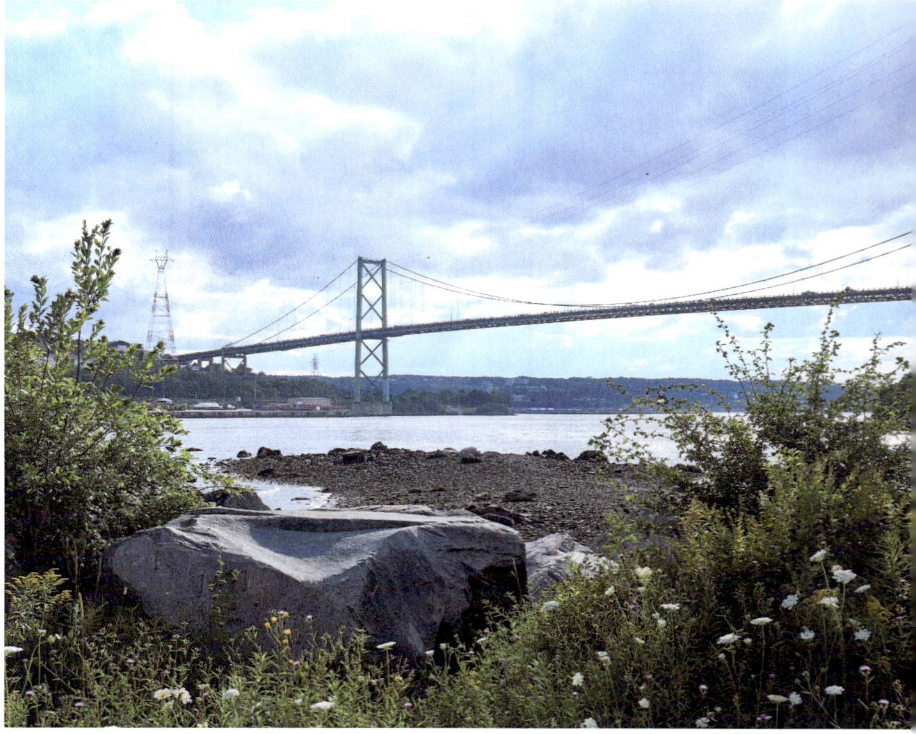

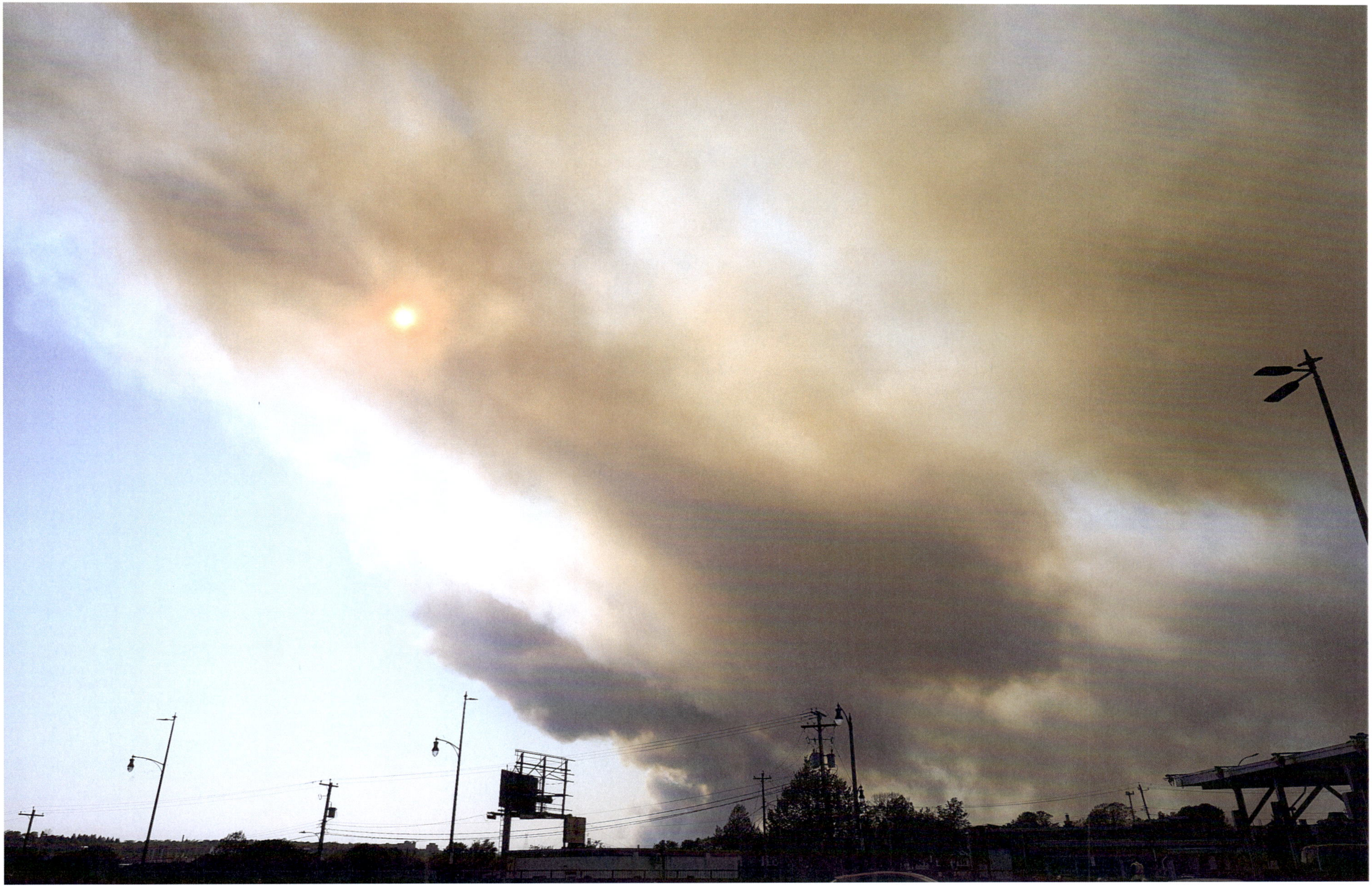

On May 28, 2023, wildfires ripped through Tantallon destroying more than 900 hectares, forcing 16,400 people out of their homes and destroying 151 homes before it was done. The smoke was visible from all over the region. This was shot from Dartmouth, as the fire was starting

Halifax is the Provincial capital, and Atlantic Canada's 'hub city'. In the last couple of years, we've really been able to see the city come back to life, after the pandemic left the streets and waterfront empty. The cruise ships have also come back, bringing with them people from all over the world. With seven universities and three college campuses bringing over 40,000 students a year, the city's downtown doesn't really have a slow season.

Taking a trip through Halifax's many neighbourhoods we can see the history of the city through its architecture, landmarks, and historical sites. Africville, York Redoubt, Point Pleasant Park and more offer a ton of information on some of what's shaped Halifax and the surrounding area. From the Citadel you can get a 360° view of the city below. And while we have our favourite haunts, we're definitely still discovering what Halifax has to offer.

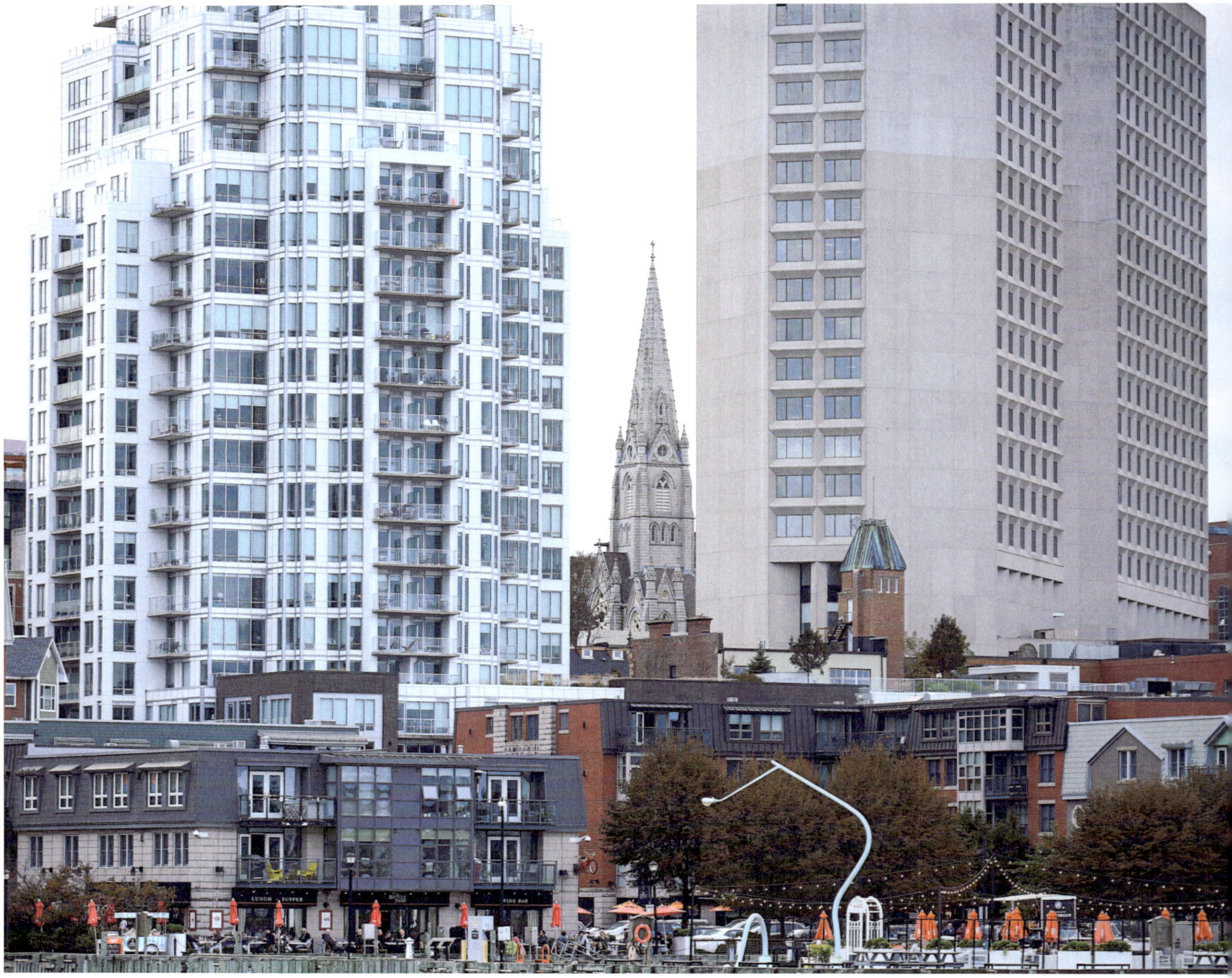

Bishop's Landing, with one of the famous 'drunken lamp pos
Opposite page: Halifax piers, casino, Purdy's Wharf, and downtov

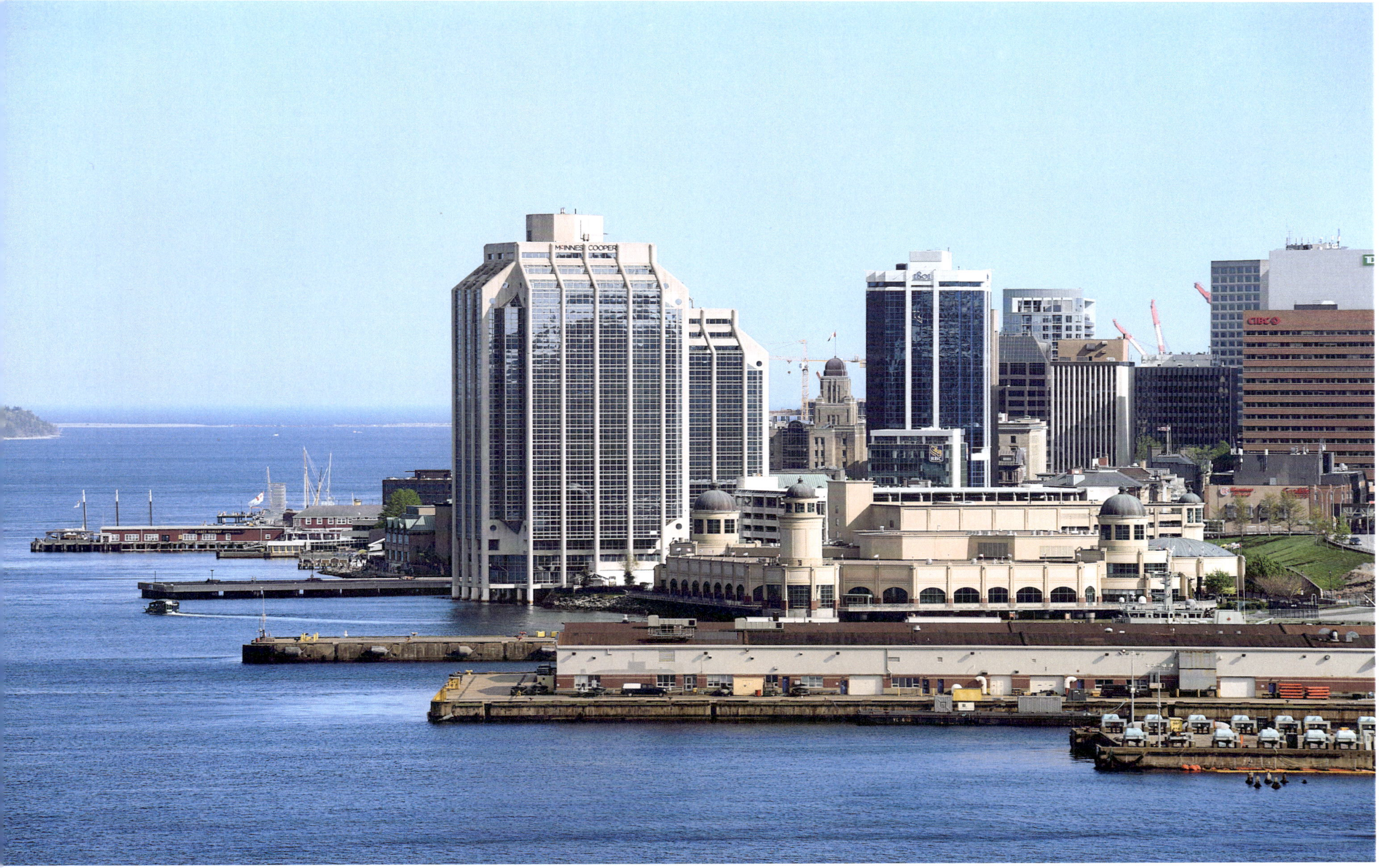
McINNES COOPER
CIBC
RBC

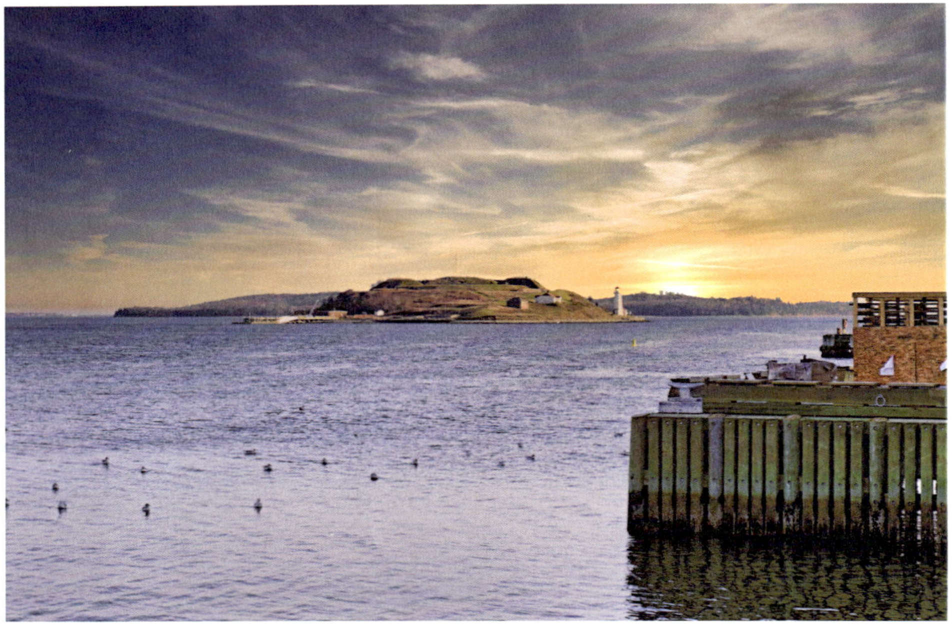
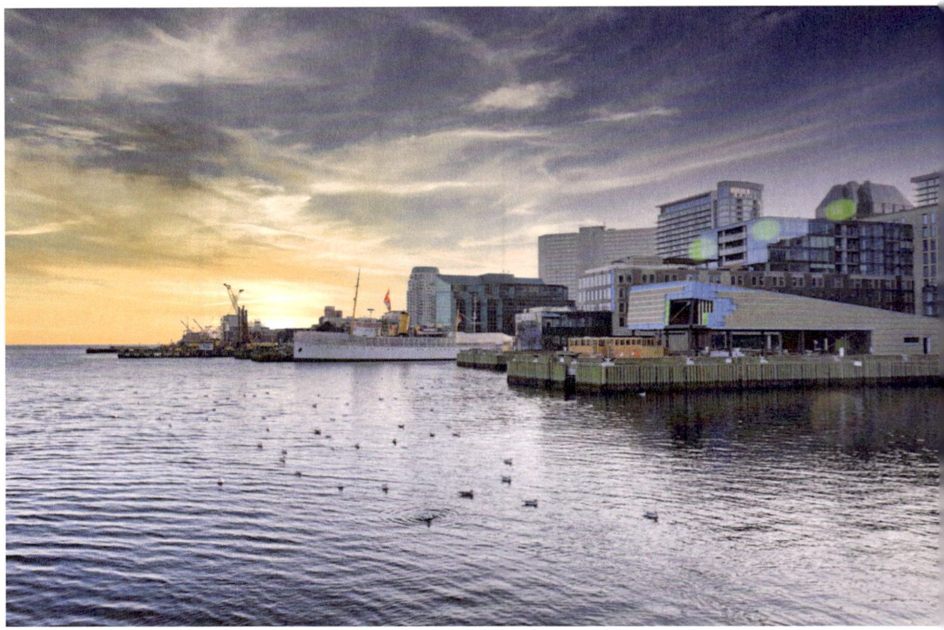
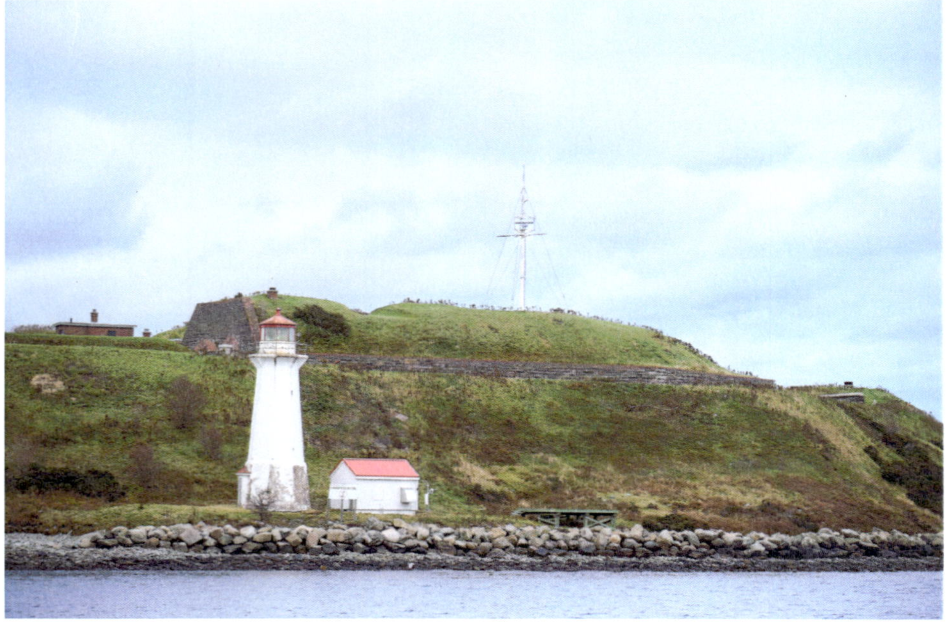
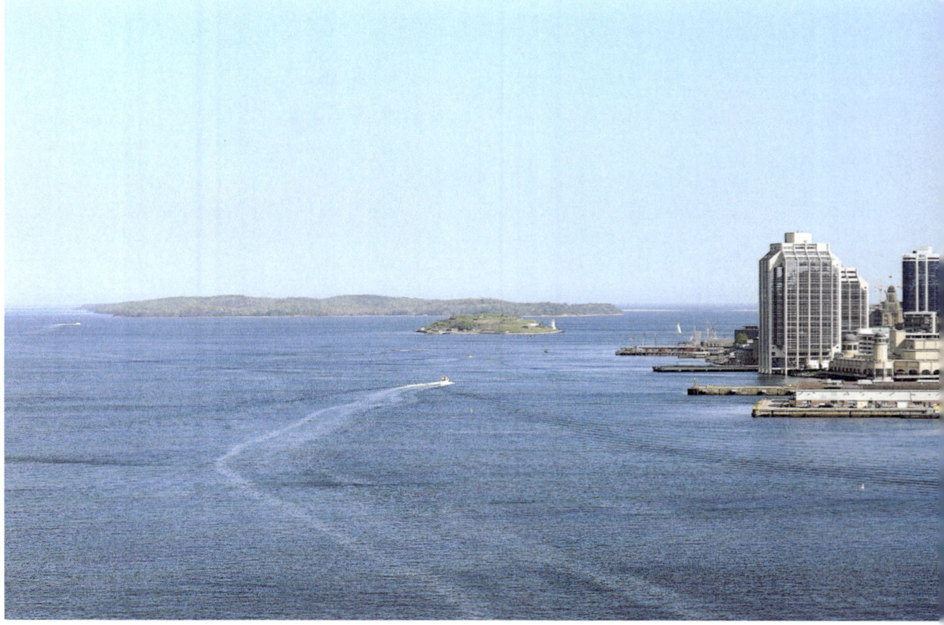

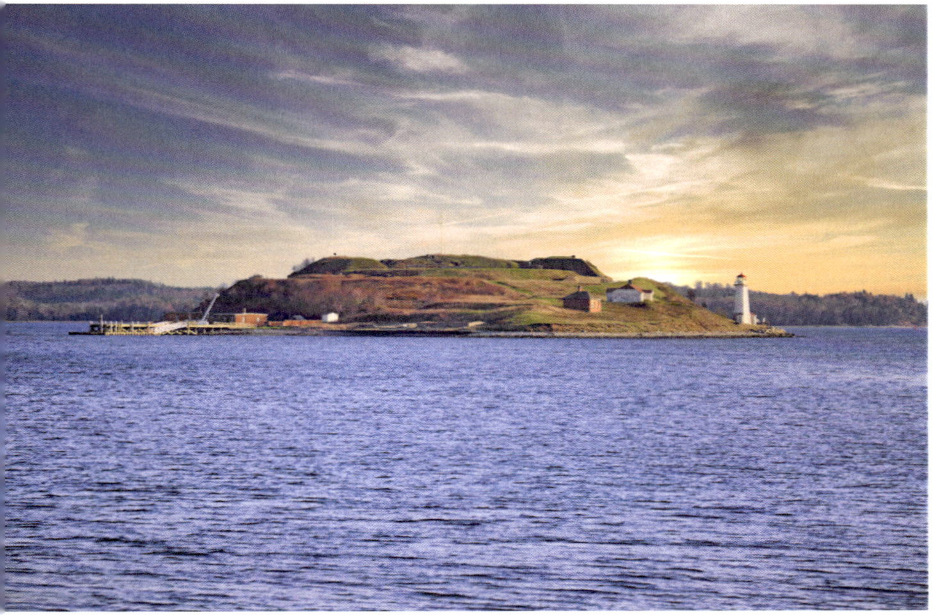

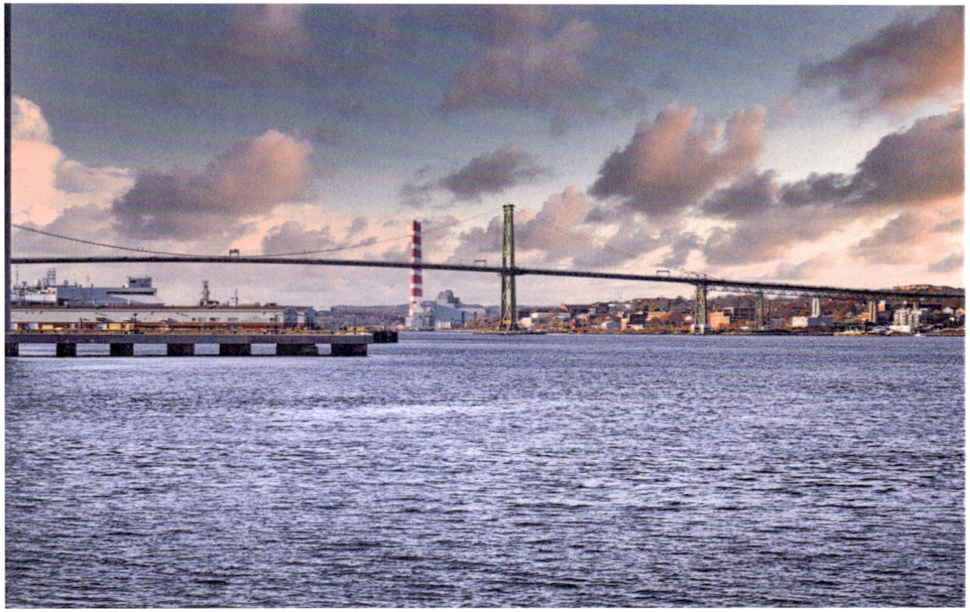

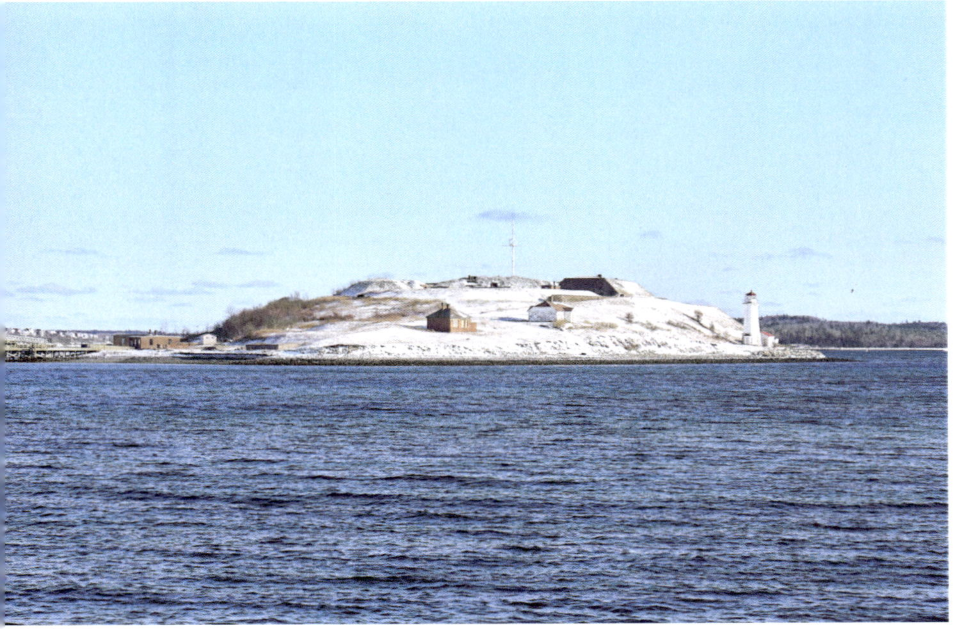

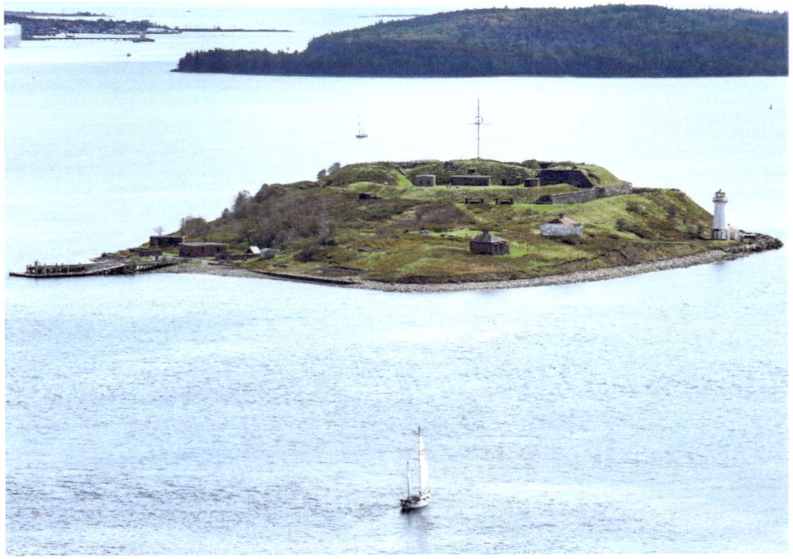

Halifax Harbour

and

Georges Island

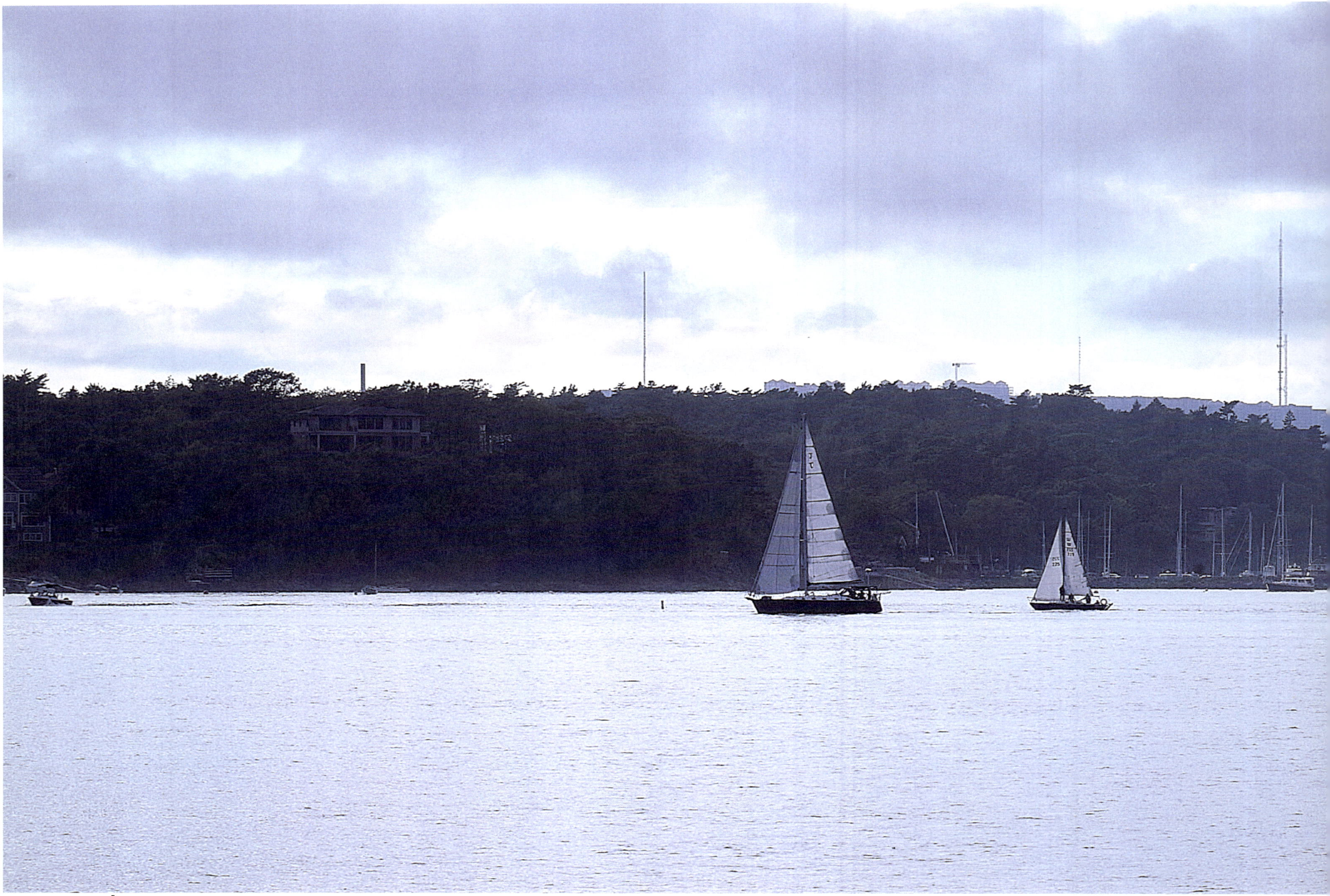

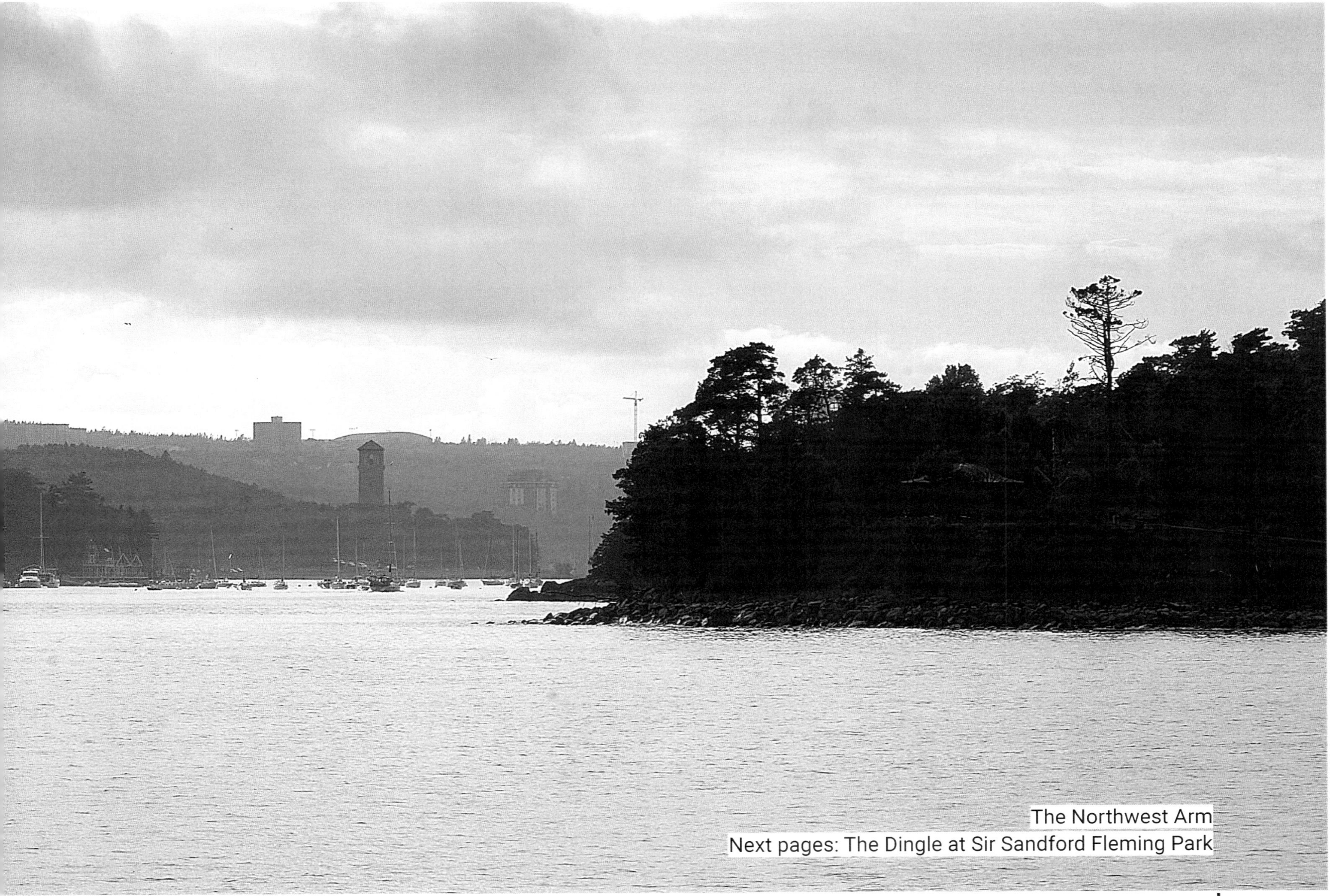

The Northwest Arm
Next pages: The Dingle at Sir Sandford Fleming Park

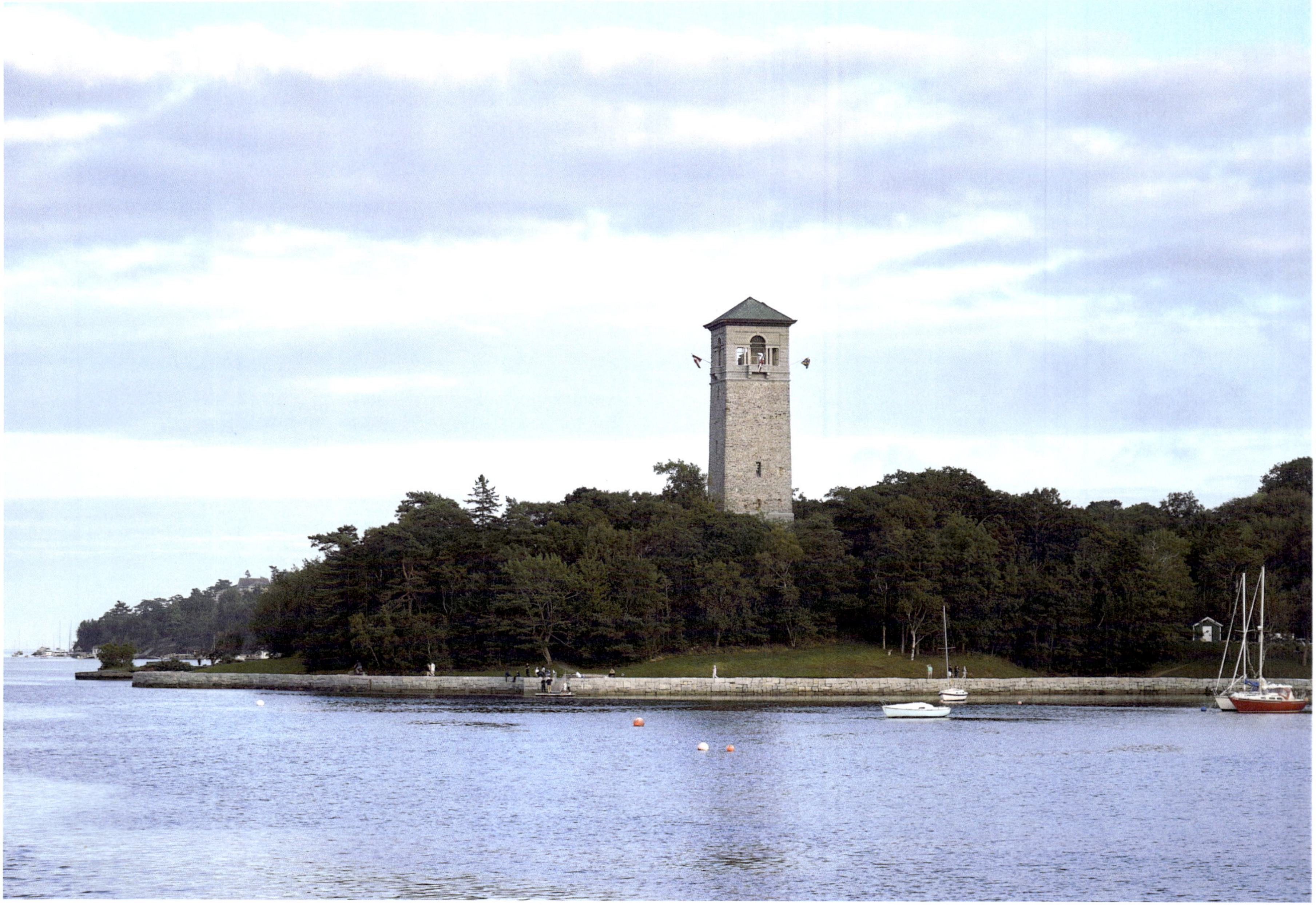

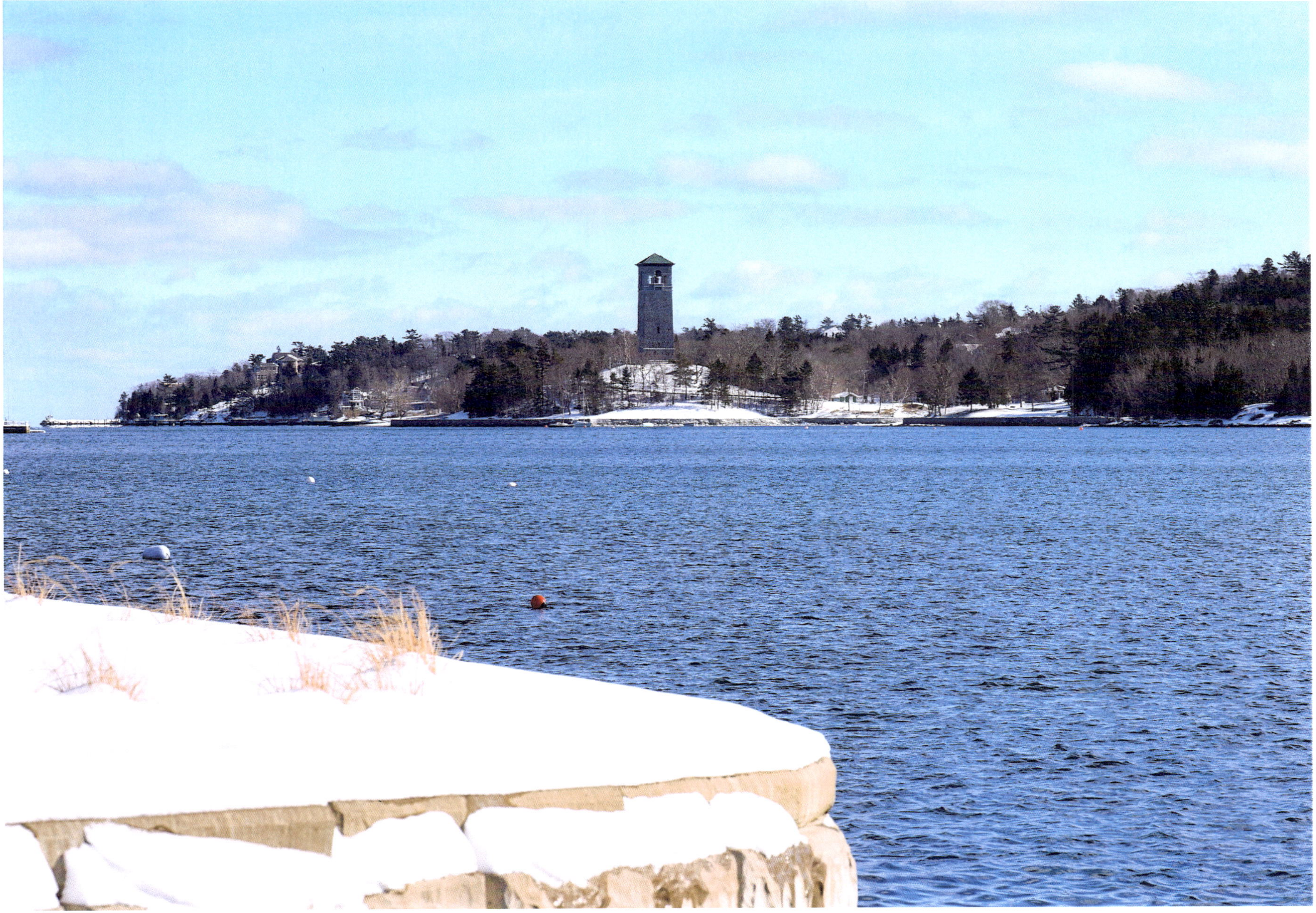

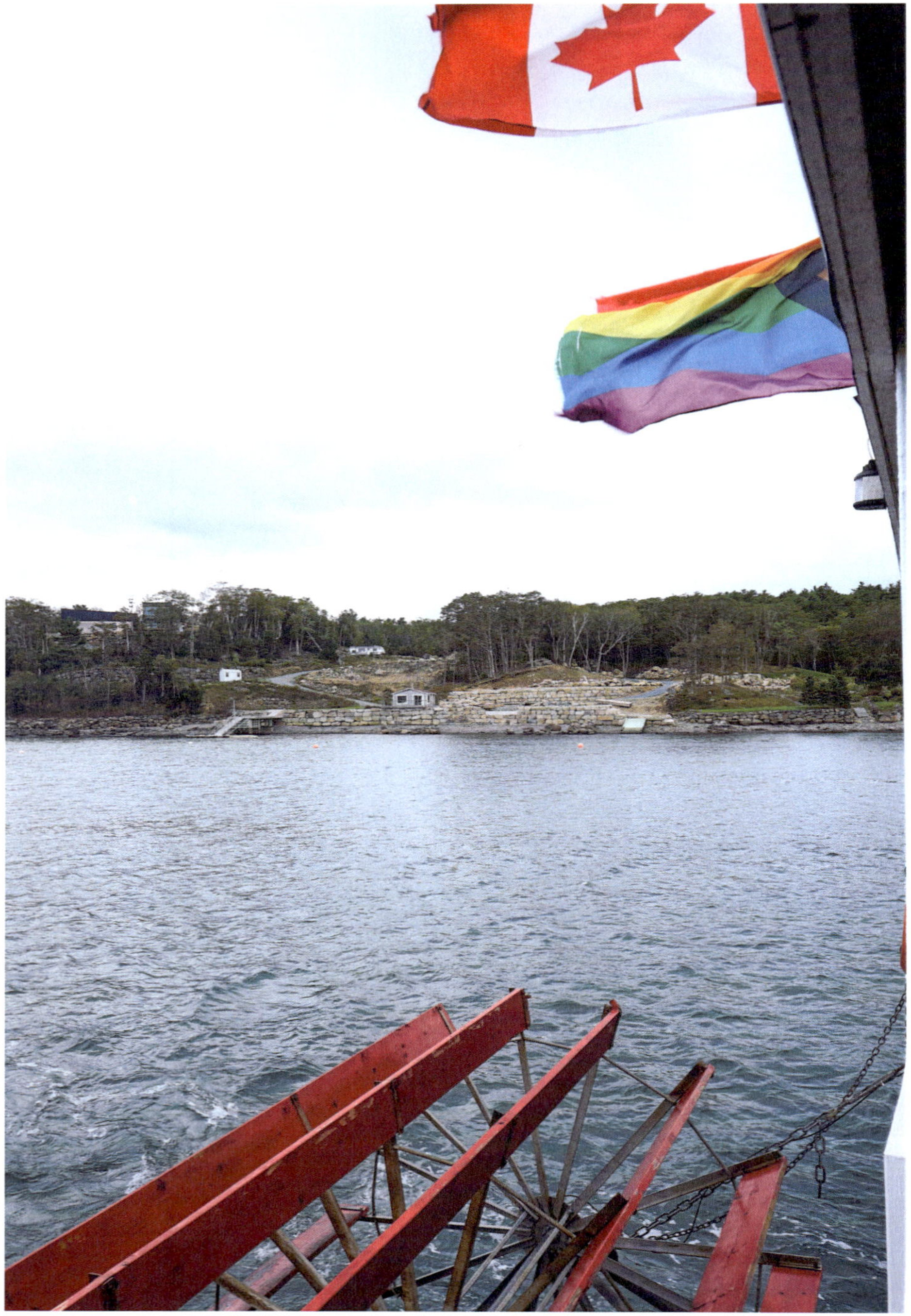

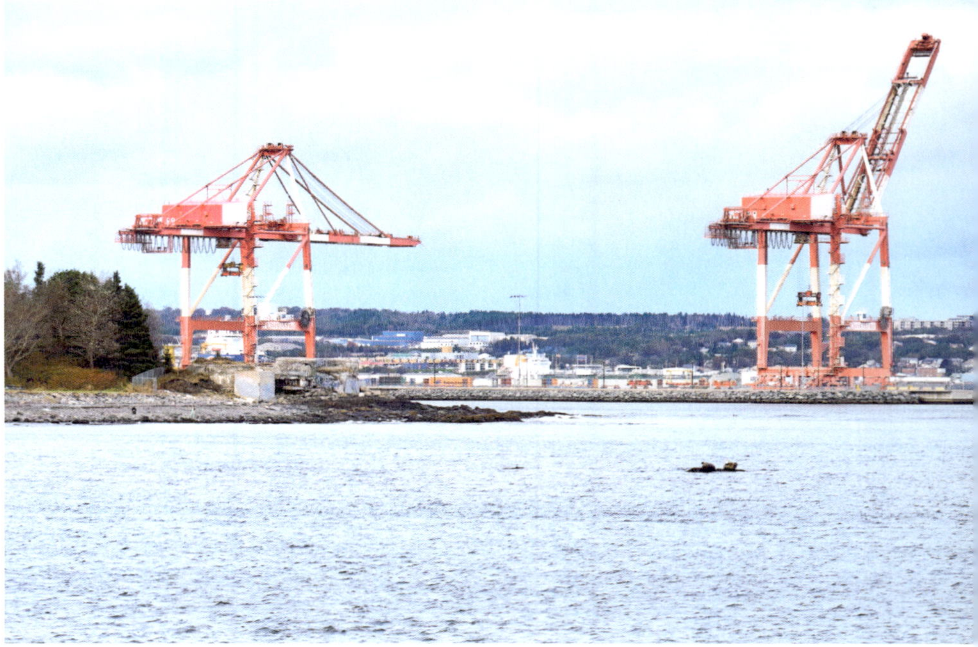

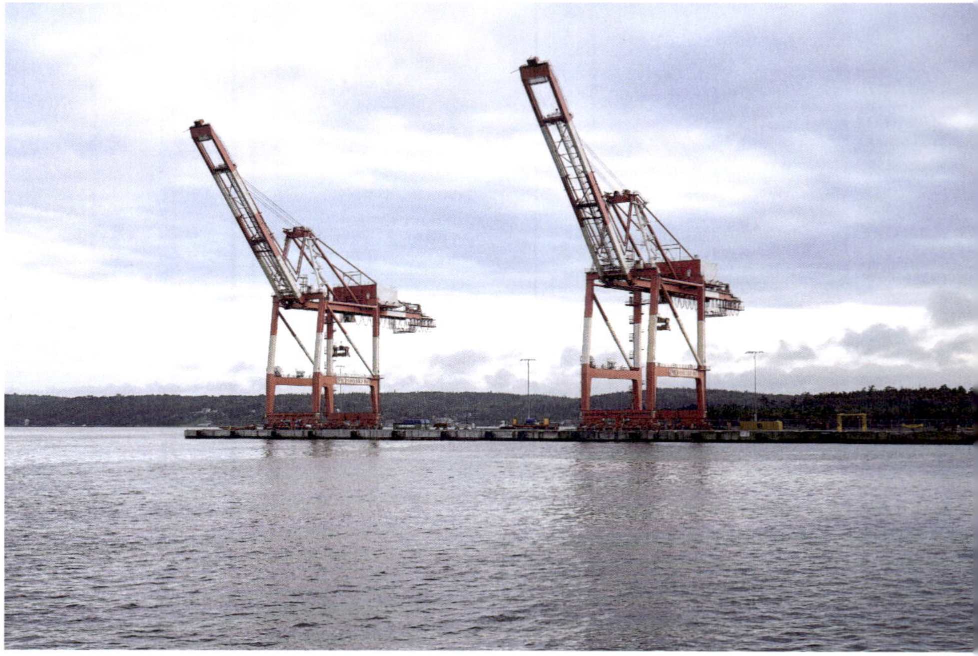

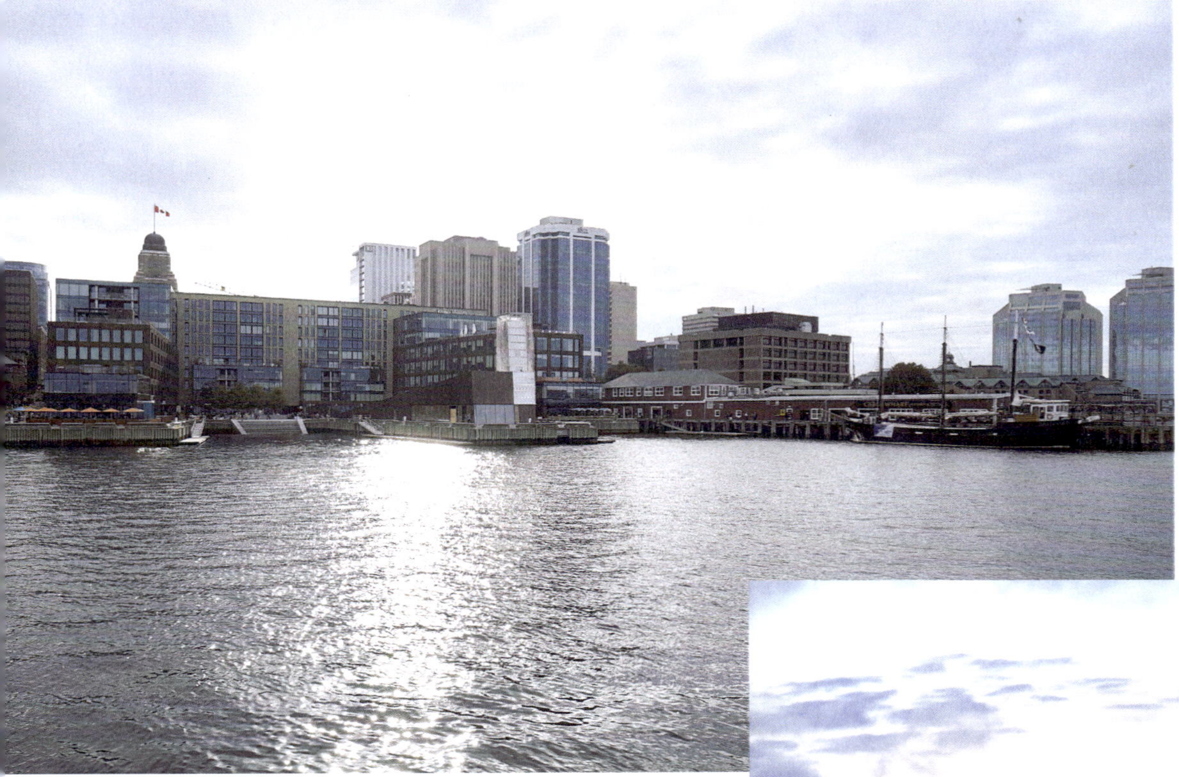

This page and opposite page:
Halifax Harbour, taken off the side of the
Harbour Queen boat

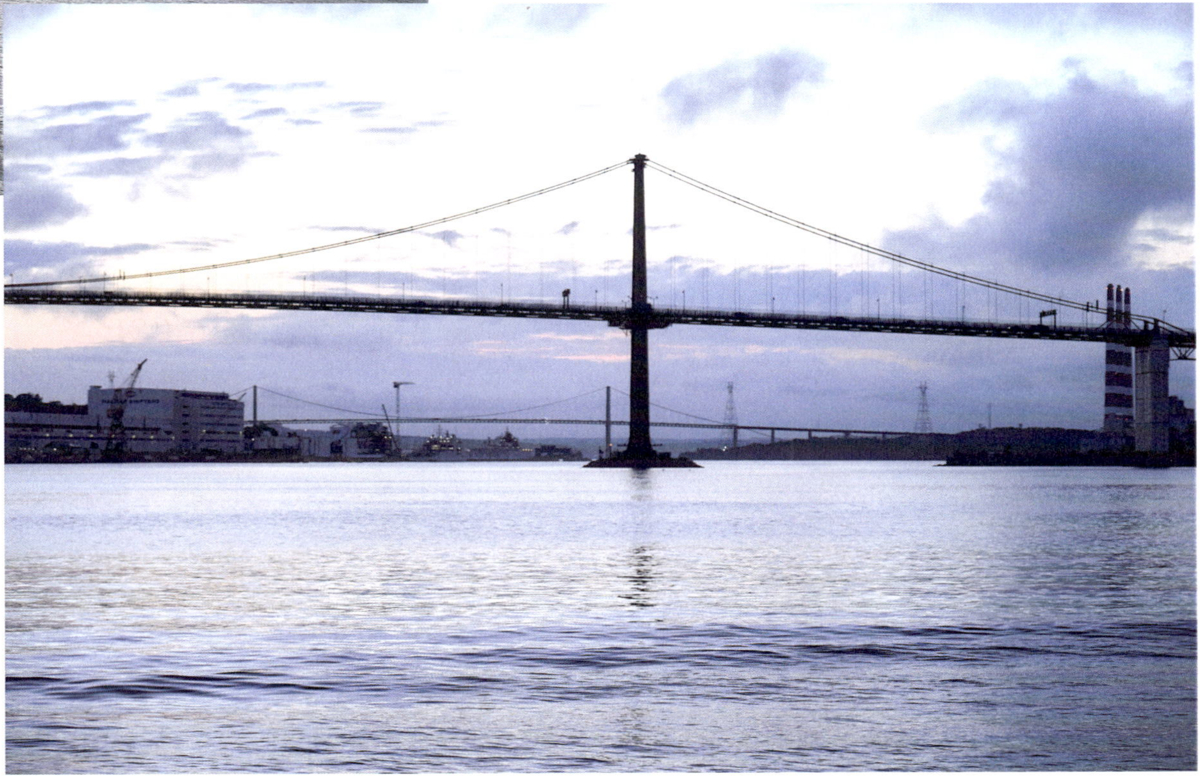

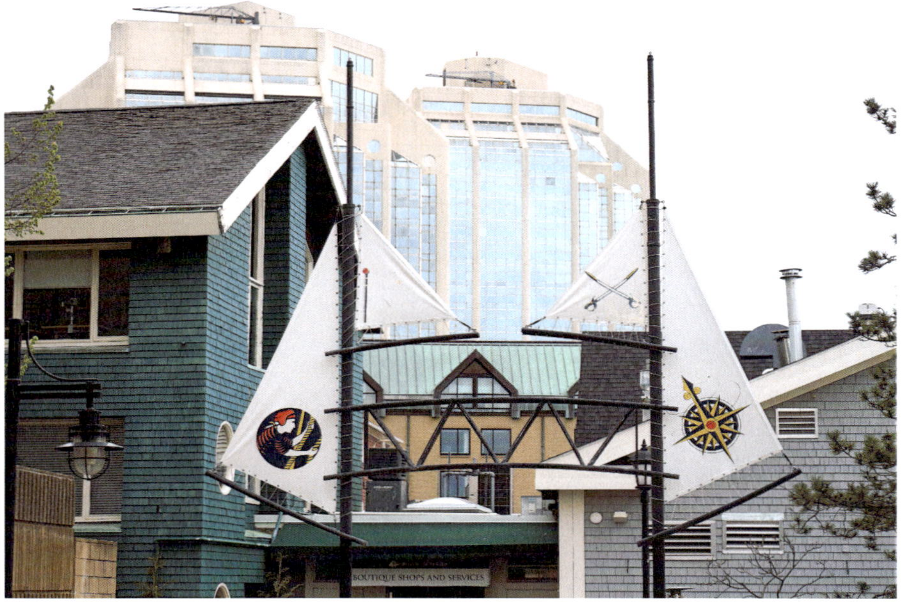
BOUTIQUE SHOPS AND SERVICES

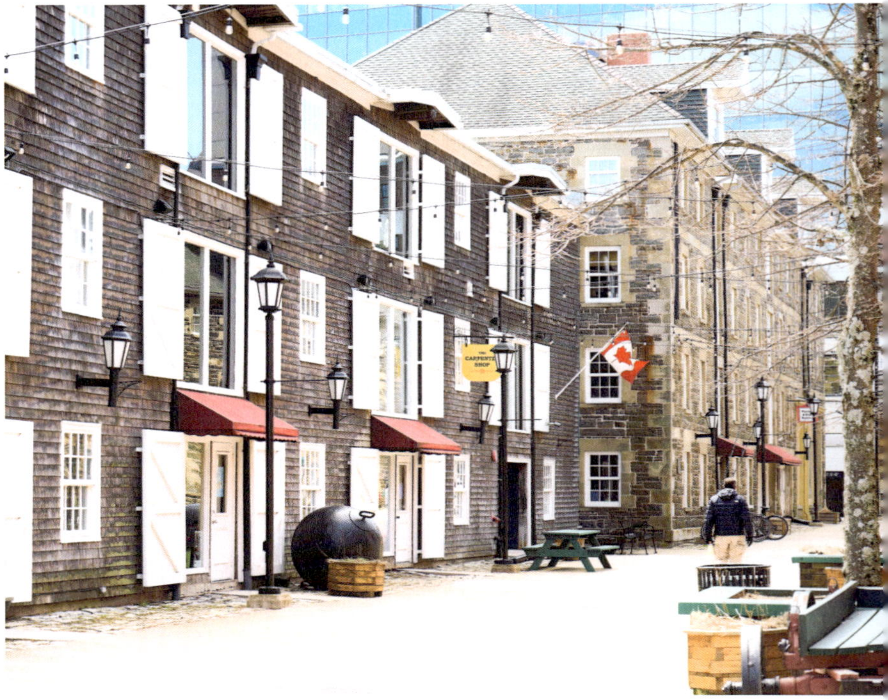

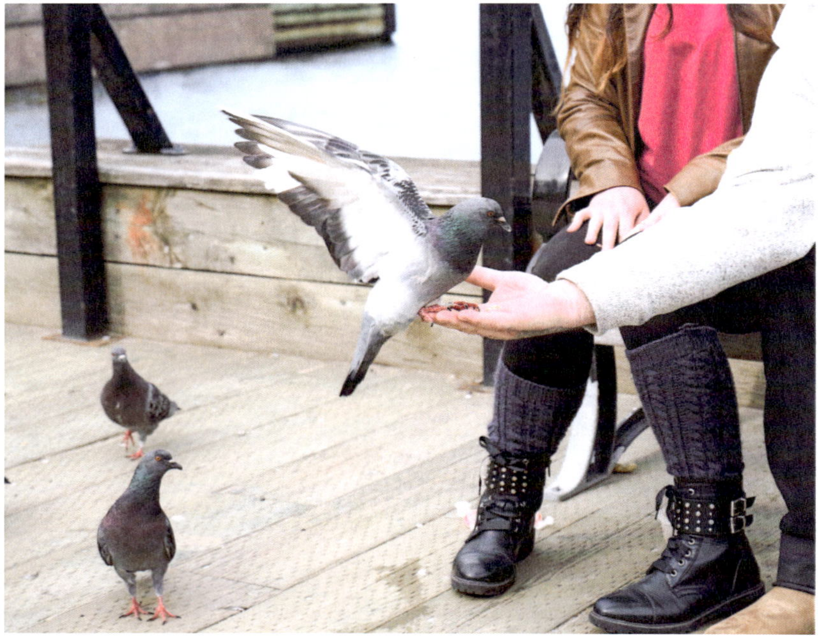

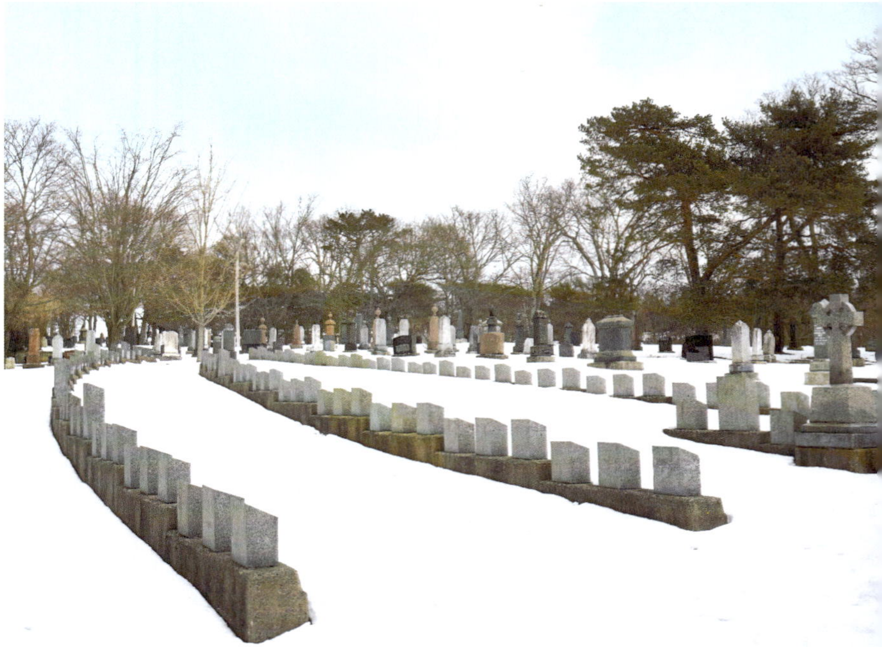

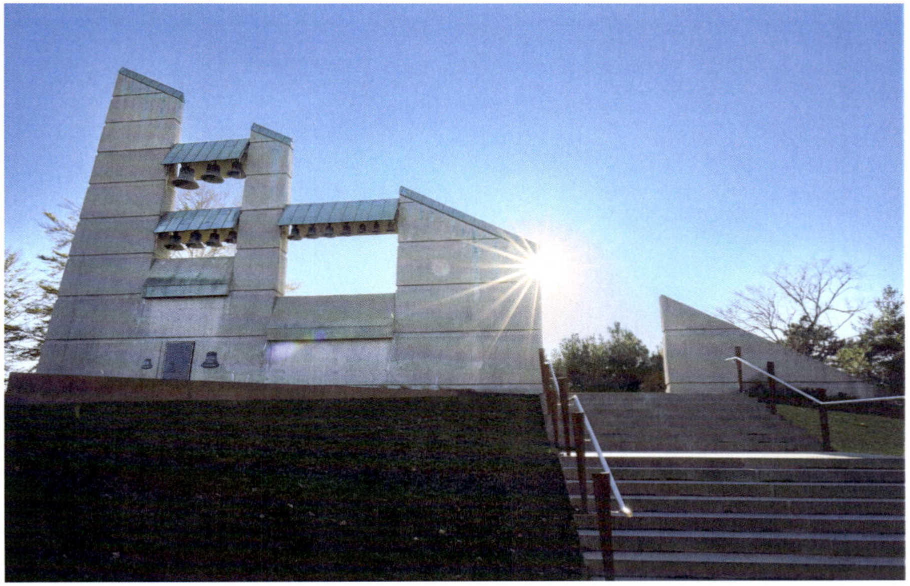

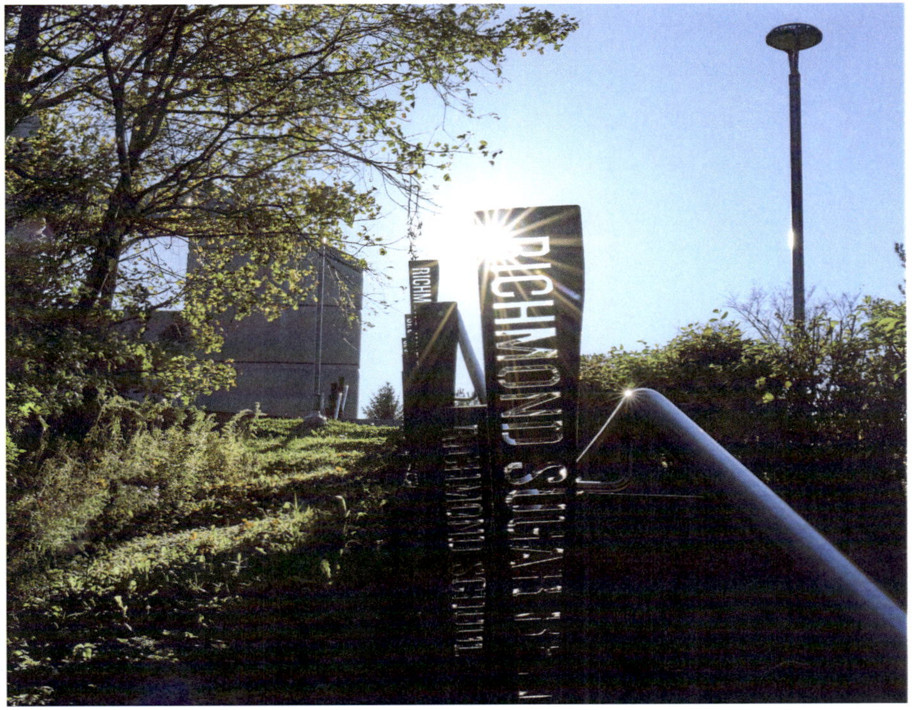

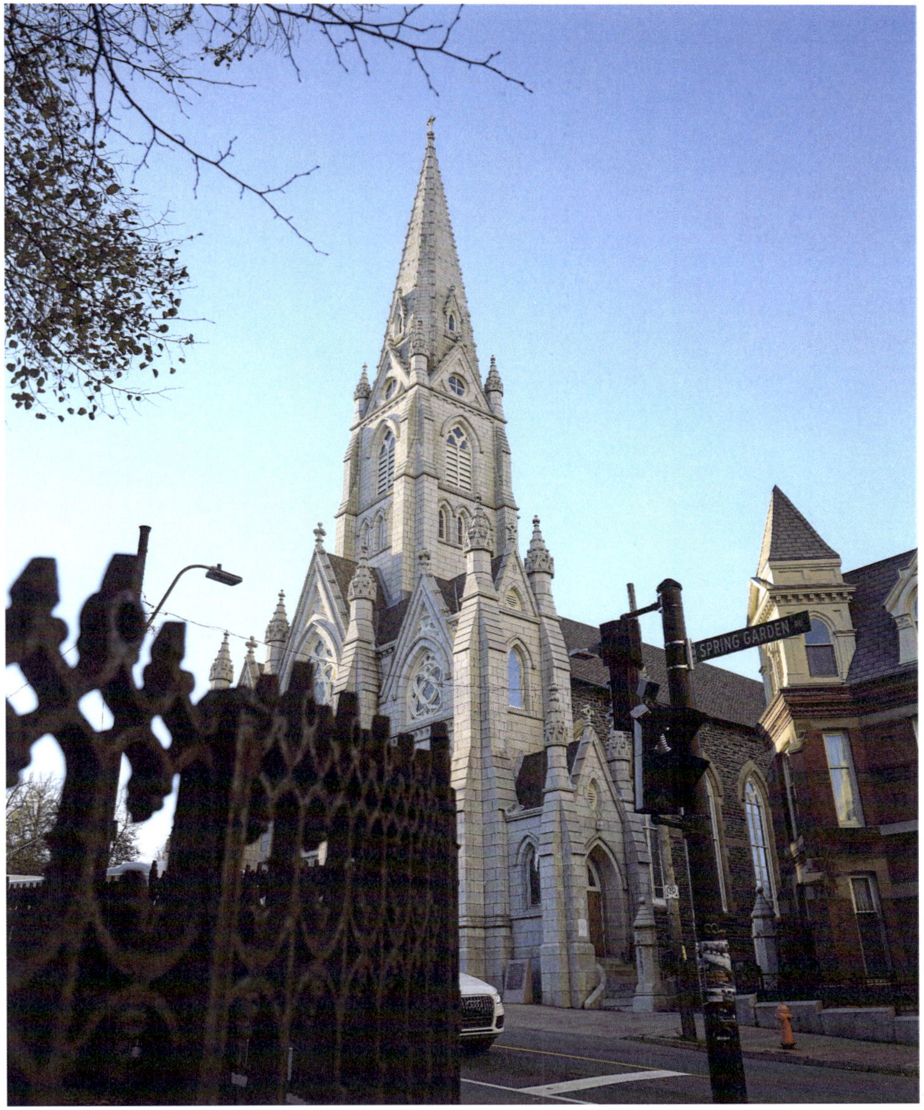

Halifax explosion memorial at Fort Needham Memorial Park
St Mary's Basilica (frescos were damaged in the explosion)

Opposite page: Halifax waterfront
Memorial for victims of the Titanic at Fairview Lawn Cemetery

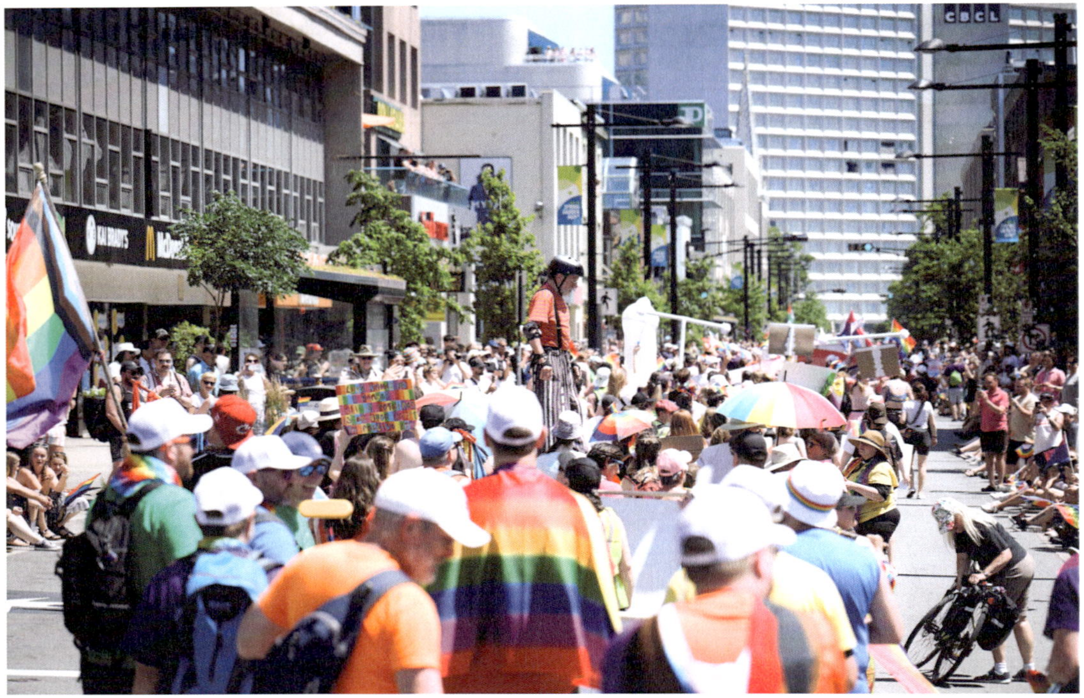

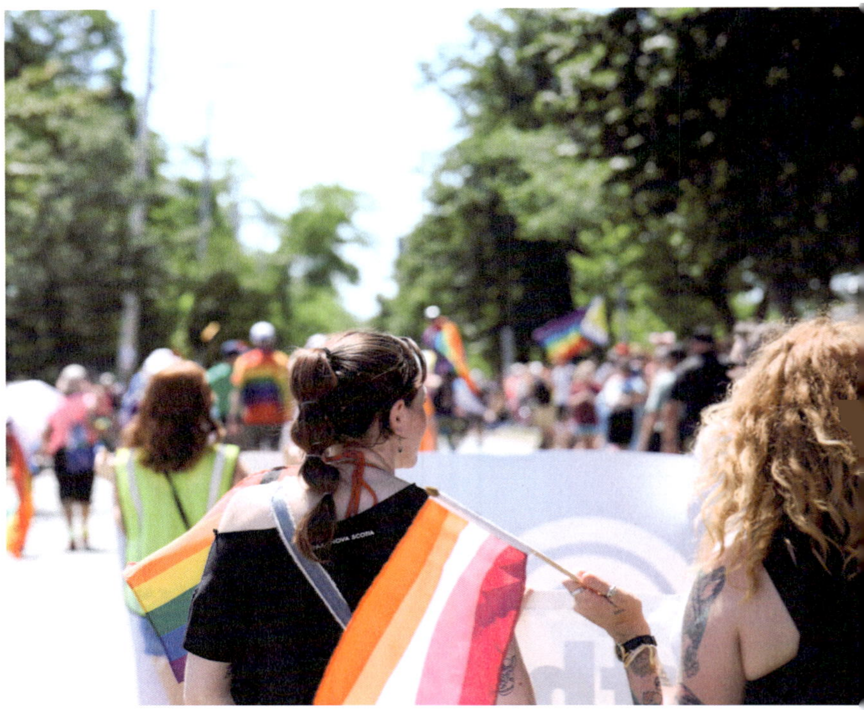

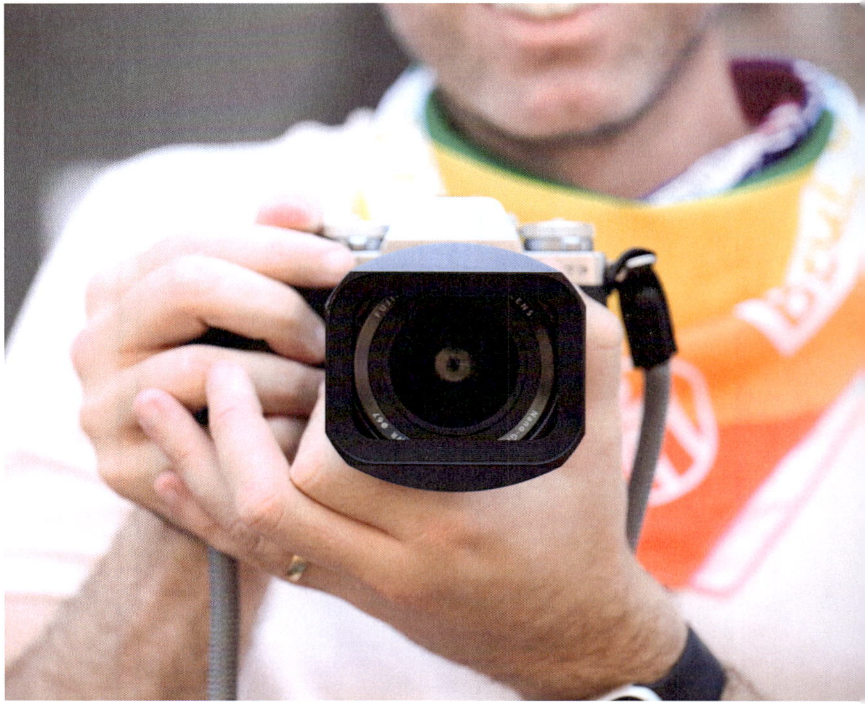

Photos from the Halifax Pride Parade
Marching in the Parade, and seeing the city awash with joy and love and support was truly heartwarming

Chapter 2
Beyond the 'Burbs -
HRM Parklands & Communities

HRM, or the Halifax Regional Municipality includes the dozens of communities of the Enfield/Airport area, Bedford, Sackville, Dartmouth, Cole Harbour, Halifax, the Eastern Shore, Musquodoboit Valley, and the Peggy's Cove Coastal Region / St Margaret's Bay area (out to Hubbards).

It's a large part of the province, with roughly half of Nova Scotia's population. HRM also provides no shortage of amazing shoreline, parks, trails, and nature, with things to do all year 'round! Some of these were the first places we explored, and some only recently. There's still a ton to go!

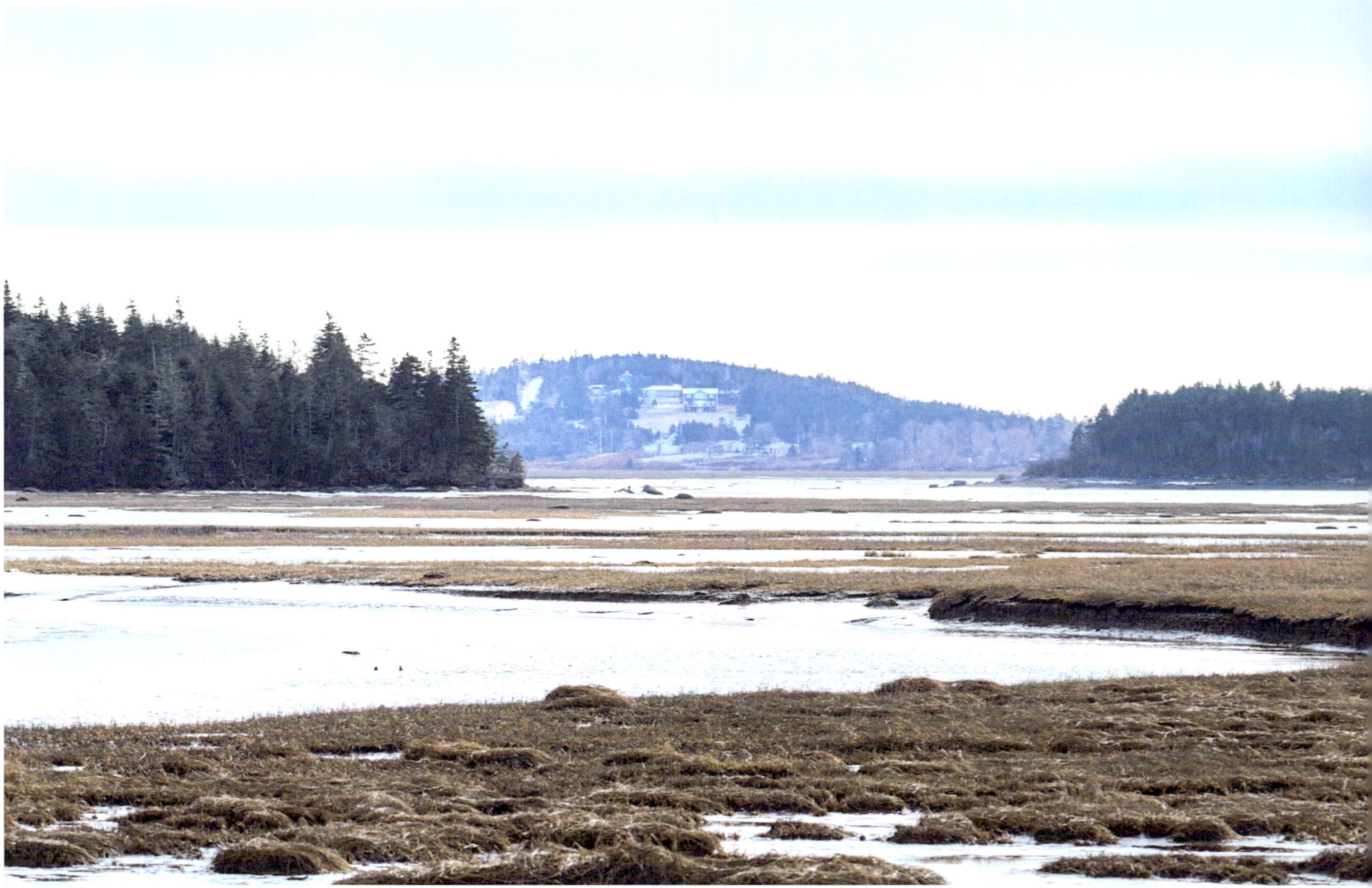

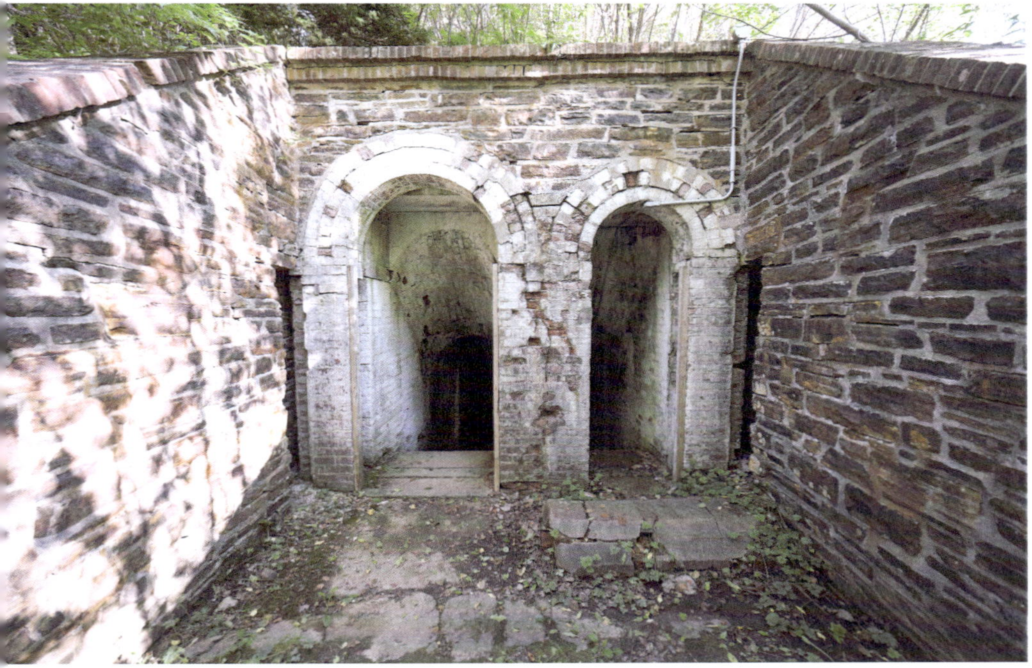

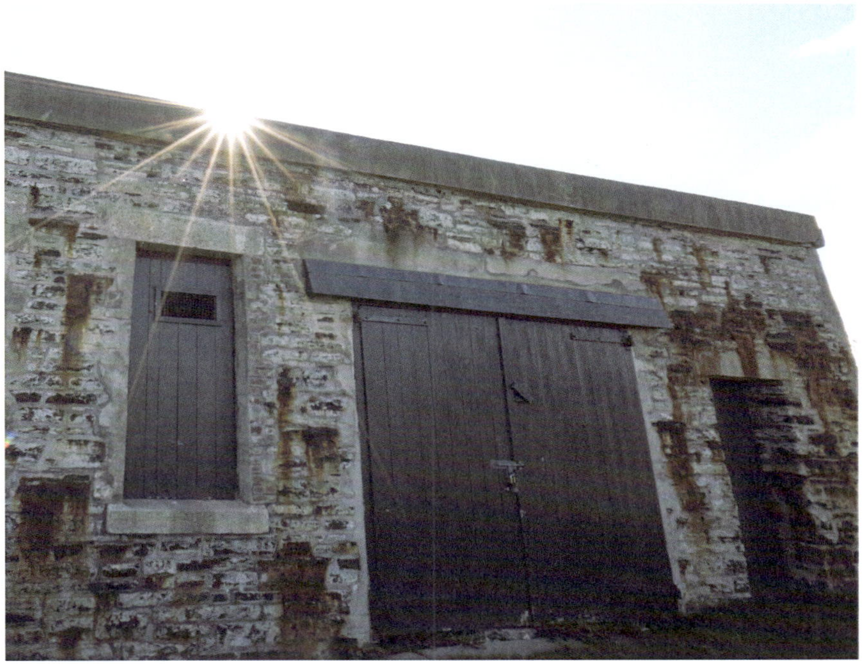

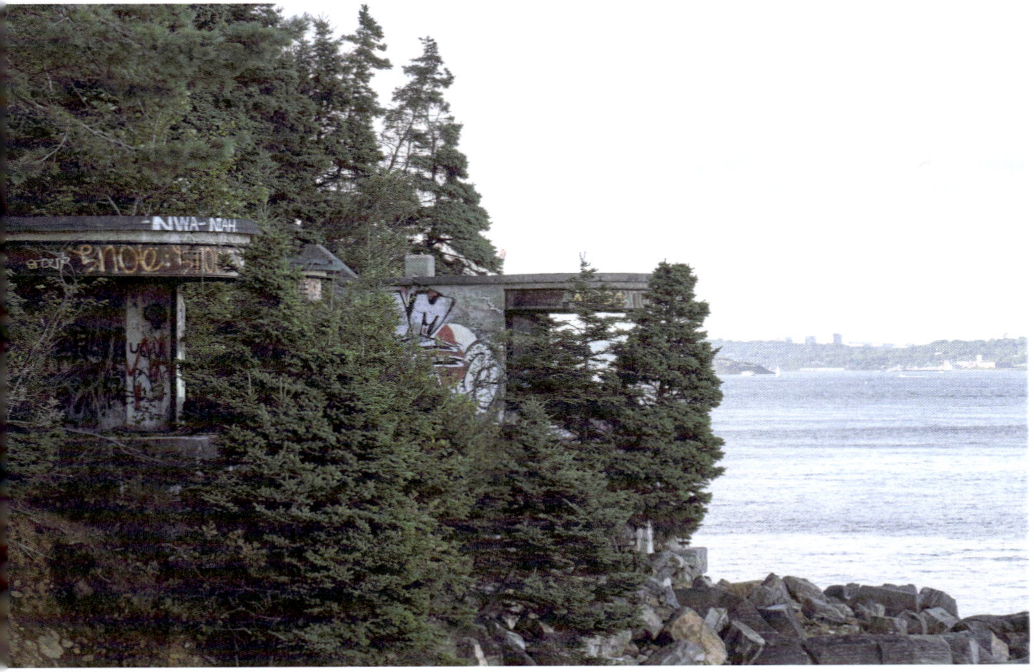

York Redoubt Historical Site

Opposite page: Chezzetcook area

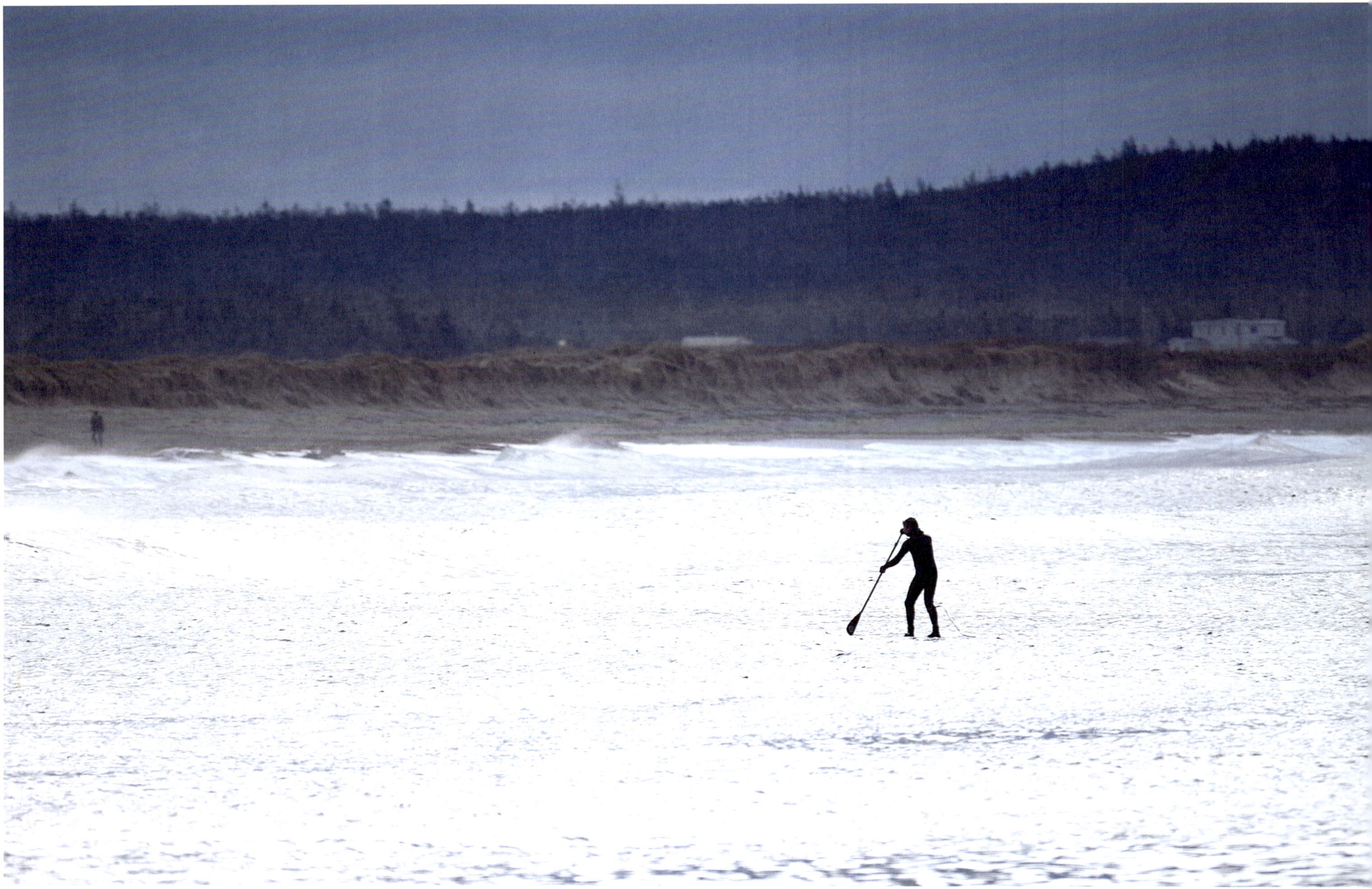

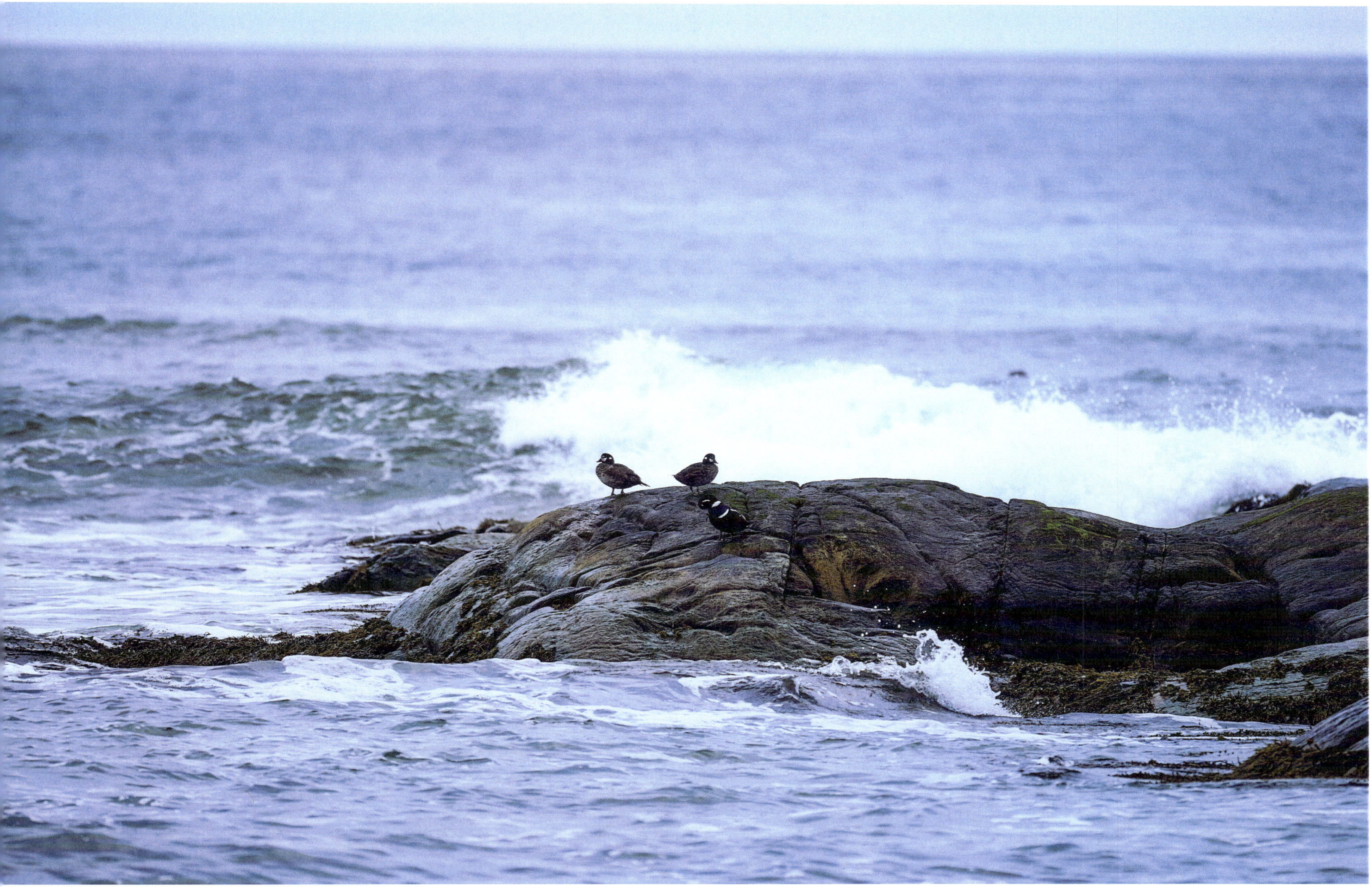

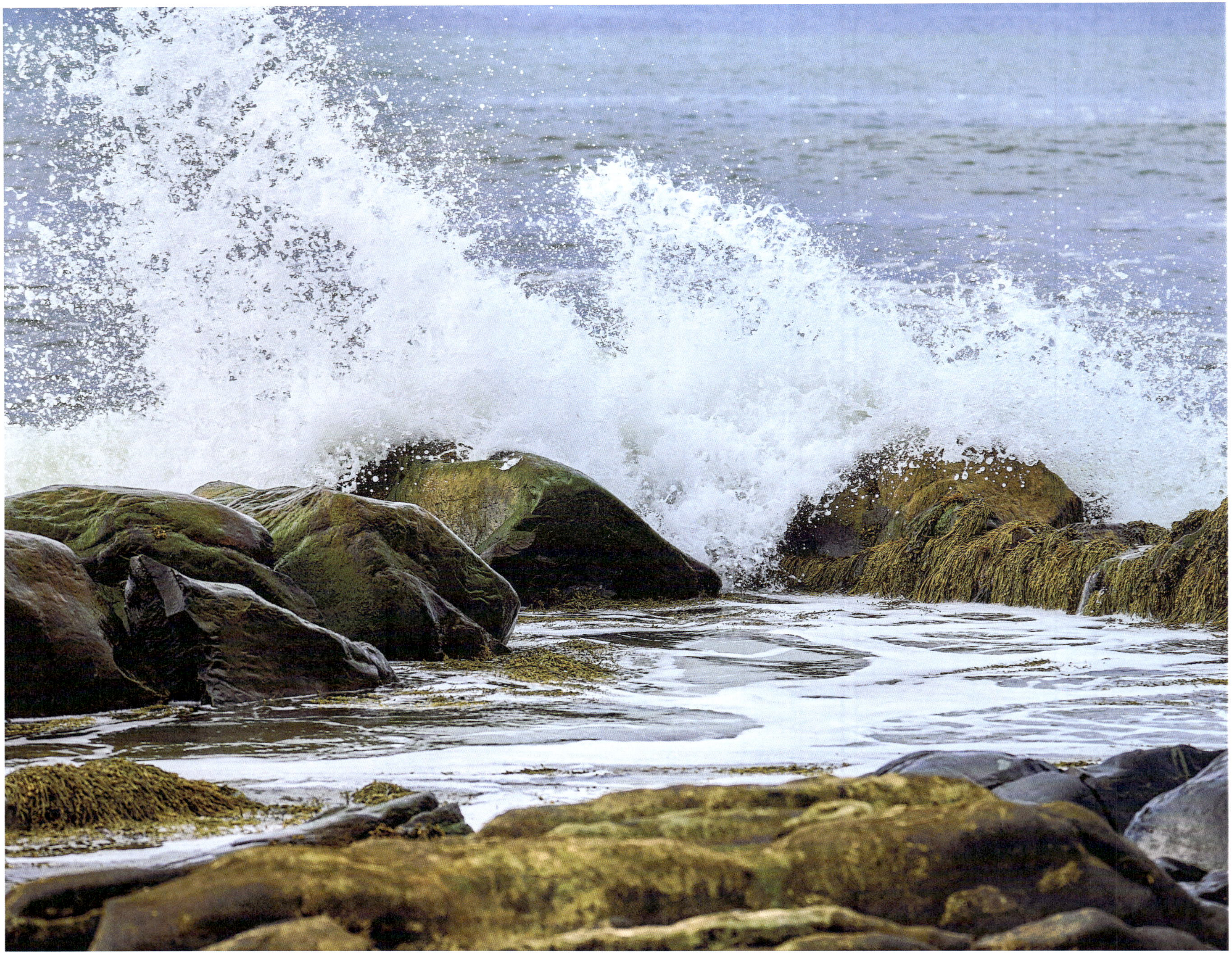

This page and Previous pages: Martinique Beach

Opposite Page: Salt Marsh Trail

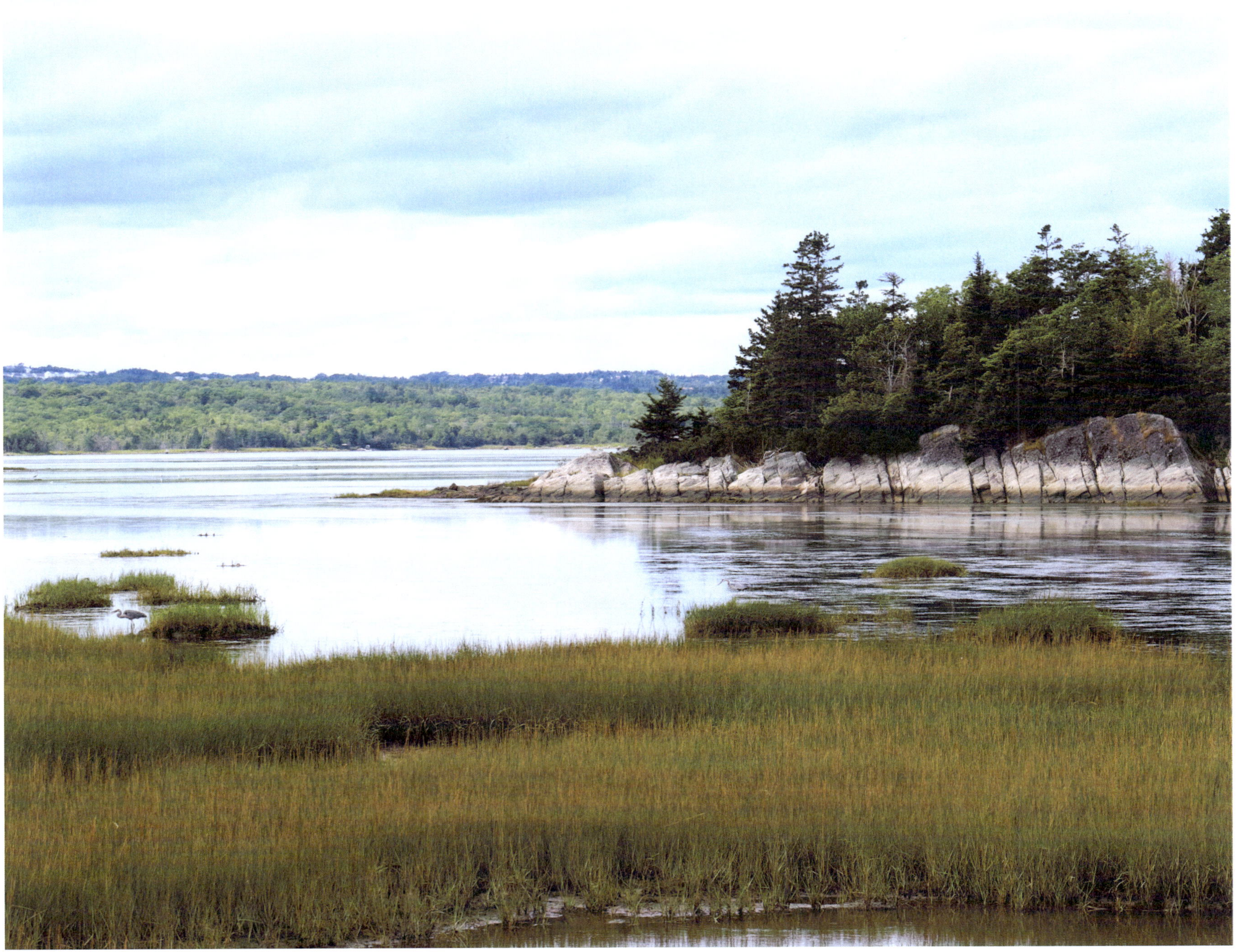

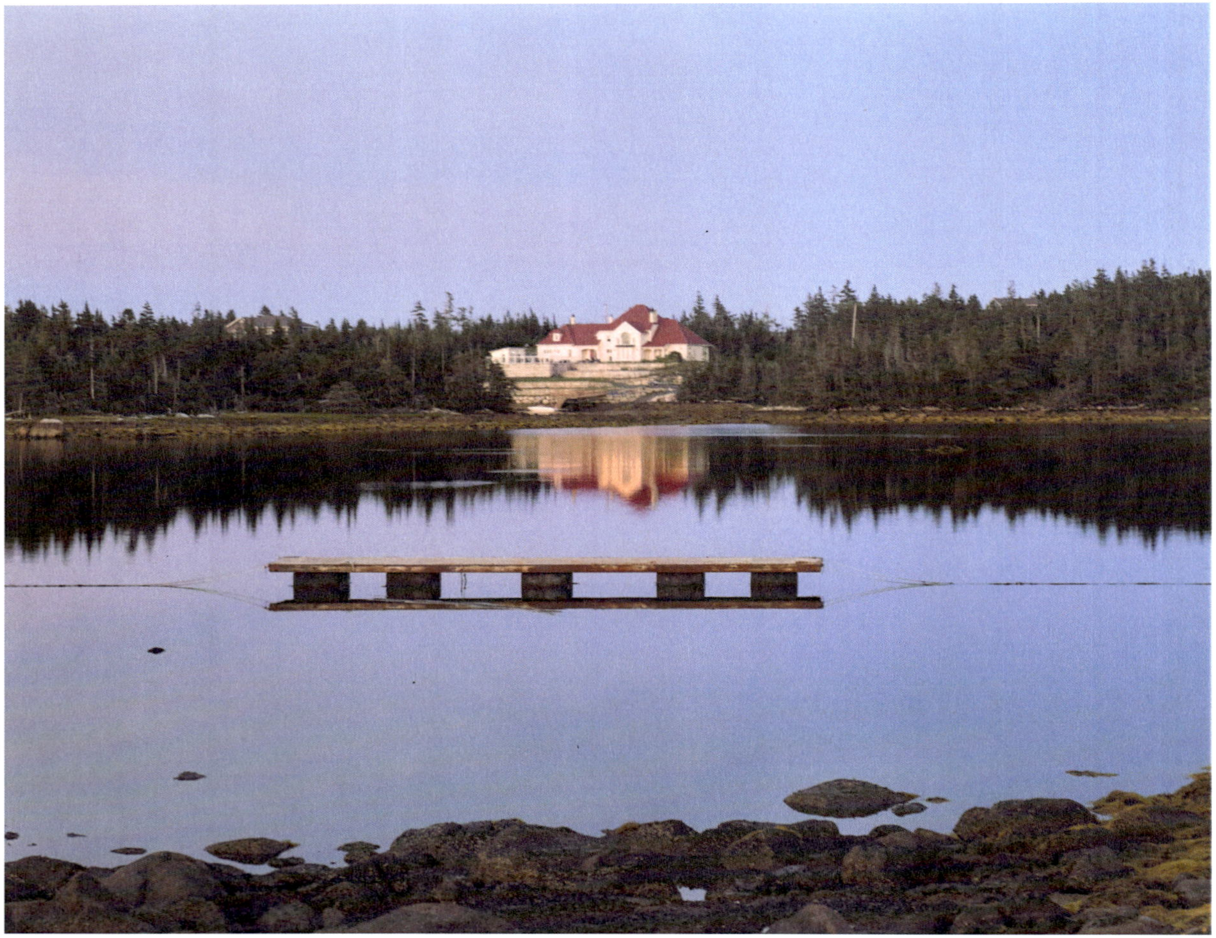

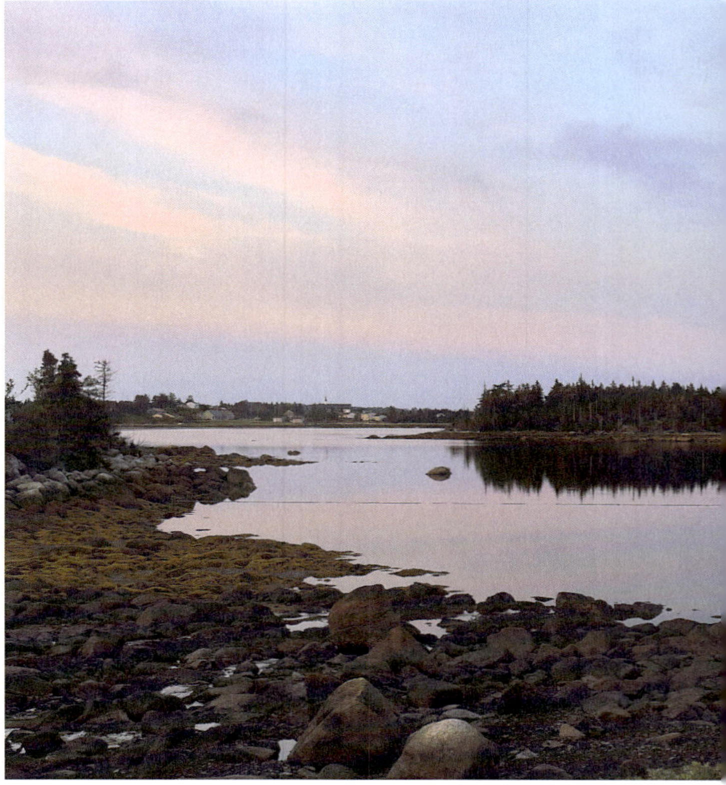

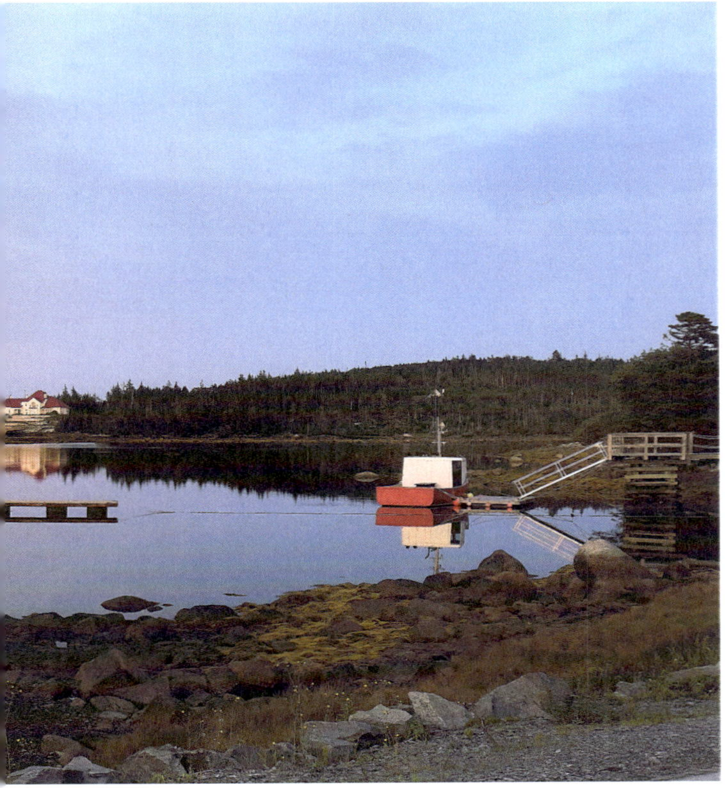

Sambro Creek

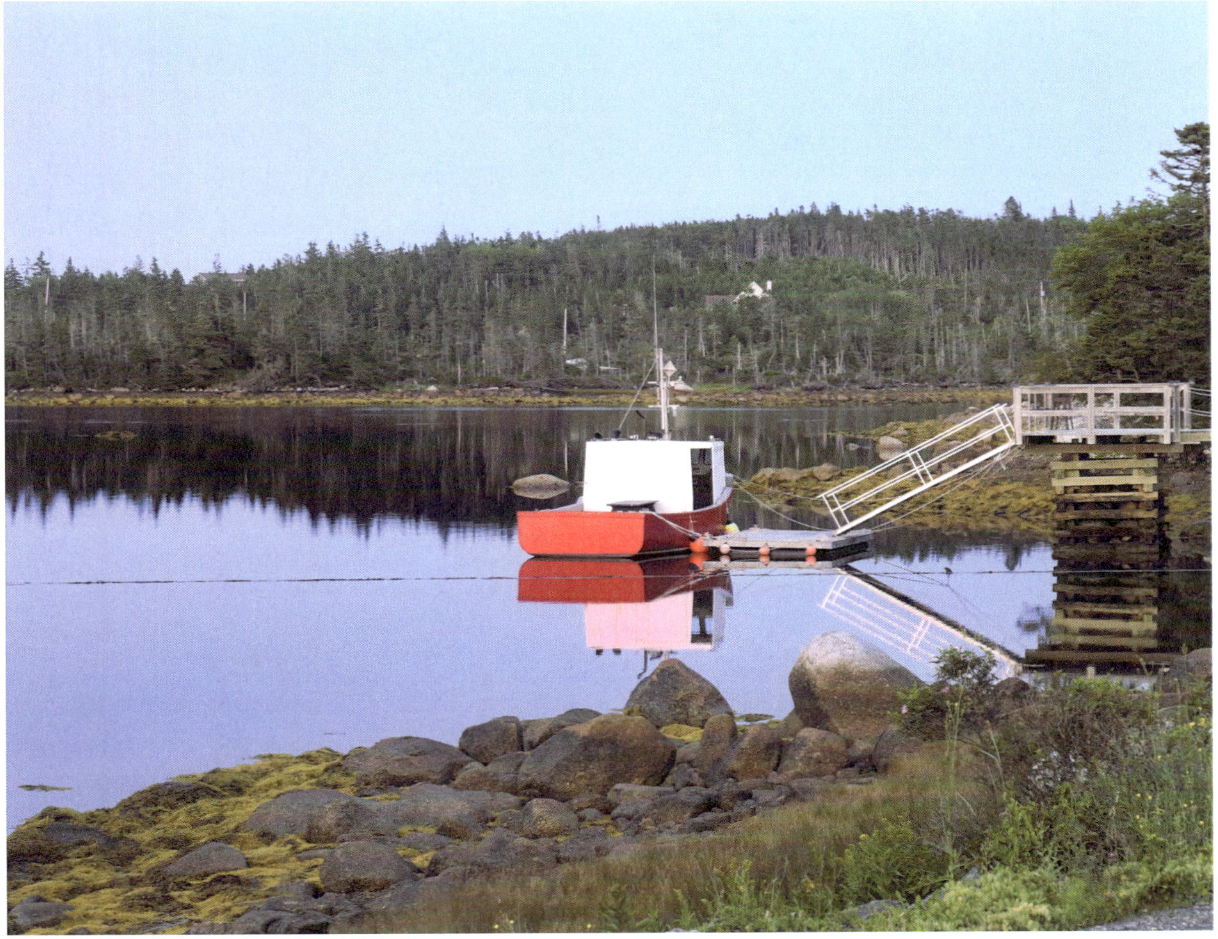

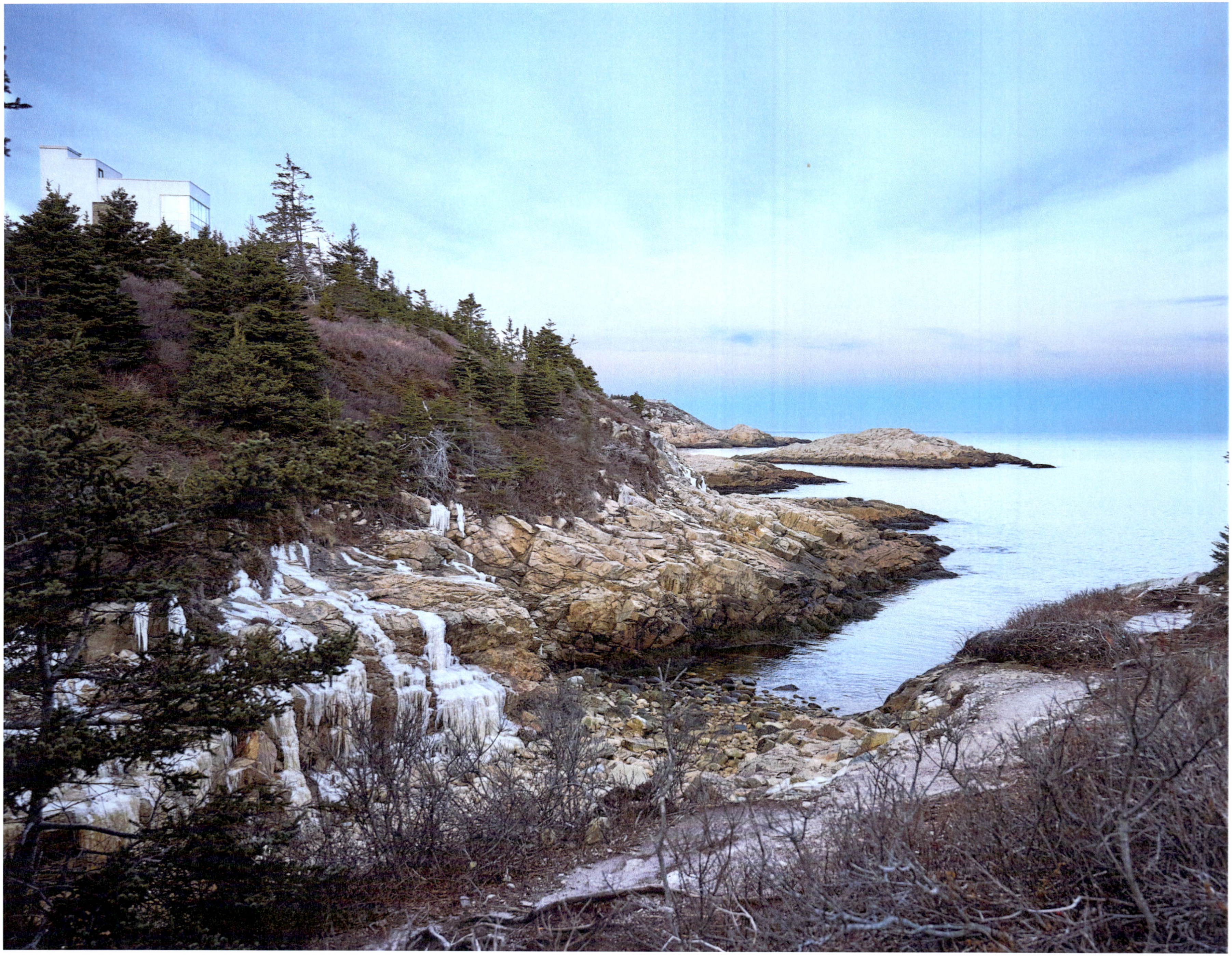

This and
Opposite page:

Duncan's Cove

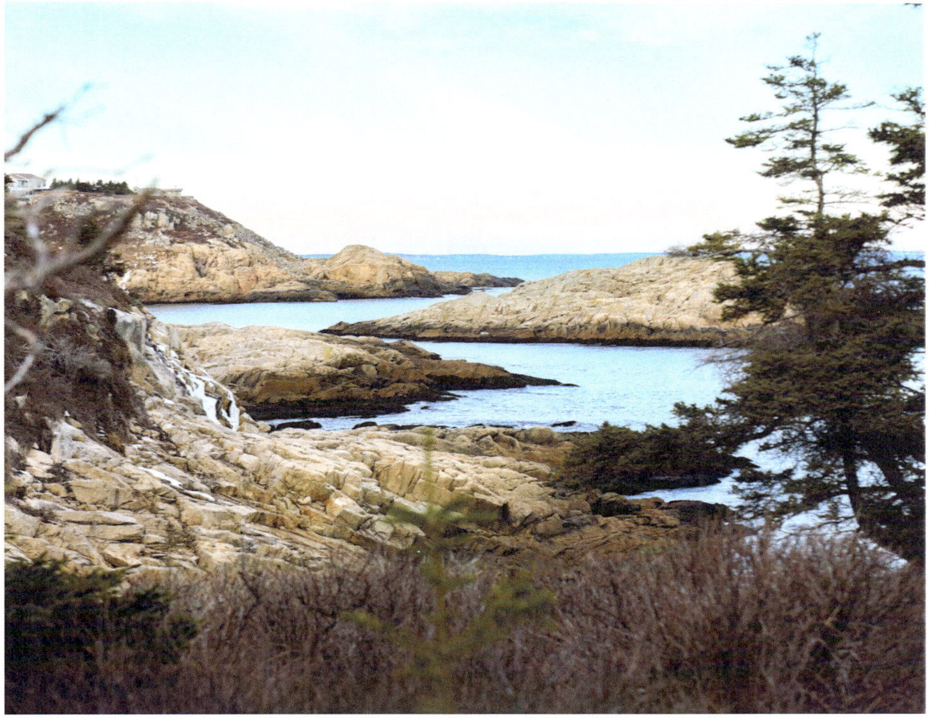

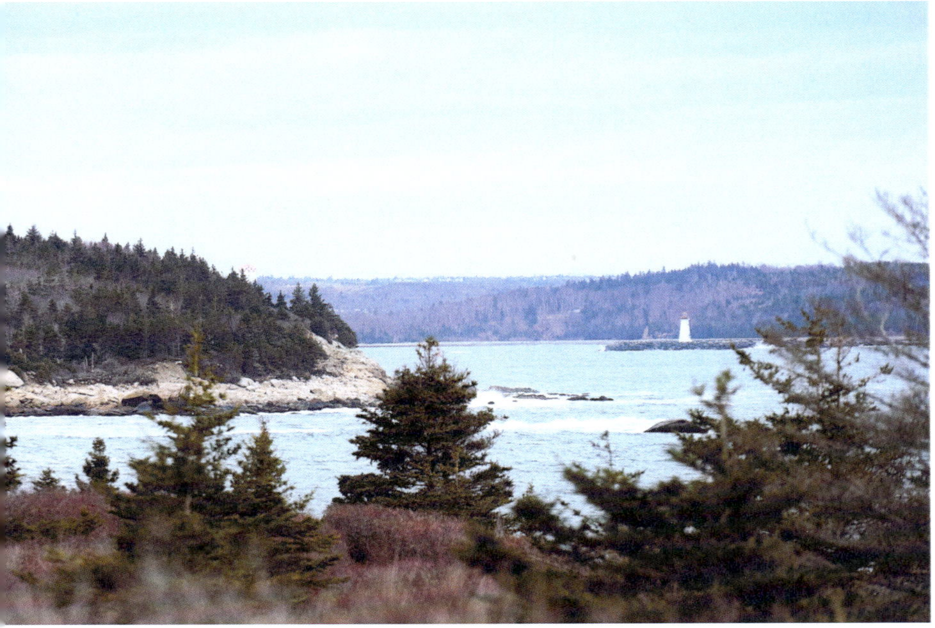

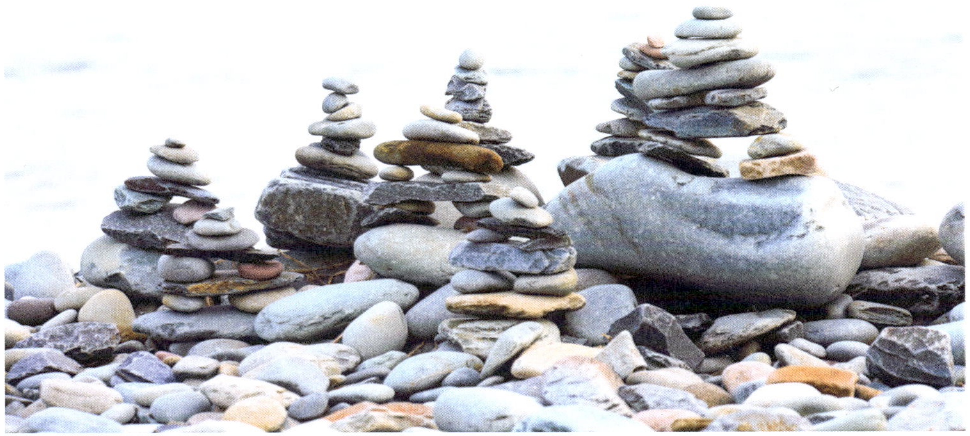

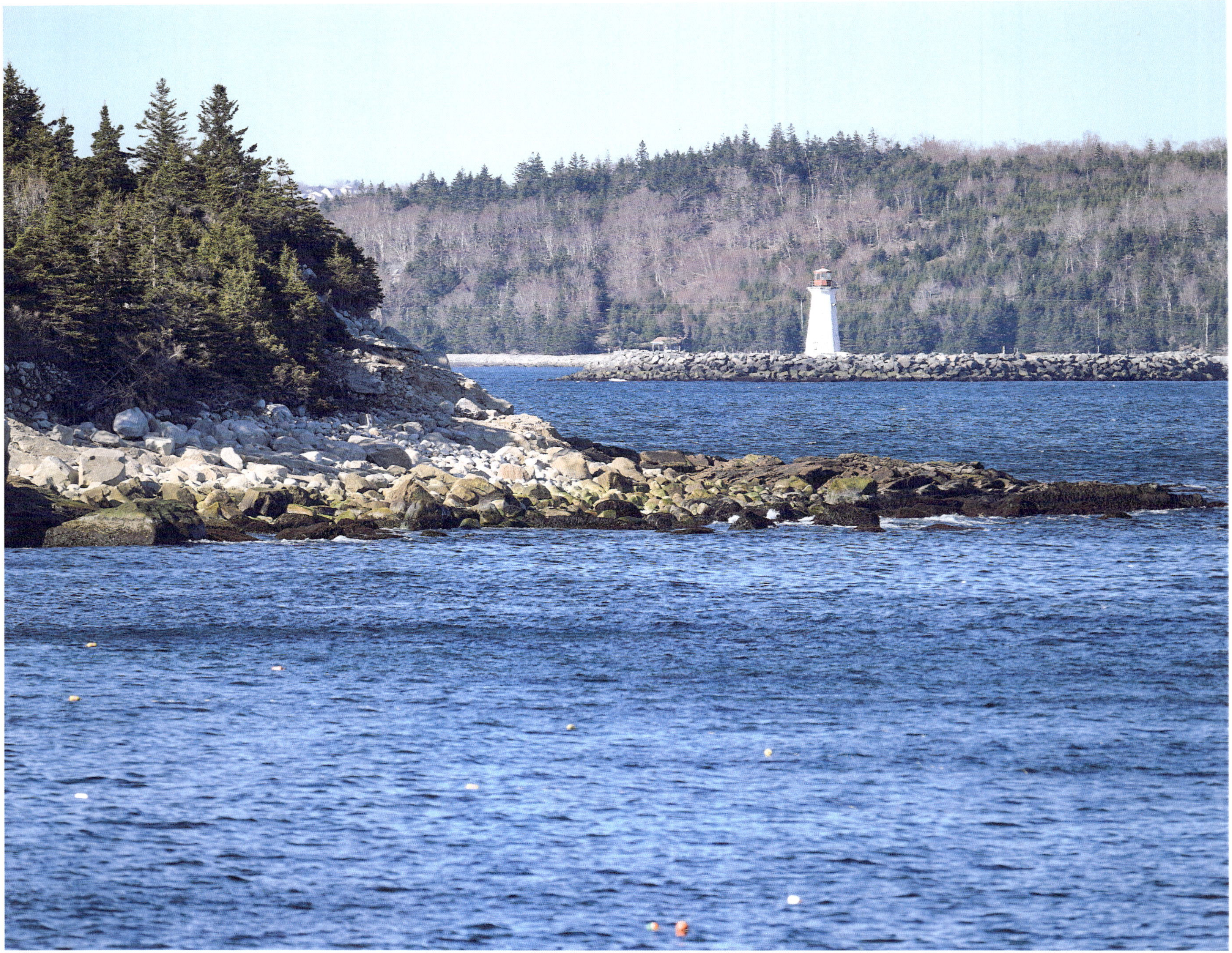

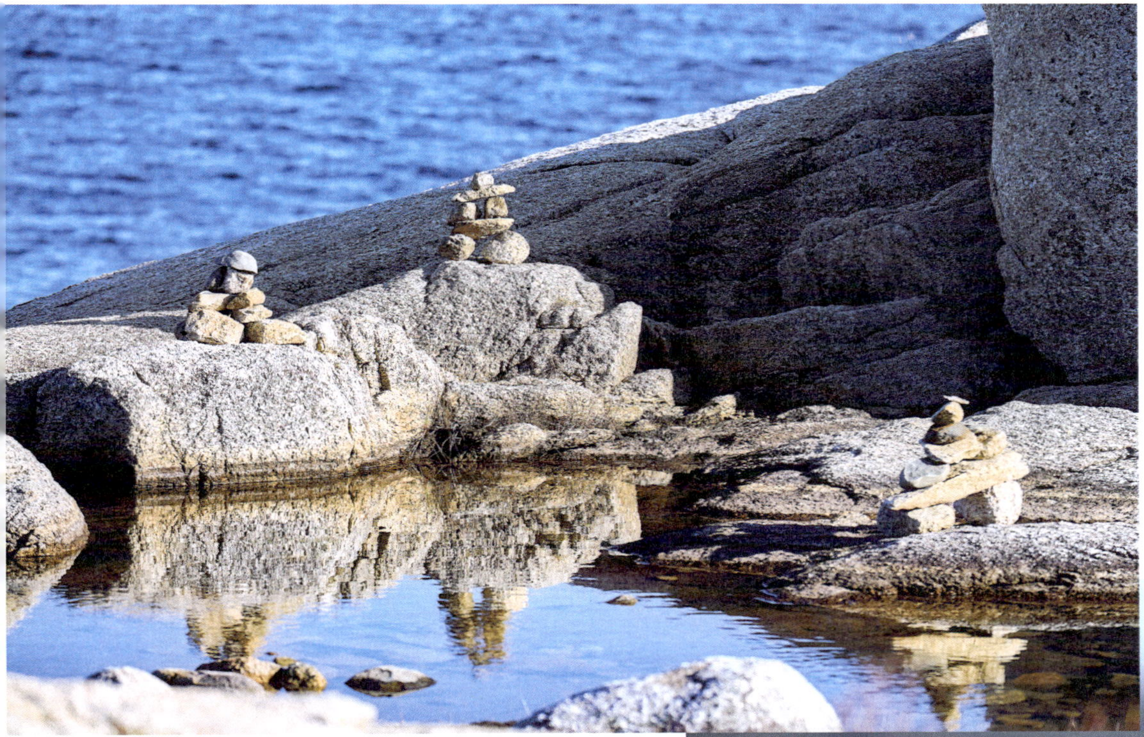

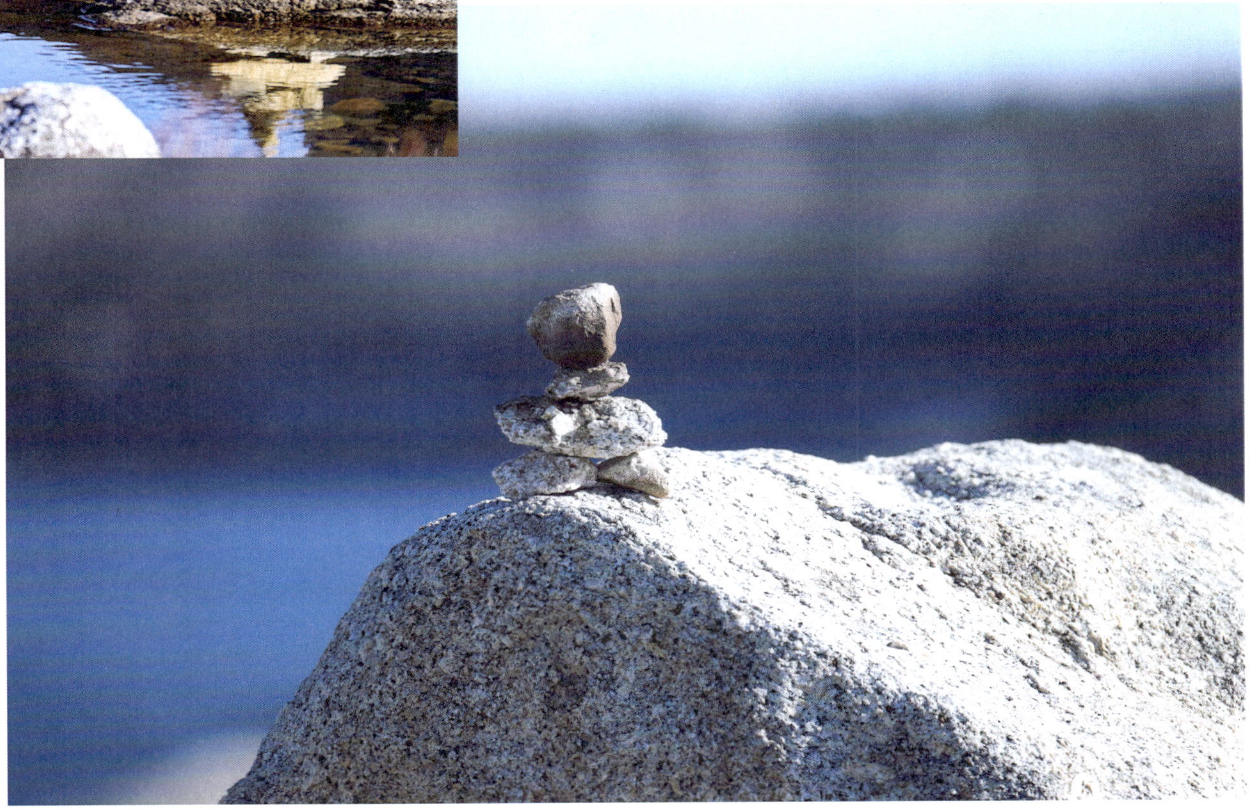

This and
Opposite page:

Herring Cove

This and opposite page:

Cole Harbour Heritage Park

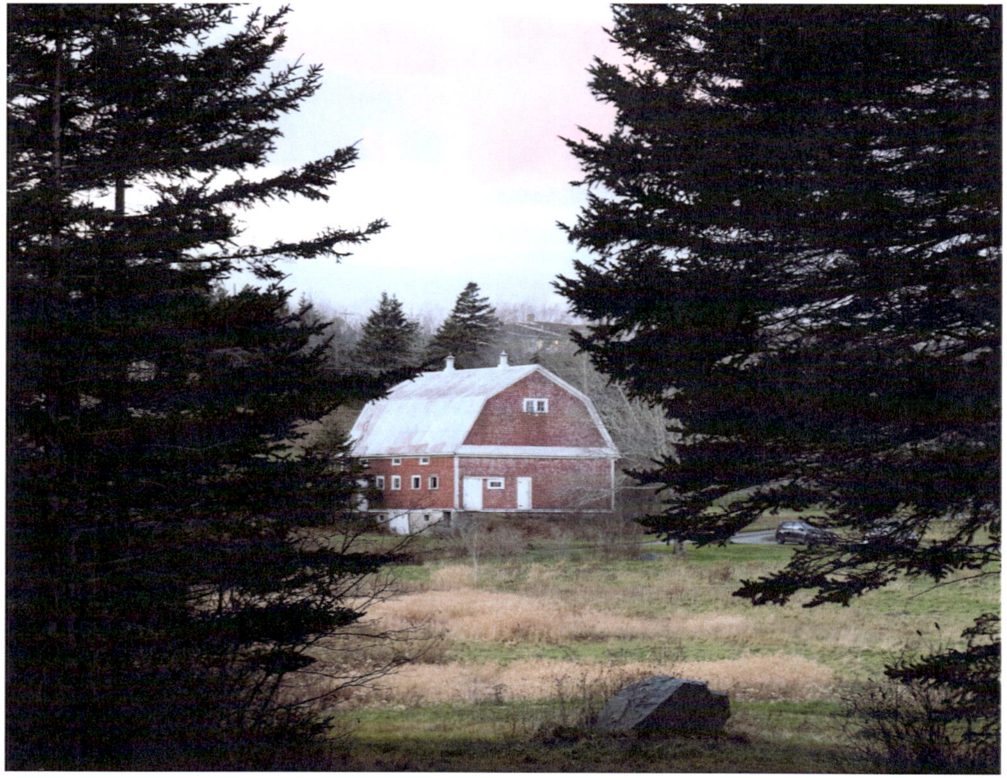

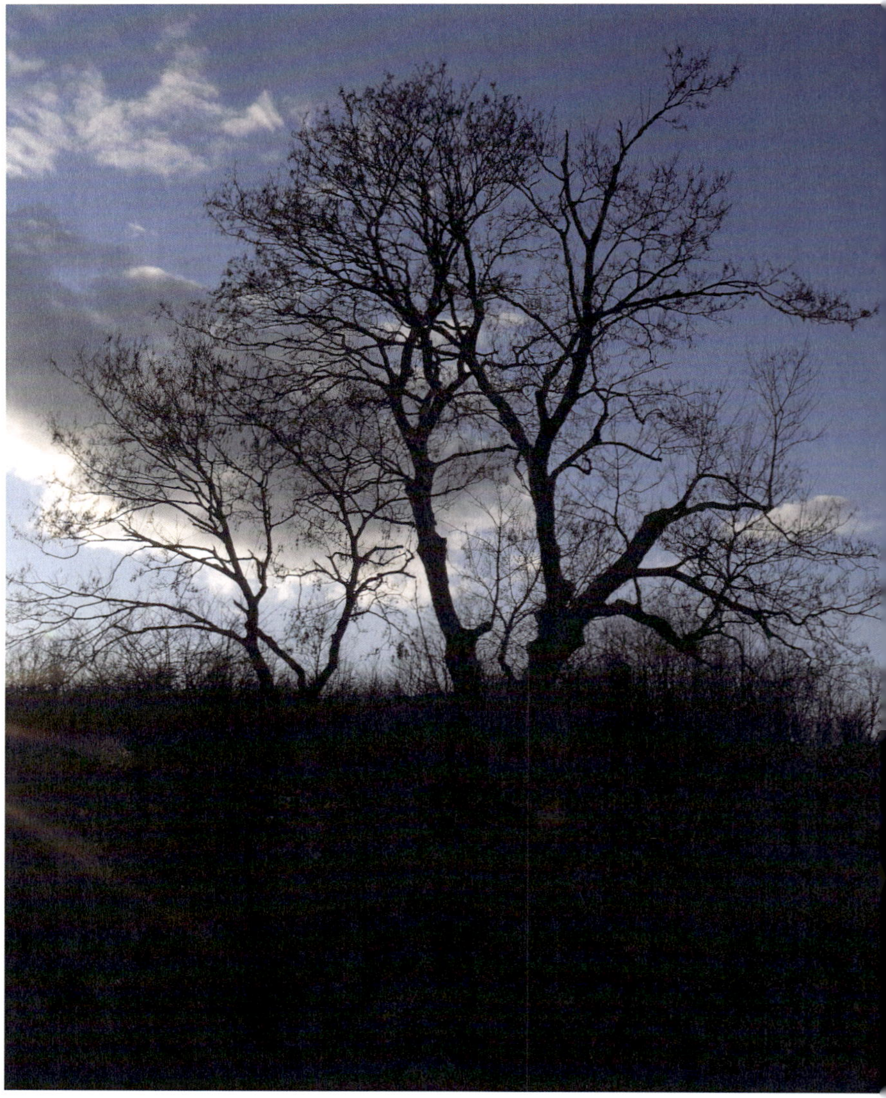

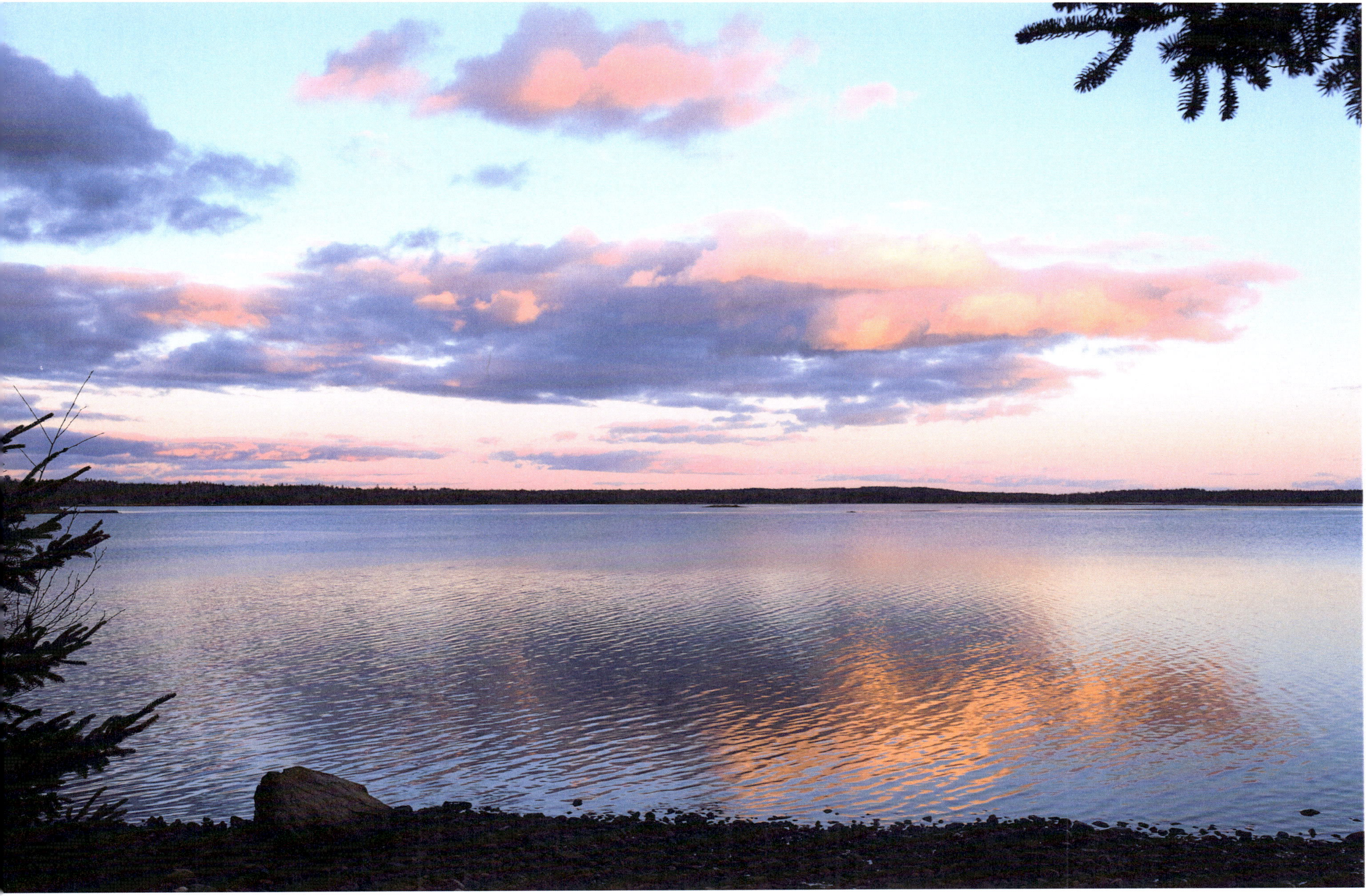

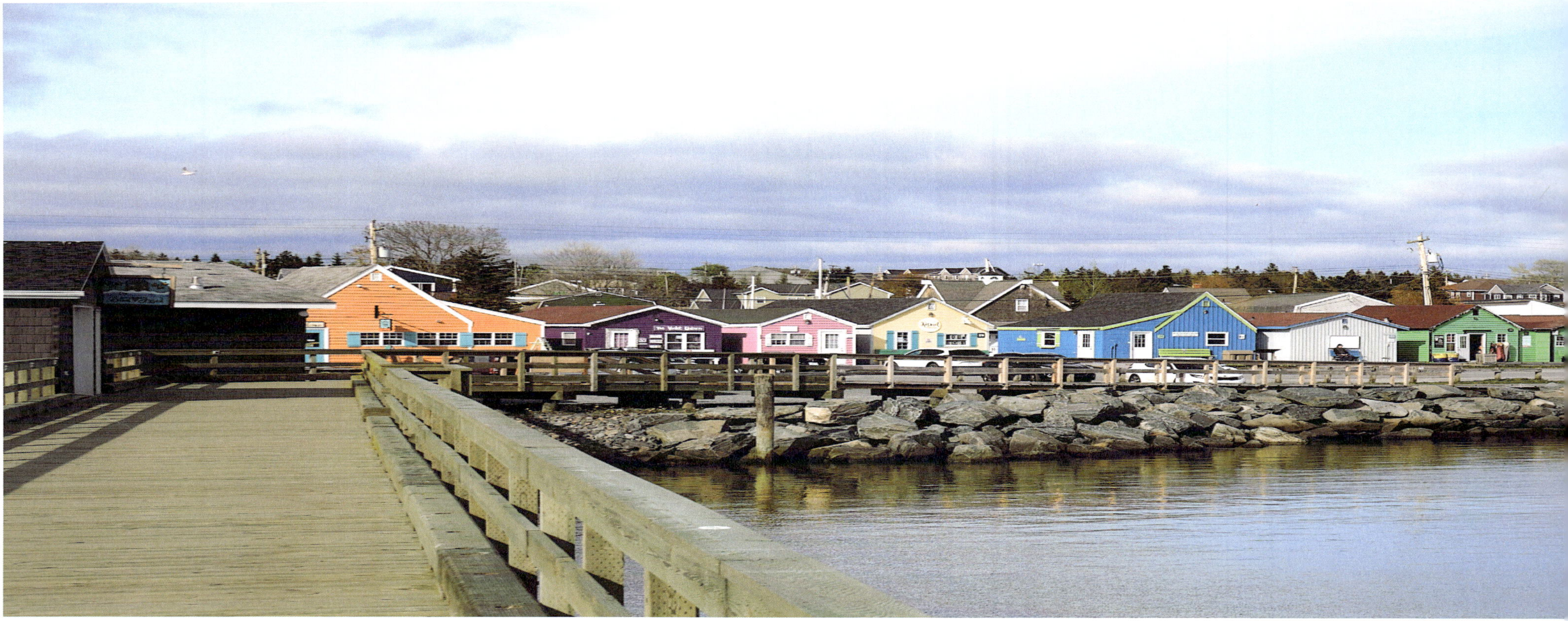

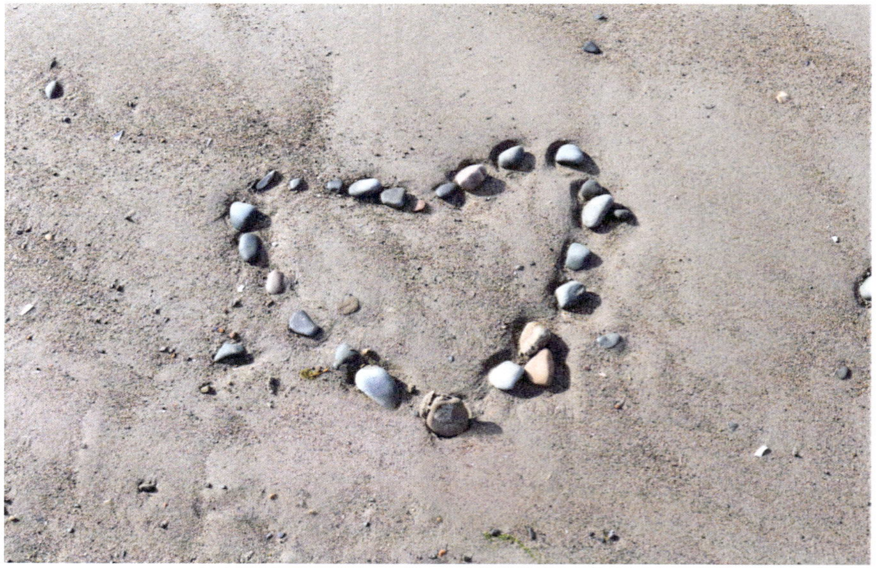

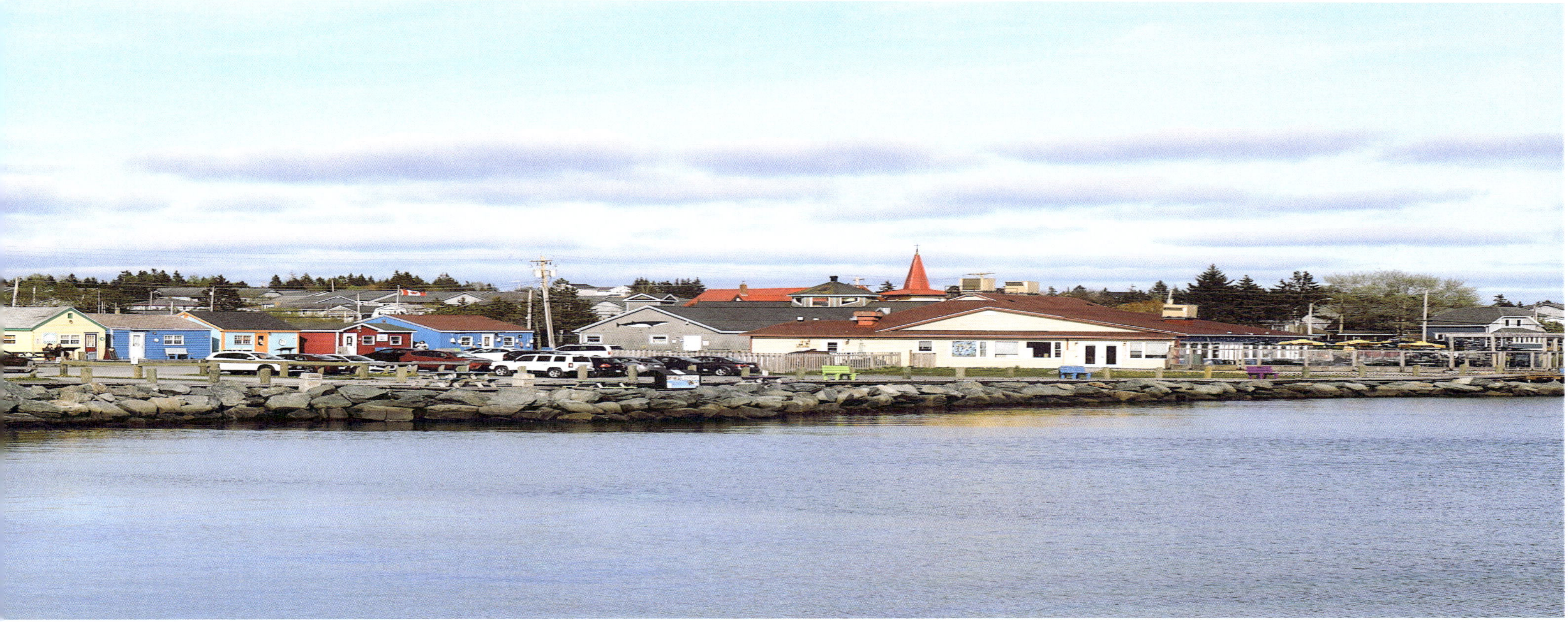

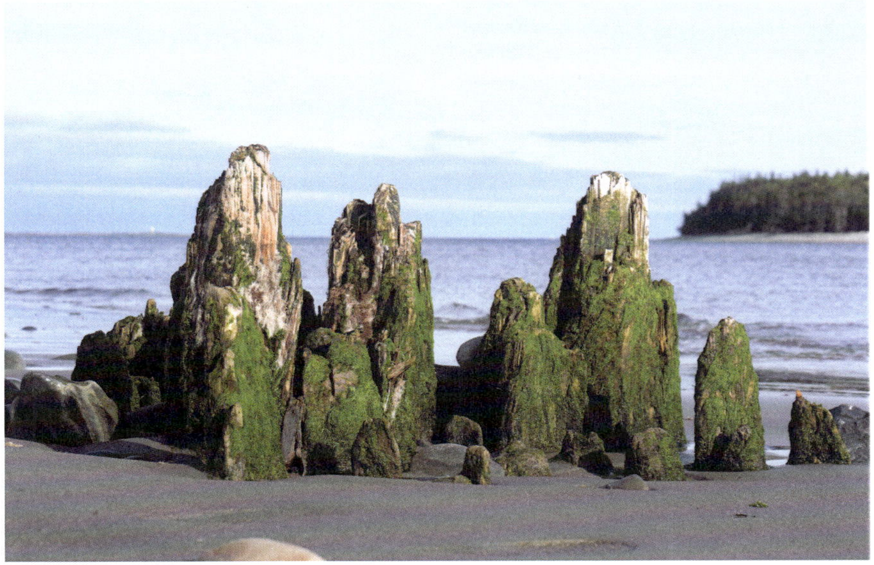

These pages and following two pages:
Fisherman's Cove

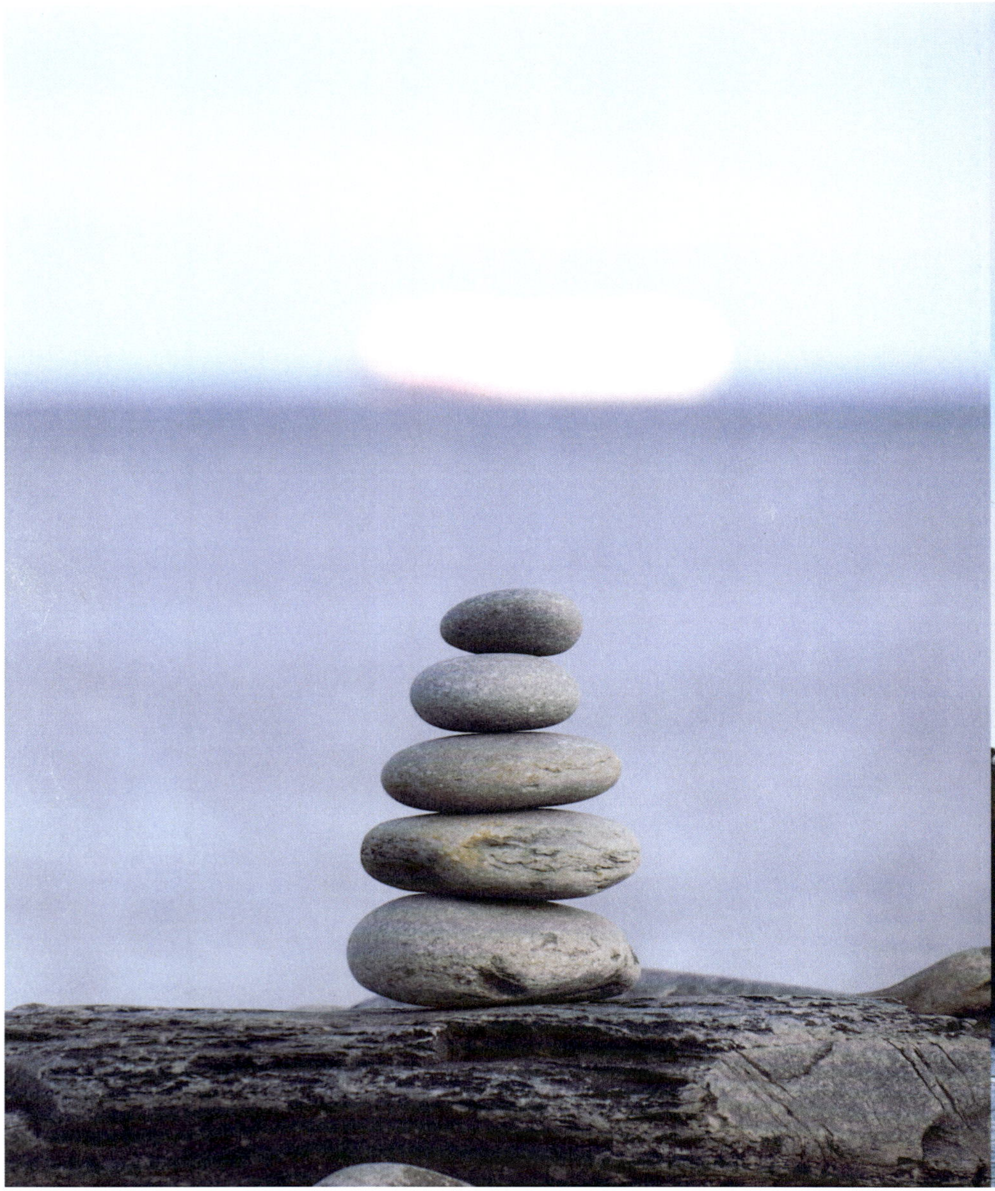

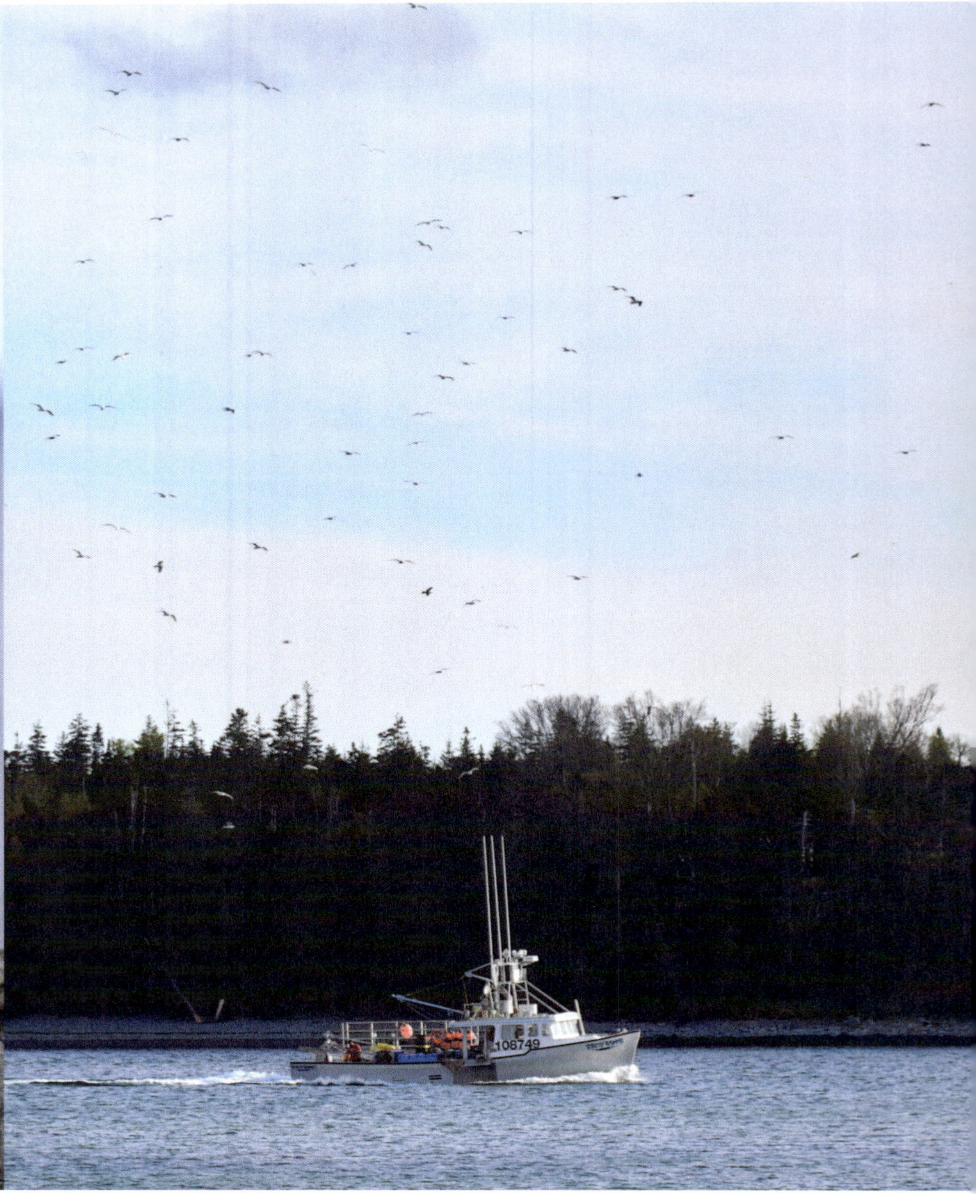
108749

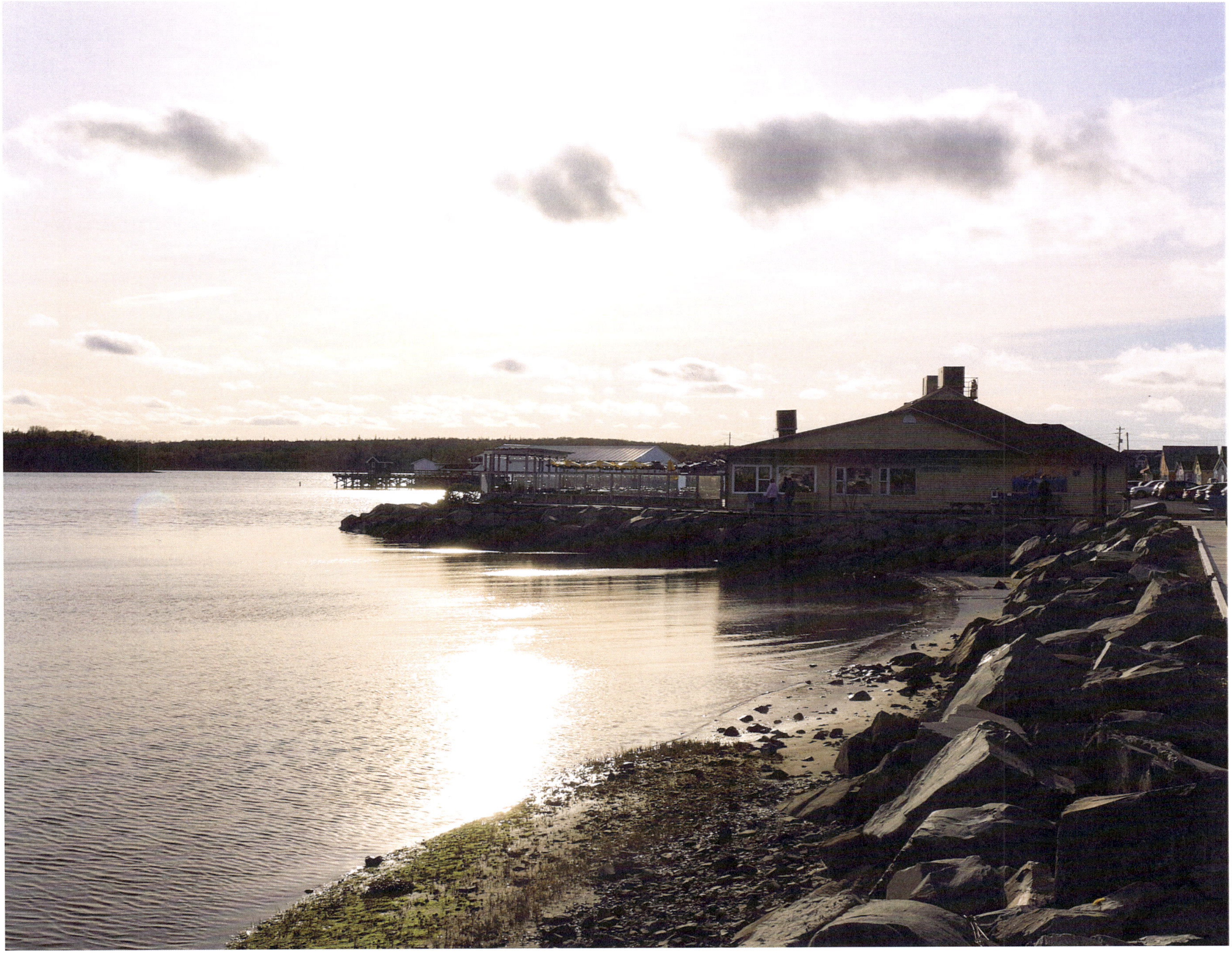

Chapter 3
The Lady & The Sea -
Peggy's Cove and St. Margaret's Bay

Is there anything more iconically Nova Scotian than the lighthouse at Peggy's Cove?

I often joke with visitors that if you come to Nova Scotia, you're legally obligated to visit. And visit they do - to the tune of about 700,000 people each year! That's a lot of "stay off the black rocks" warnings given.

We spent our first New Year's Day as Nova Scotians down at Peggy's Cove. Since then, we've made it our annual tradition to make it down there at some point on Jan 1 to welcome in the new year. It might be one of the spots we've visited most in our time here, and so gets a dedicated chapter. Okay, there are a few photos of St Margaret's Bay in here as well, but one can hardly separate the two.

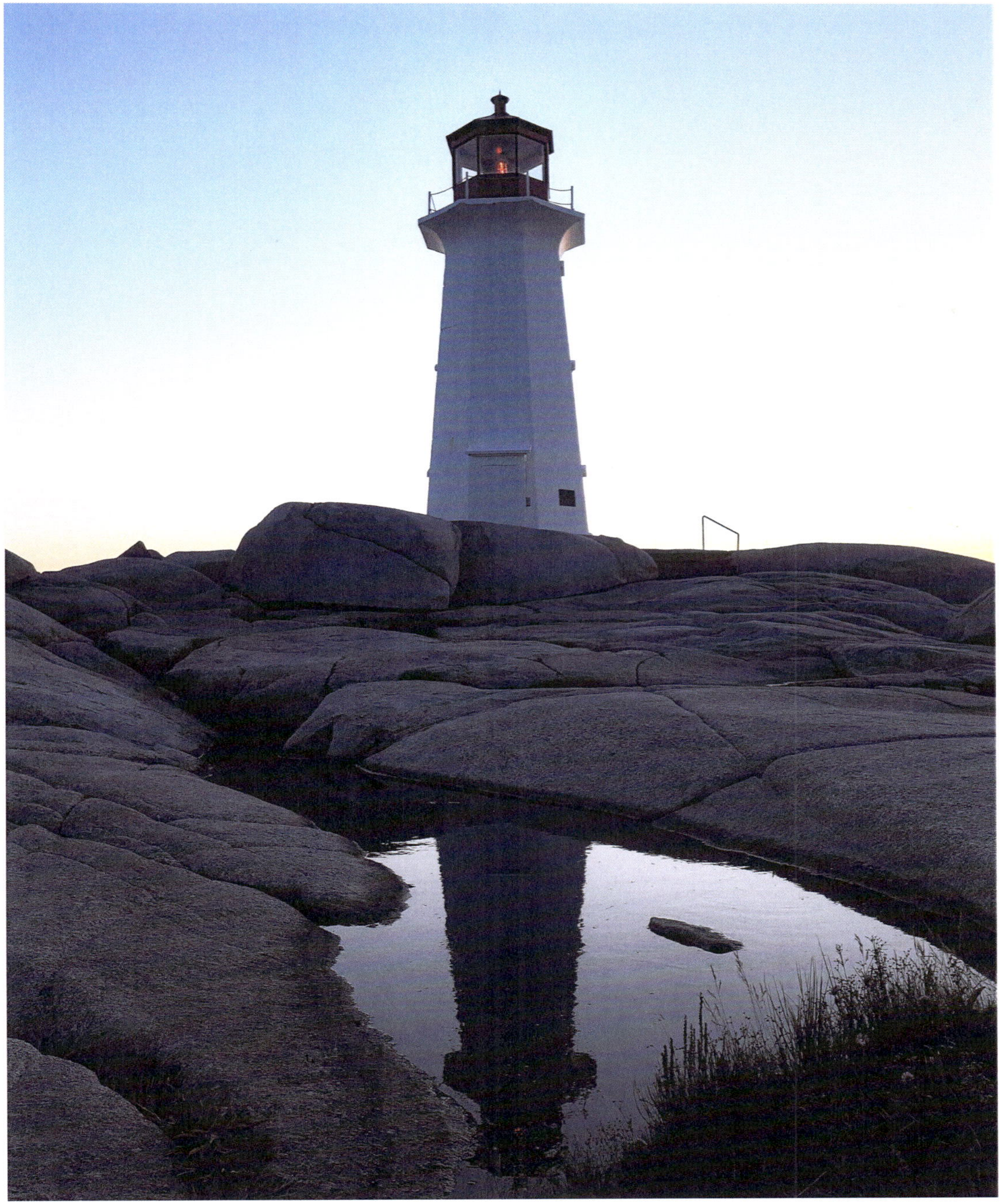

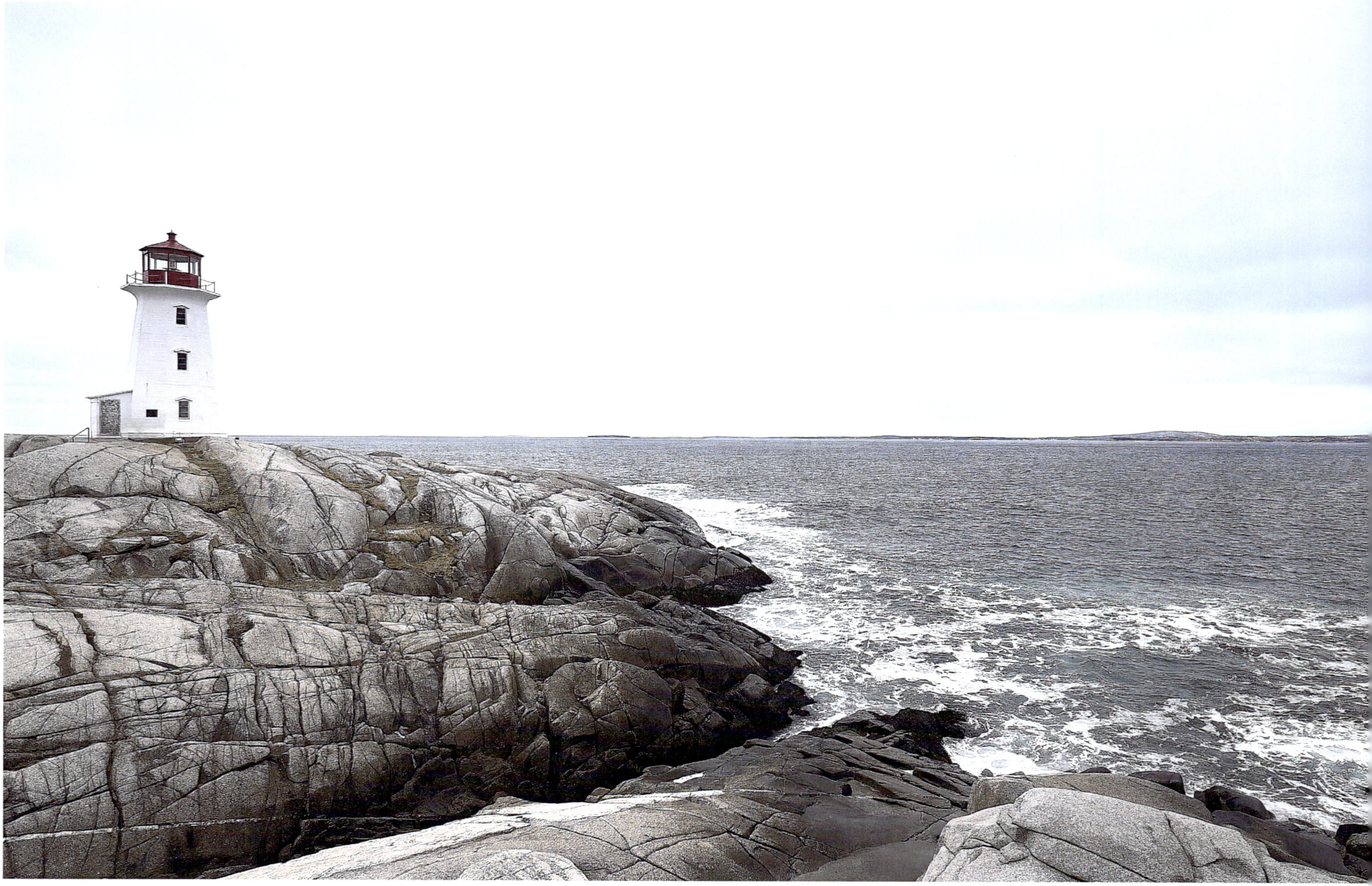

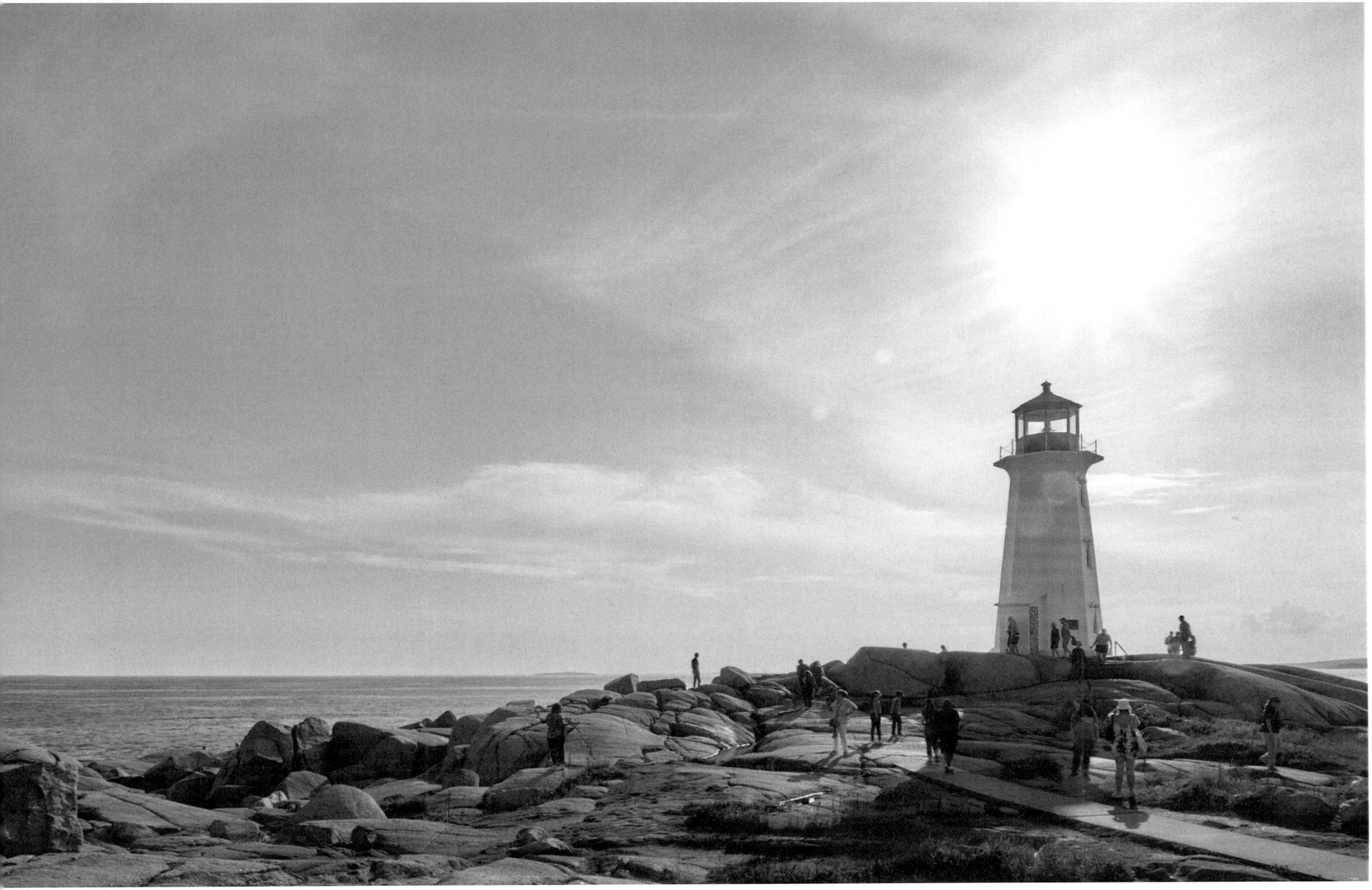

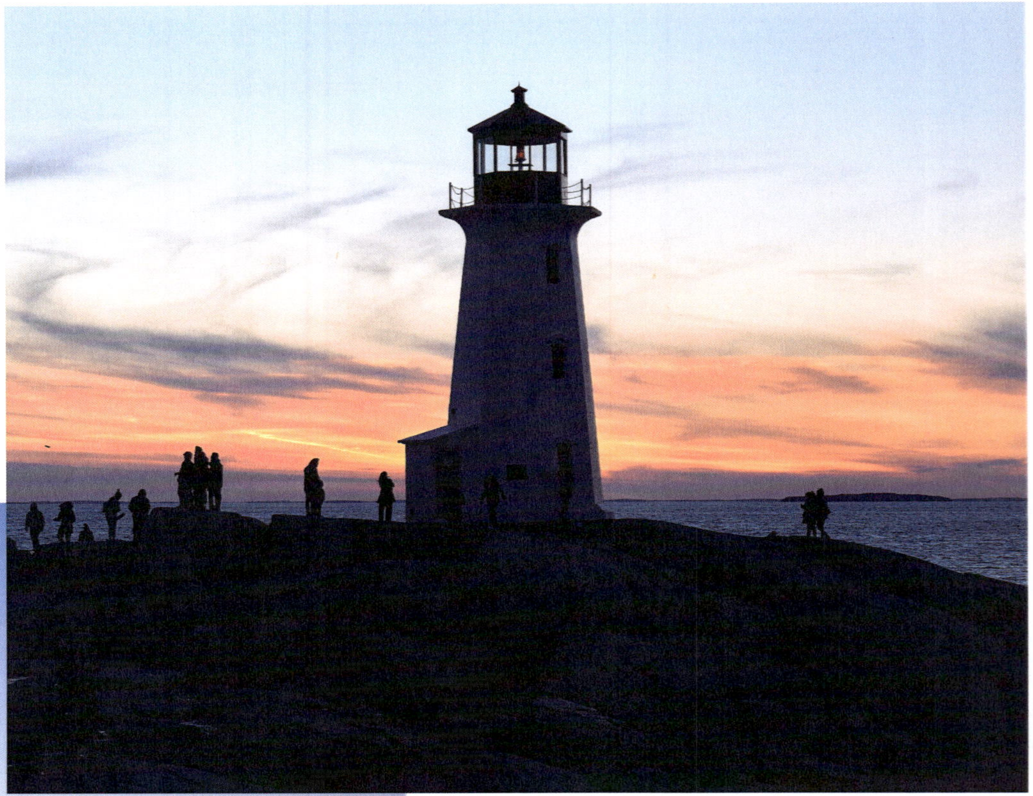

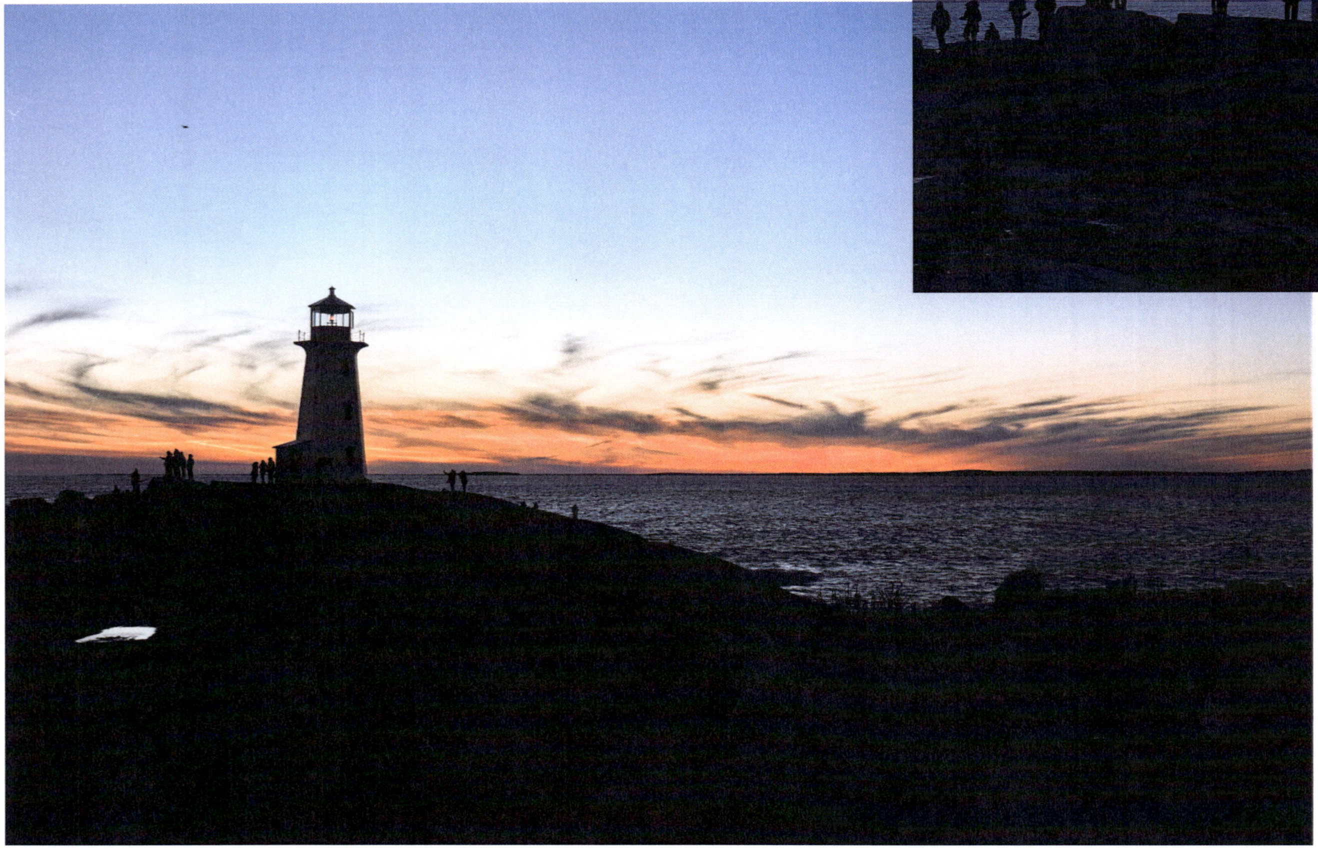

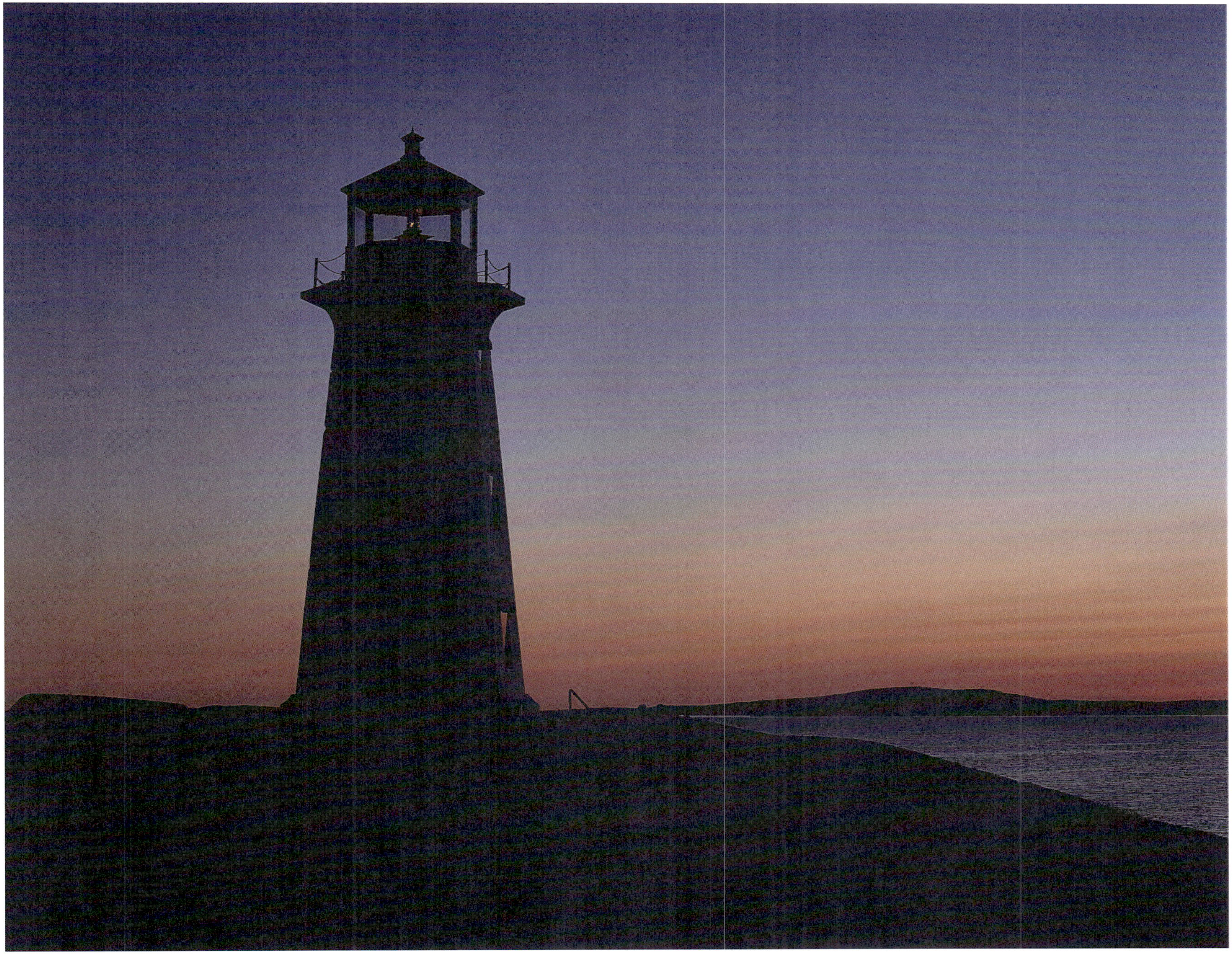

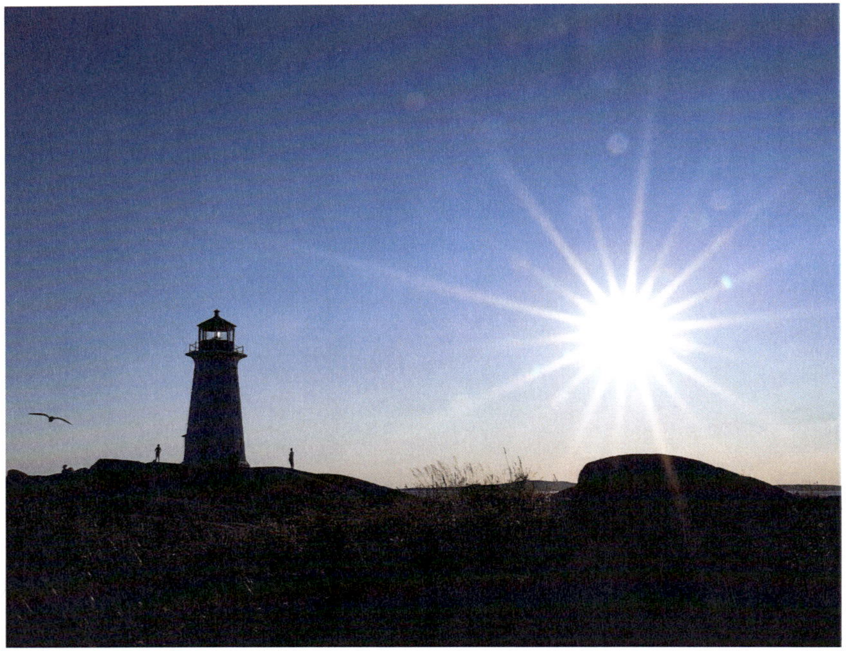

Previous pages: Some of my favourite shots of the iconic lighthouse

This page: The lighthouse at sunset, the neighbouring fishing village, and the famous Sou'Wester Restaurant and Gift Shop

Opposite page: The village surrounding the cove

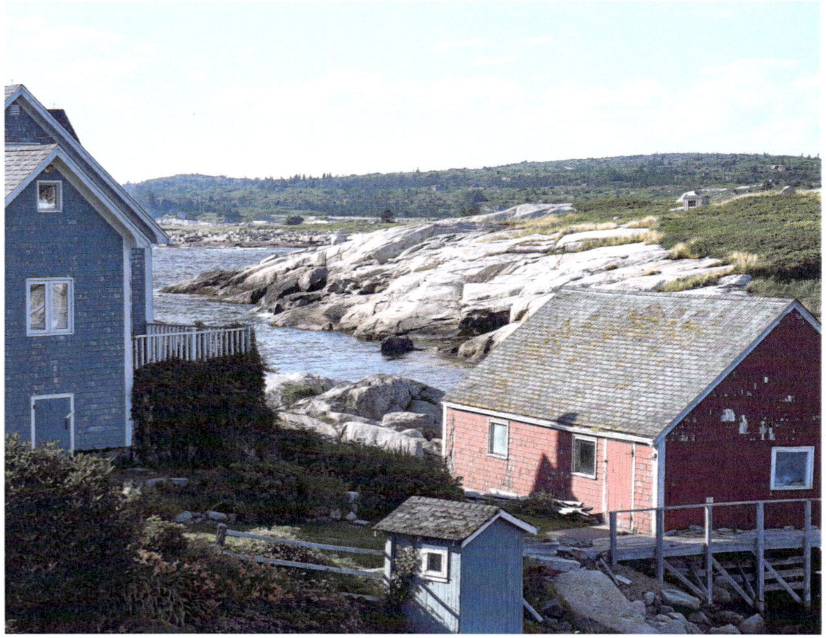

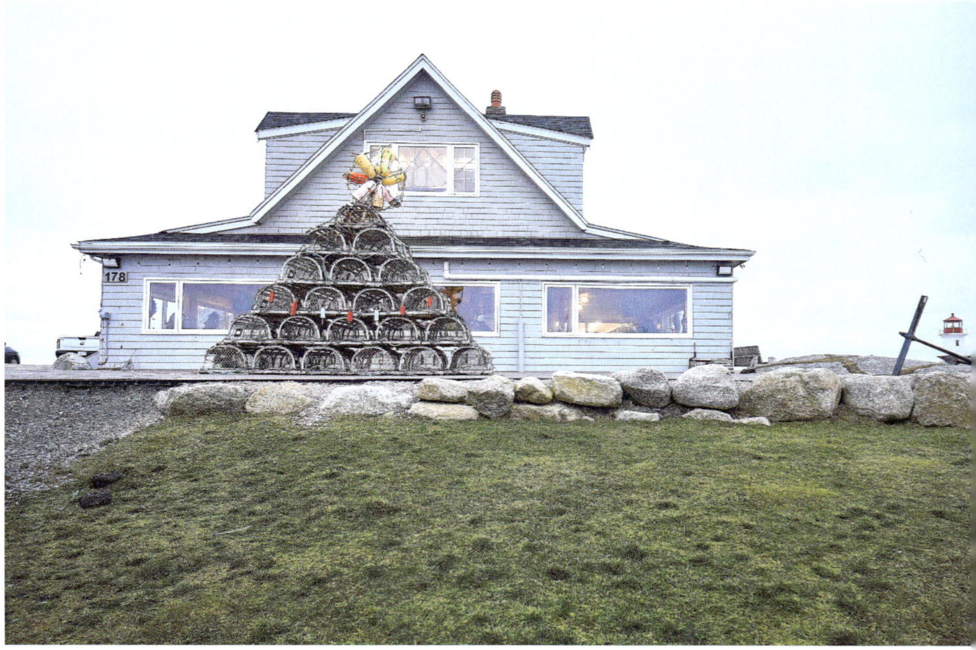

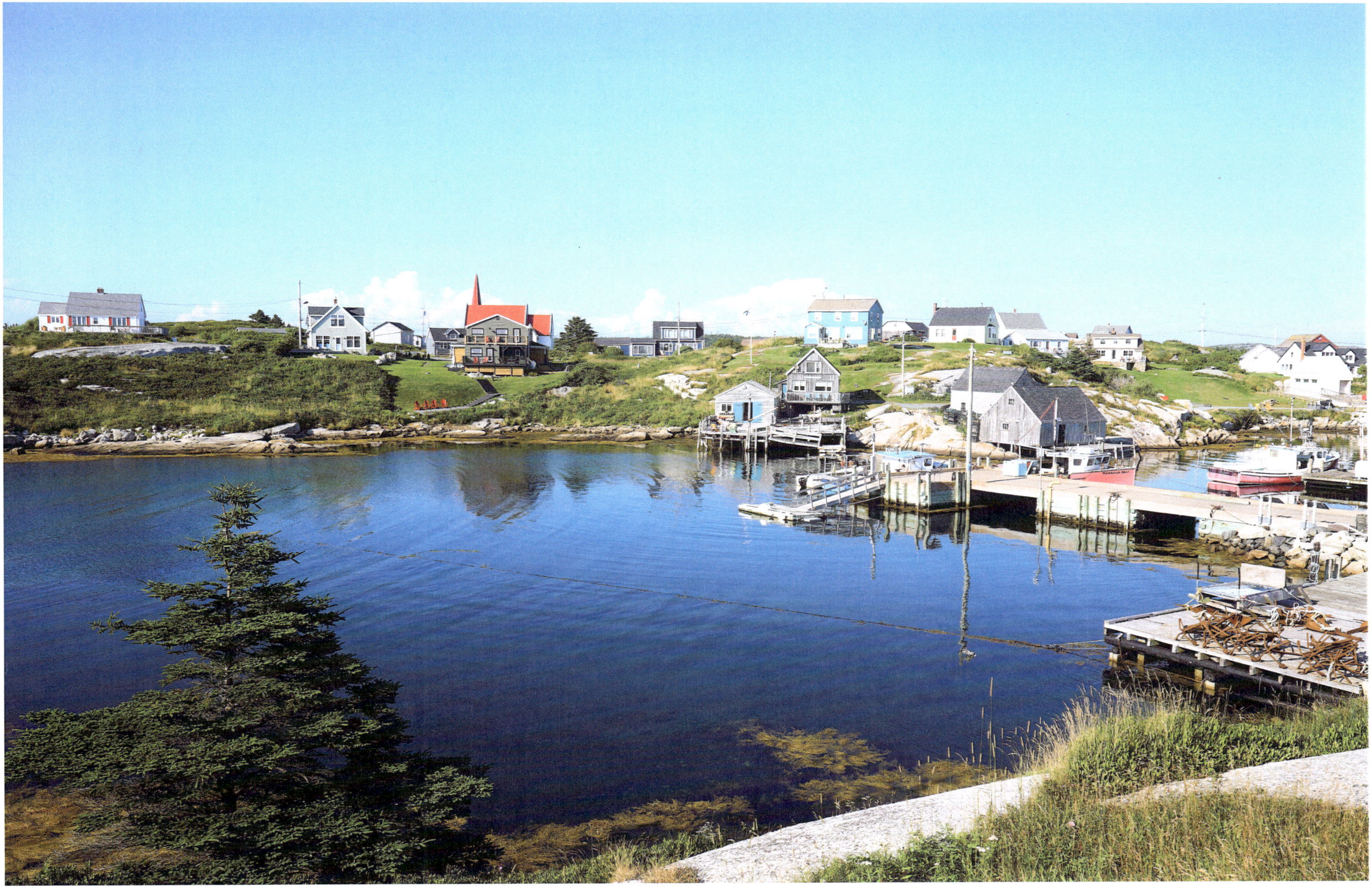

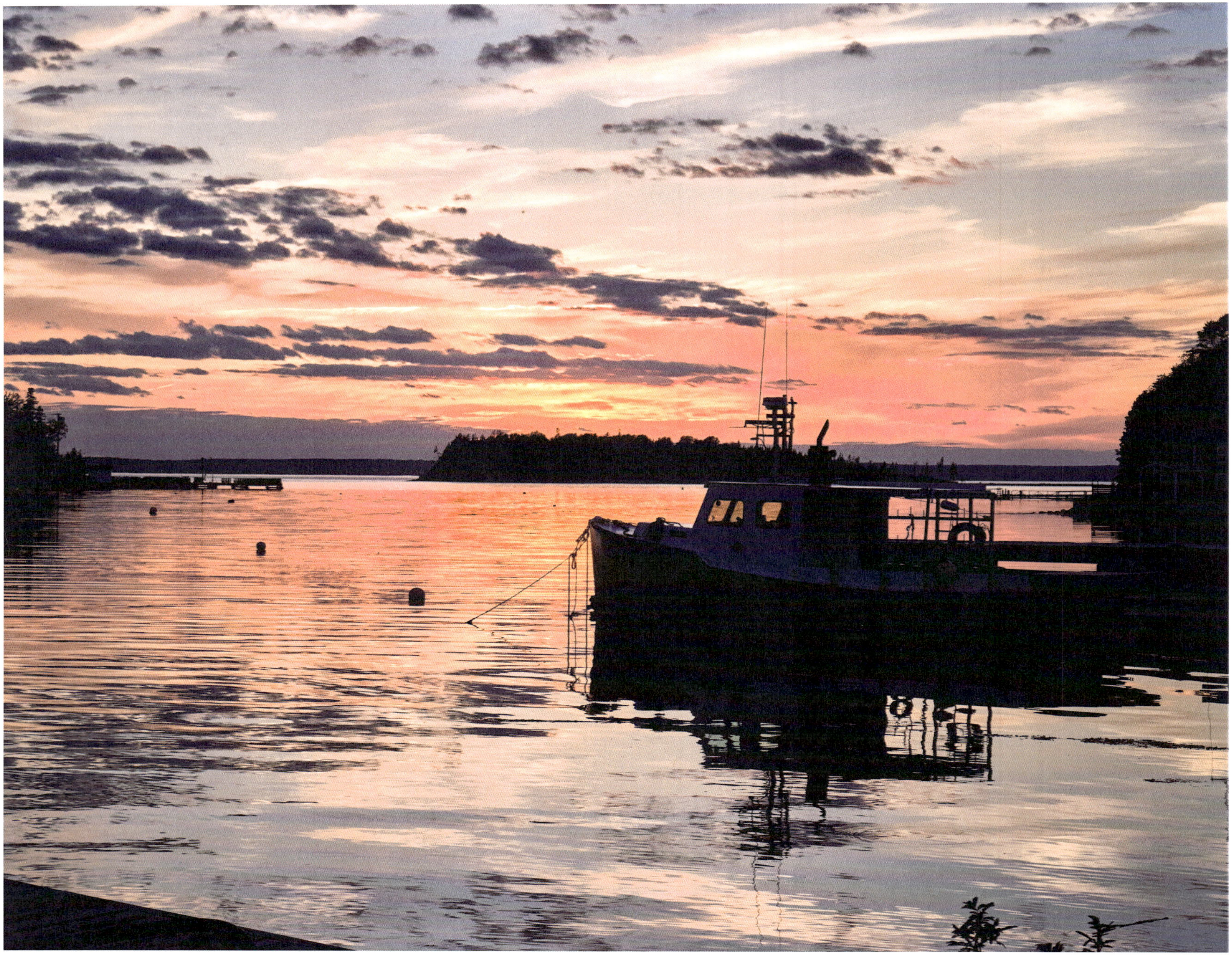

Sunset on St. Margaret's Bay

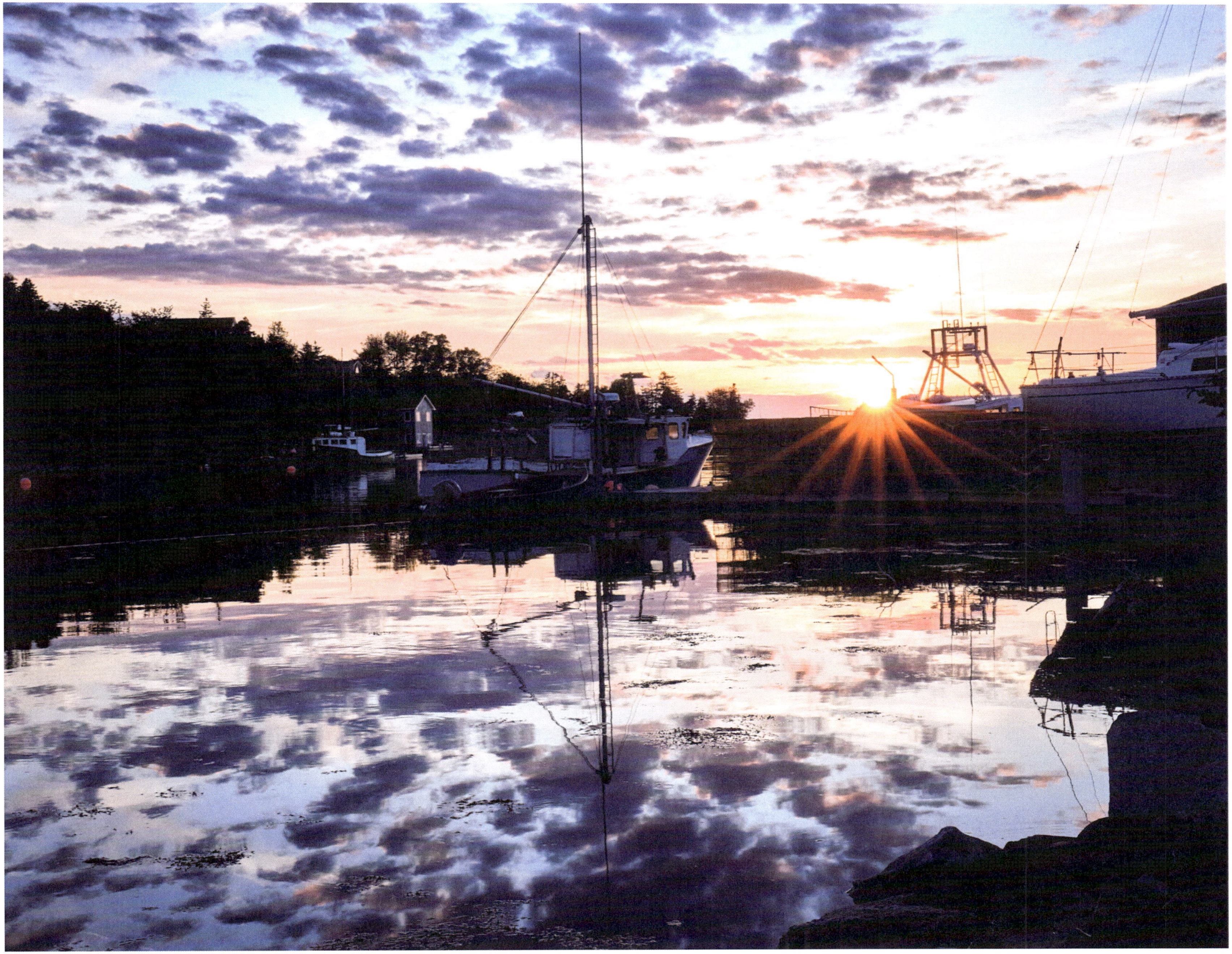

Chapter 4
Privateers & The Picturesque - The South Shore

Someone once told me that the South Shore was basically built for postcards. I can't really argue with that. From the mysteries of Oak Island, to the picturesque Mahone Bay, to the iconic Lunenburg & the Bluenose II, to the Privateer past of Liverpool, this area of Nova Scotia offers enough to keep you busy exploring for as long as you like.

There's a reason that so many movies and TV shows are filmed down here - you've probably seen some without realizing it! The South Shore offers a ton of natural beauty, and just enough of that quintessential seaside town that both the big screen and the small screen love to feature.

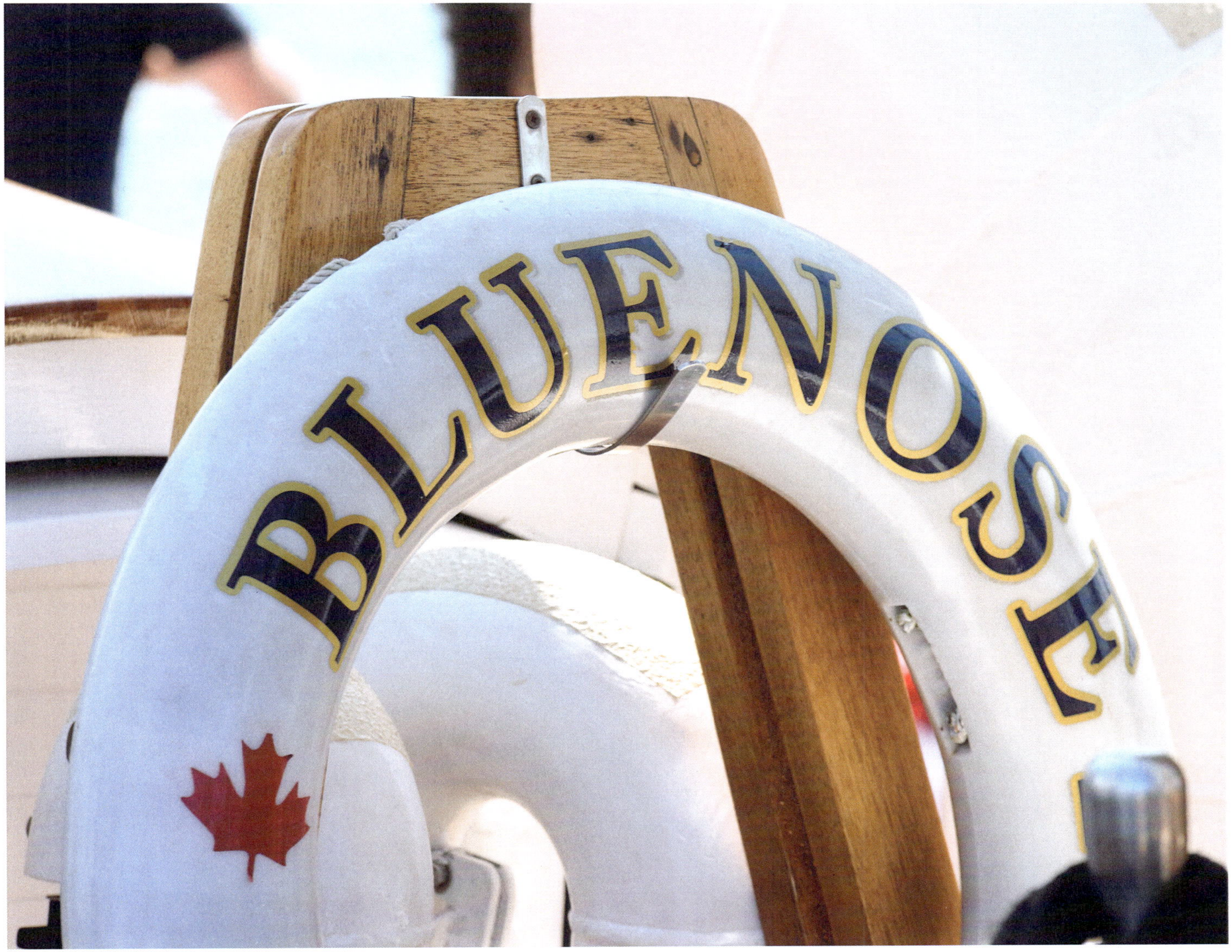

Previous page:

Life ring from the
Bluenose II

This page:

Sunset over the
shore near
Oak Island

Opposite page:

Mahone Bay

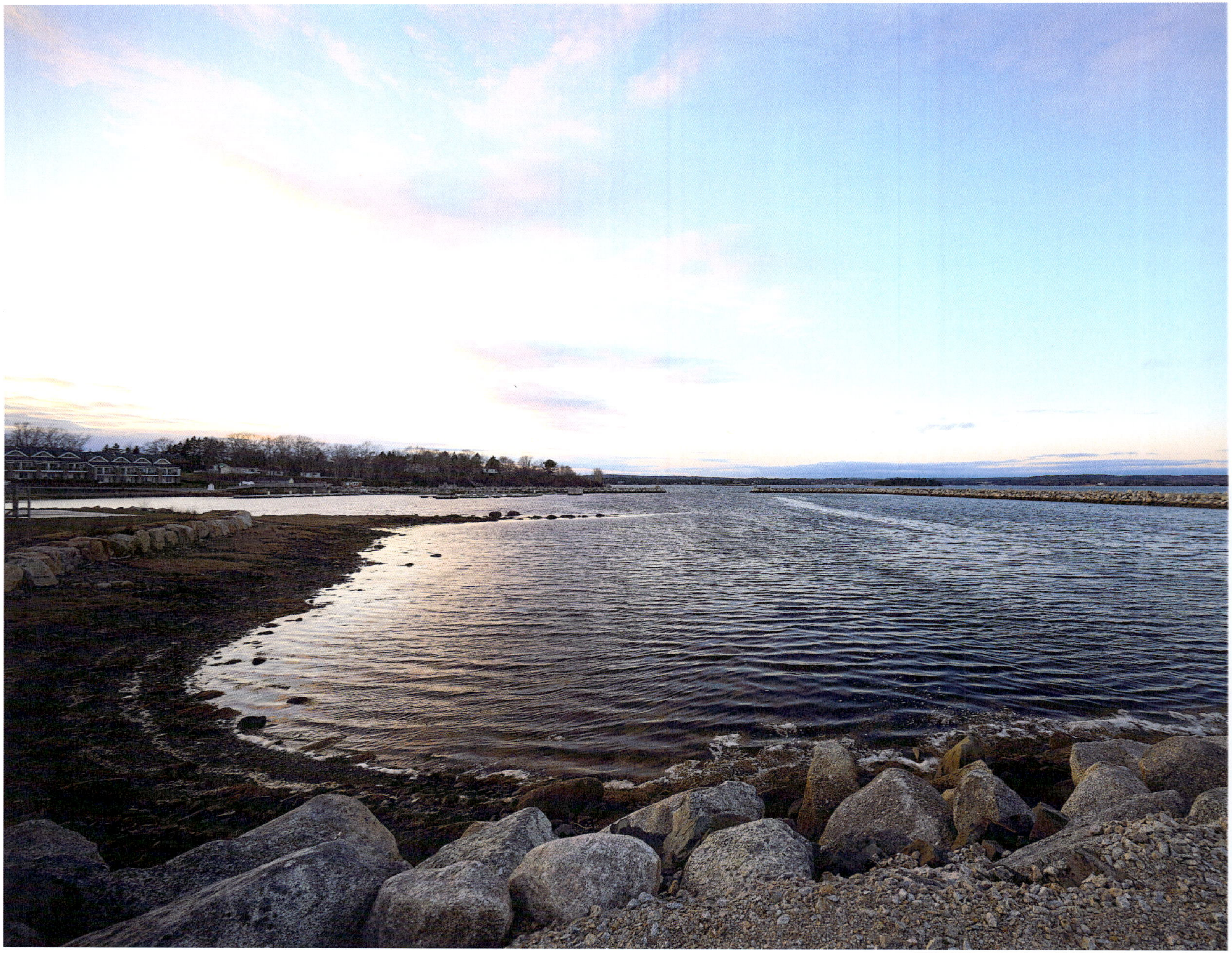

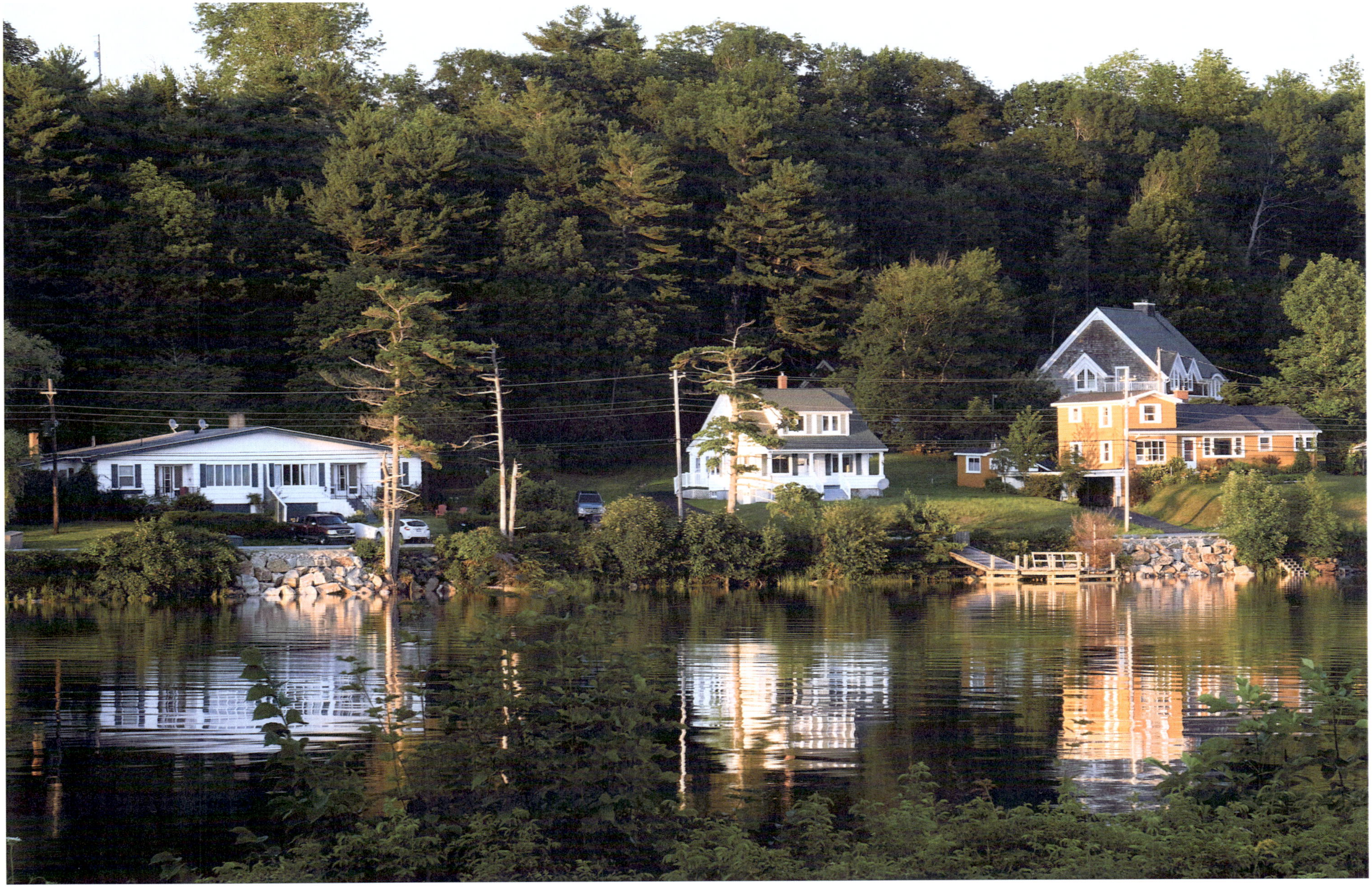

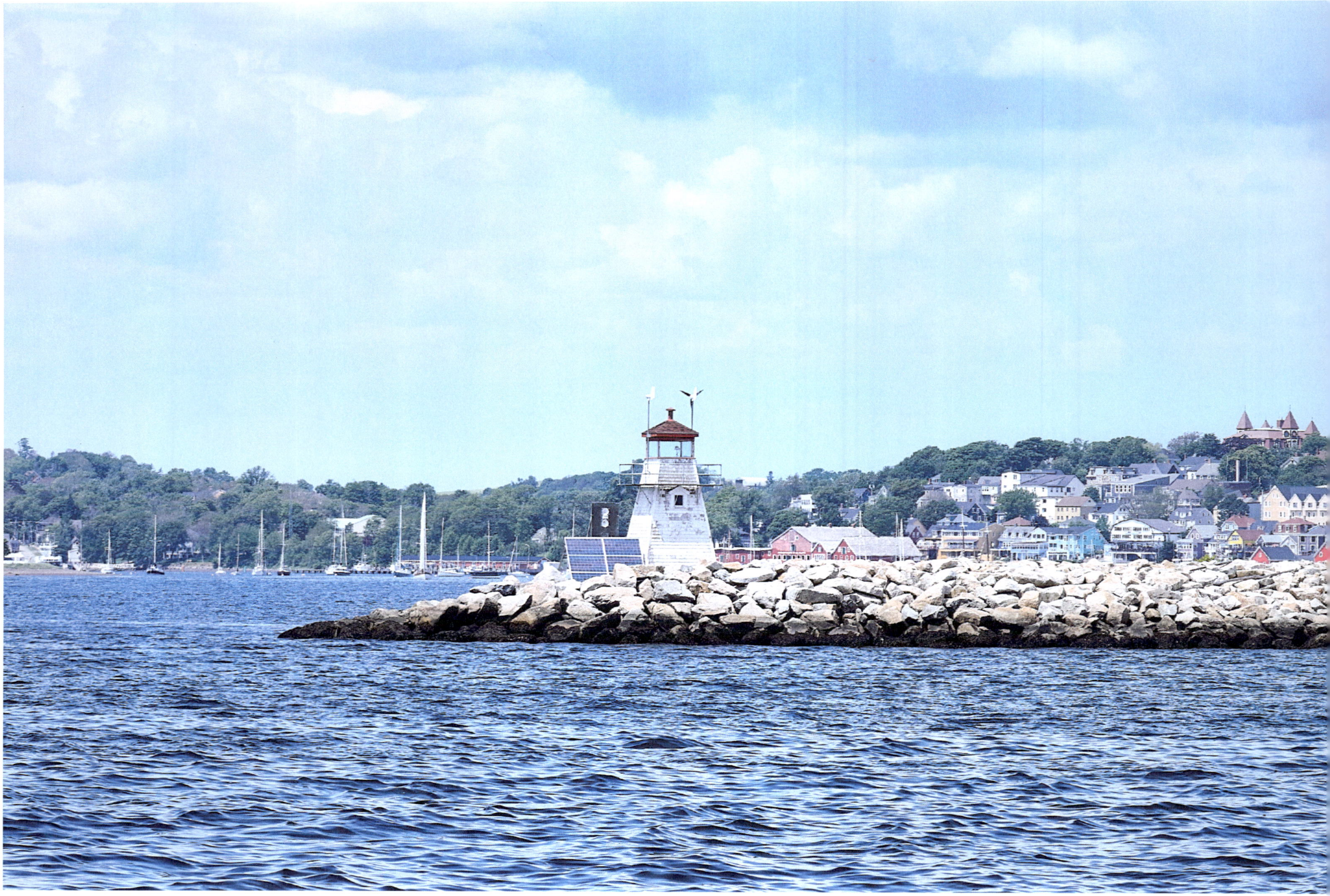

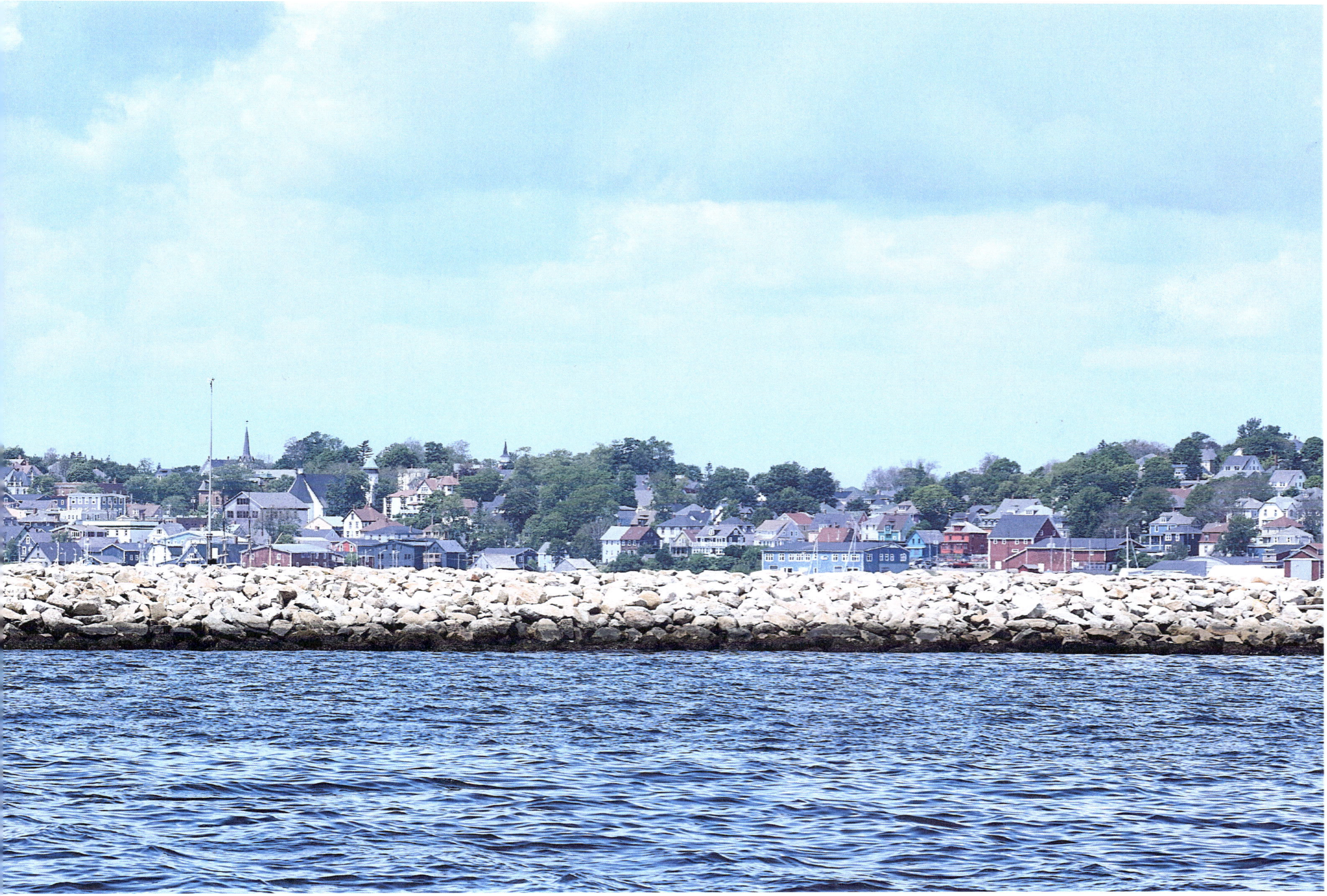

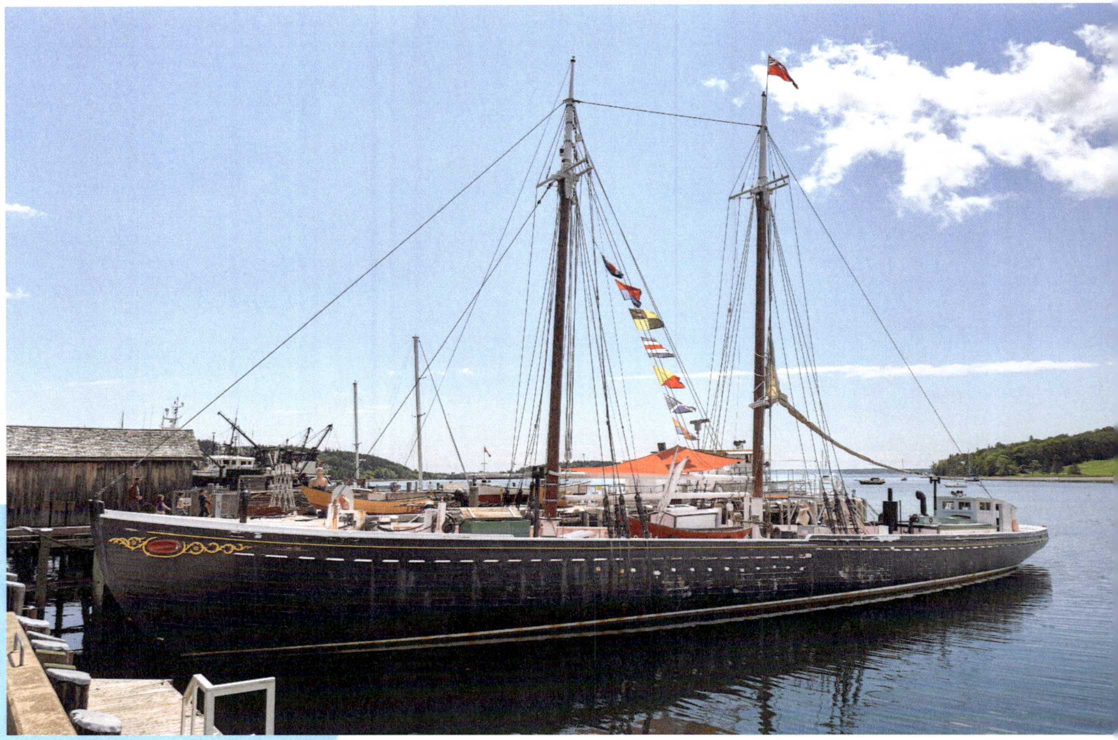

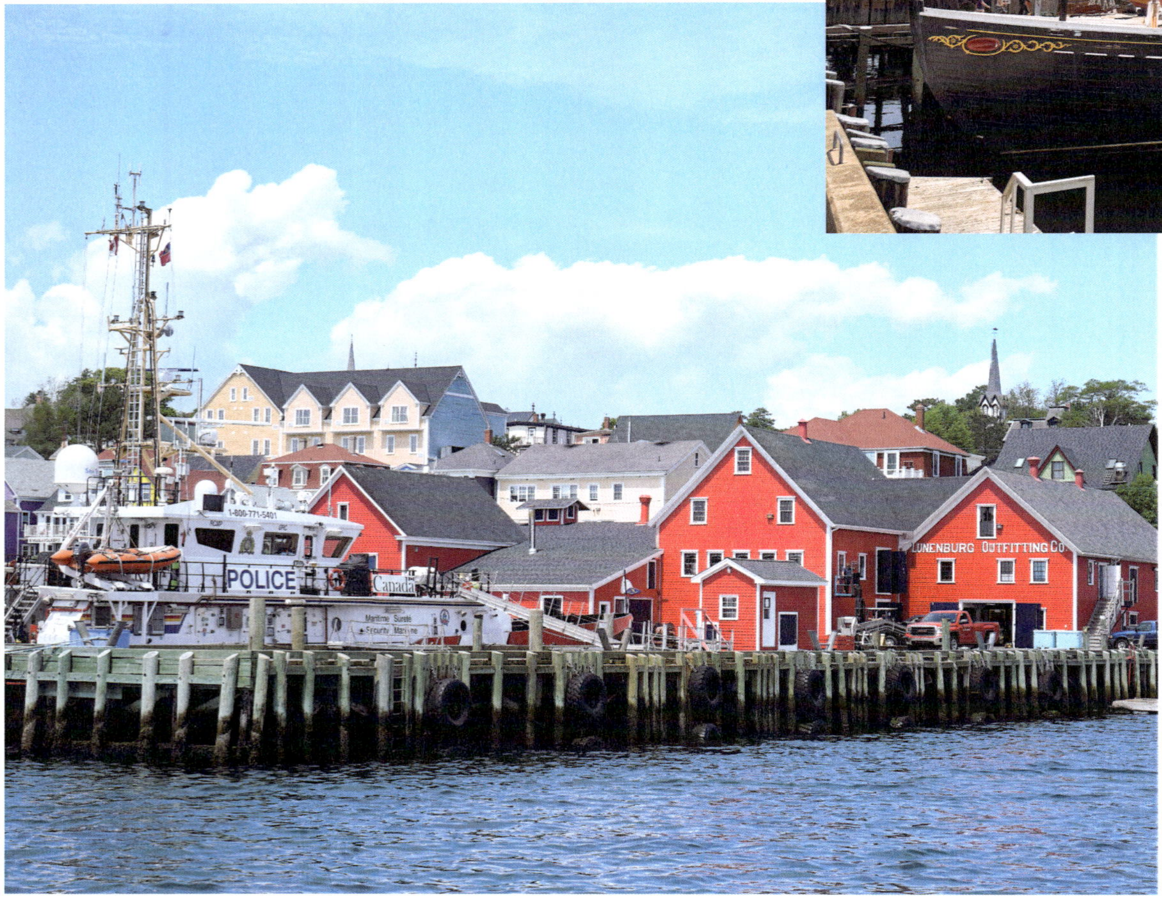

Previous pages: Looking toward Lunenburg

This page: Lunenburg Waterfront

Opposite page: The main mast from the Bluenose II

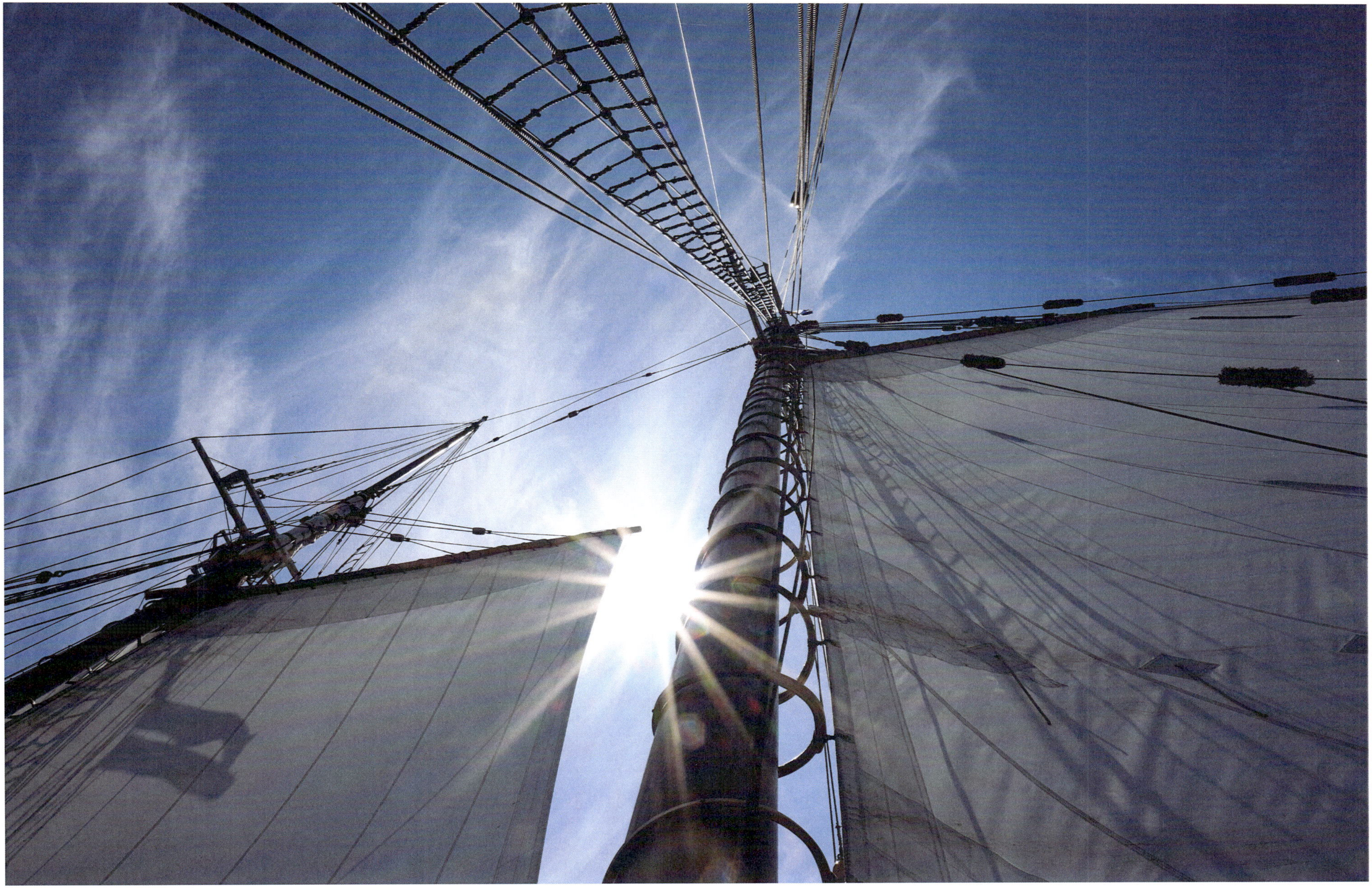

This page:

White Point Resort
Main building

Opposite page:

Waves crashing on
the rocks at
White Point

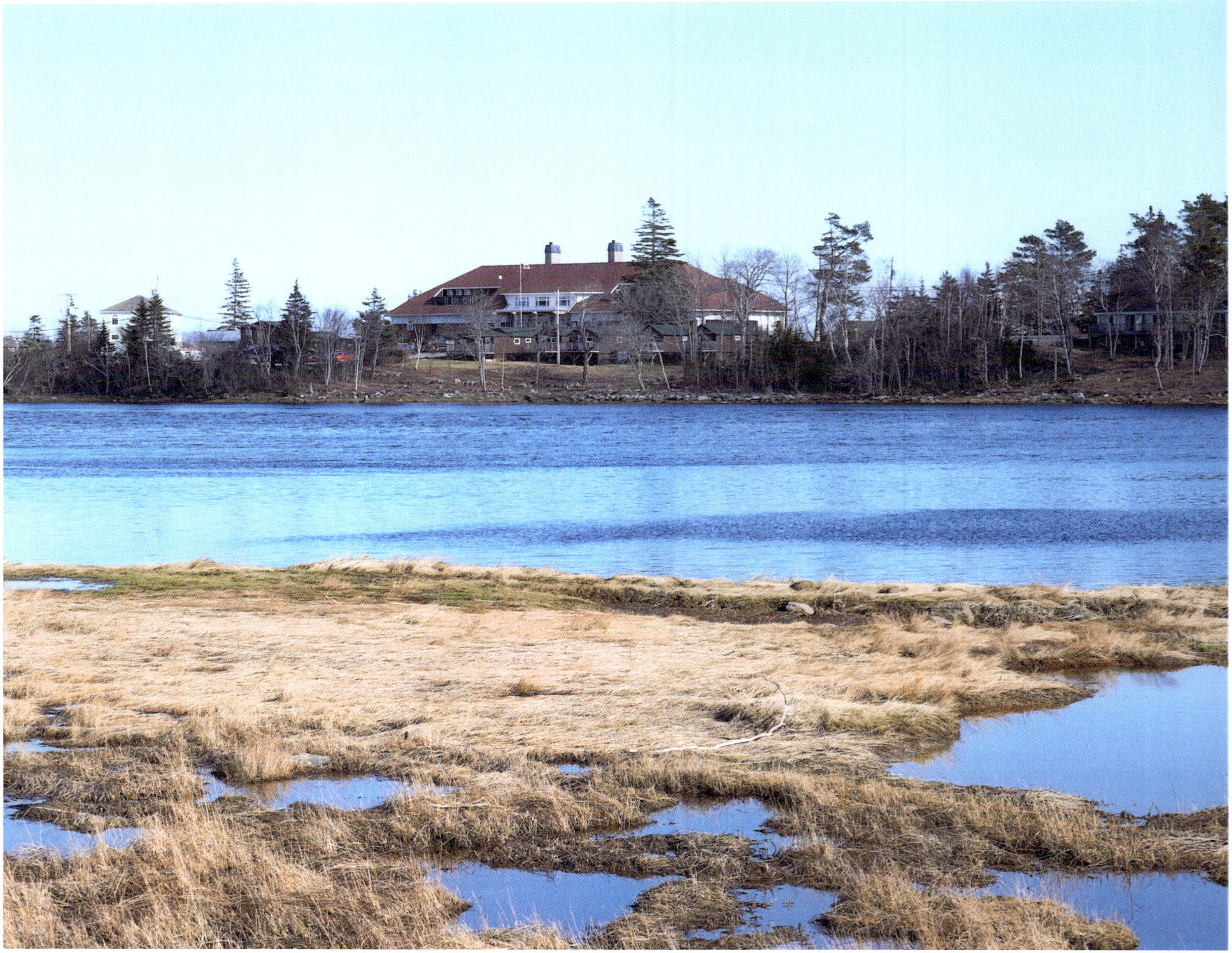

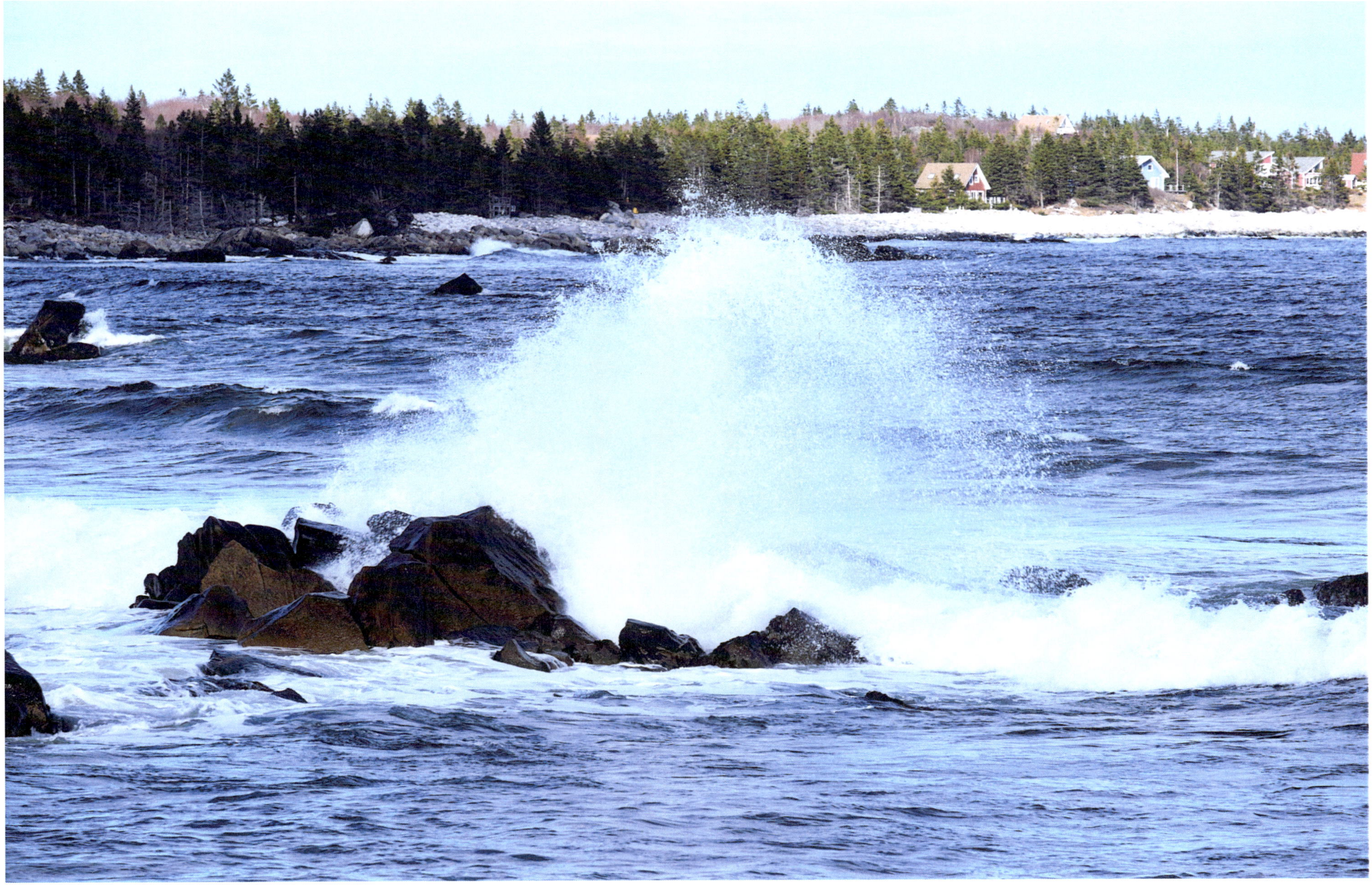

The mast in Liverpool Harbour. Liverpool was, at one point, considered the Privateer capital of North America. The town is rife with history that includes ship building, rum running, and it celebrates Privateer Days annually

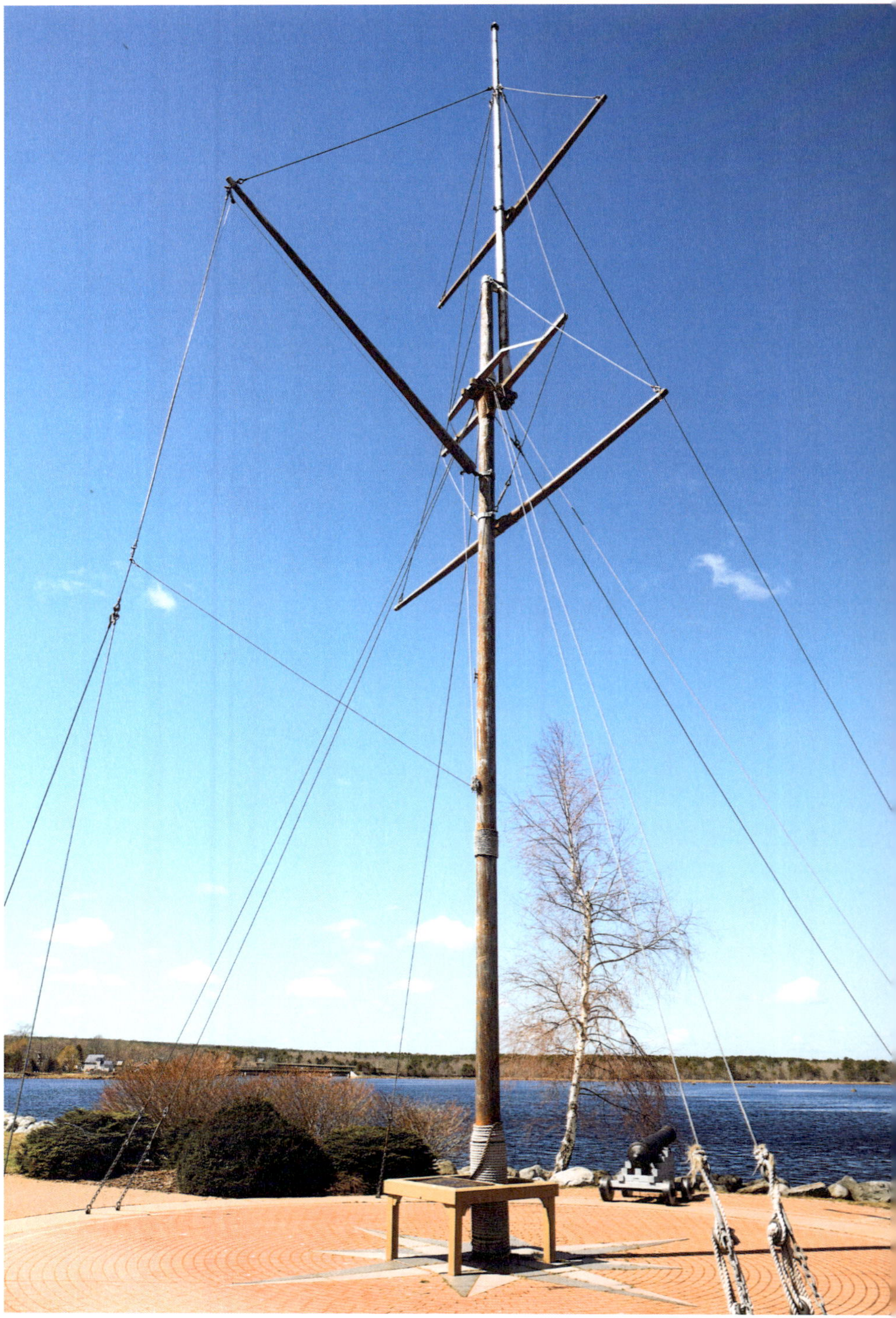

Chapter 5
Eat, Drink & Be Merry - The Annapolis Valley

The Annapolis Valley could be described as the heartland of Nova Scotia. Vineyards and farms span across the countryside, meeting the sea in the world famous Bay of Fundy.

From the heights of Blomidon, you get a breathtaking view of rolling hills on one side, and the Fundy tidal bore on the other. It's hard to paint the area with one brush as far as its landscapes because there's so much variety. Stretching from the Minas Basin to the Digby Neck, the Valley features an amazing assortment of wineries, distilleries, restaurants, parklands, and is home to Acadia University.

Note: Digby was originally going to get its own chapter, but, alas, those photos are part of the hundreds of missing photos from my travels (along with many South Shore photos). Hopefully they'll be found for a new edition!

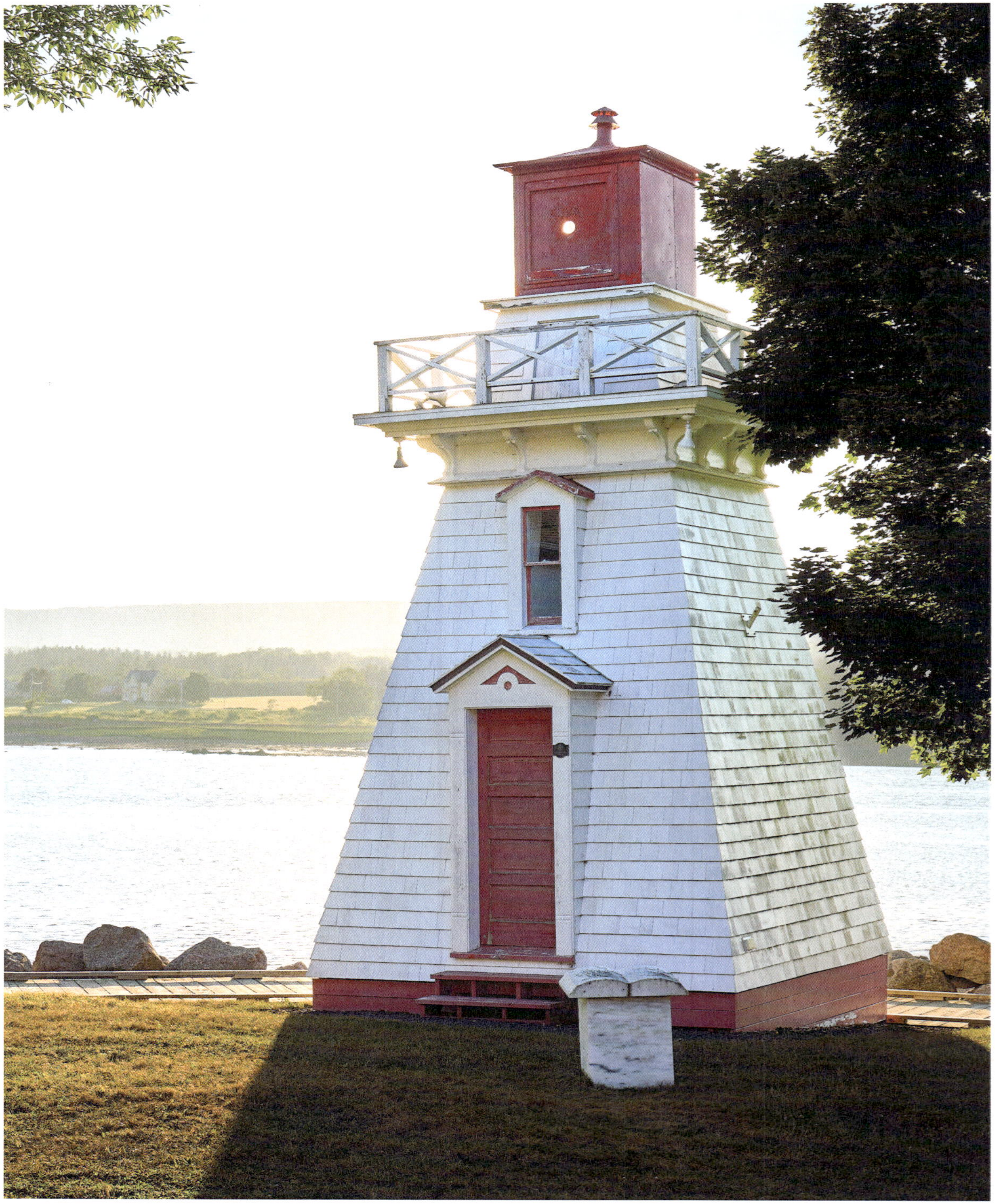

Lighthouse in Annapolis Royal

Opposite page: Canon from the old fortress of Annapolis Royal

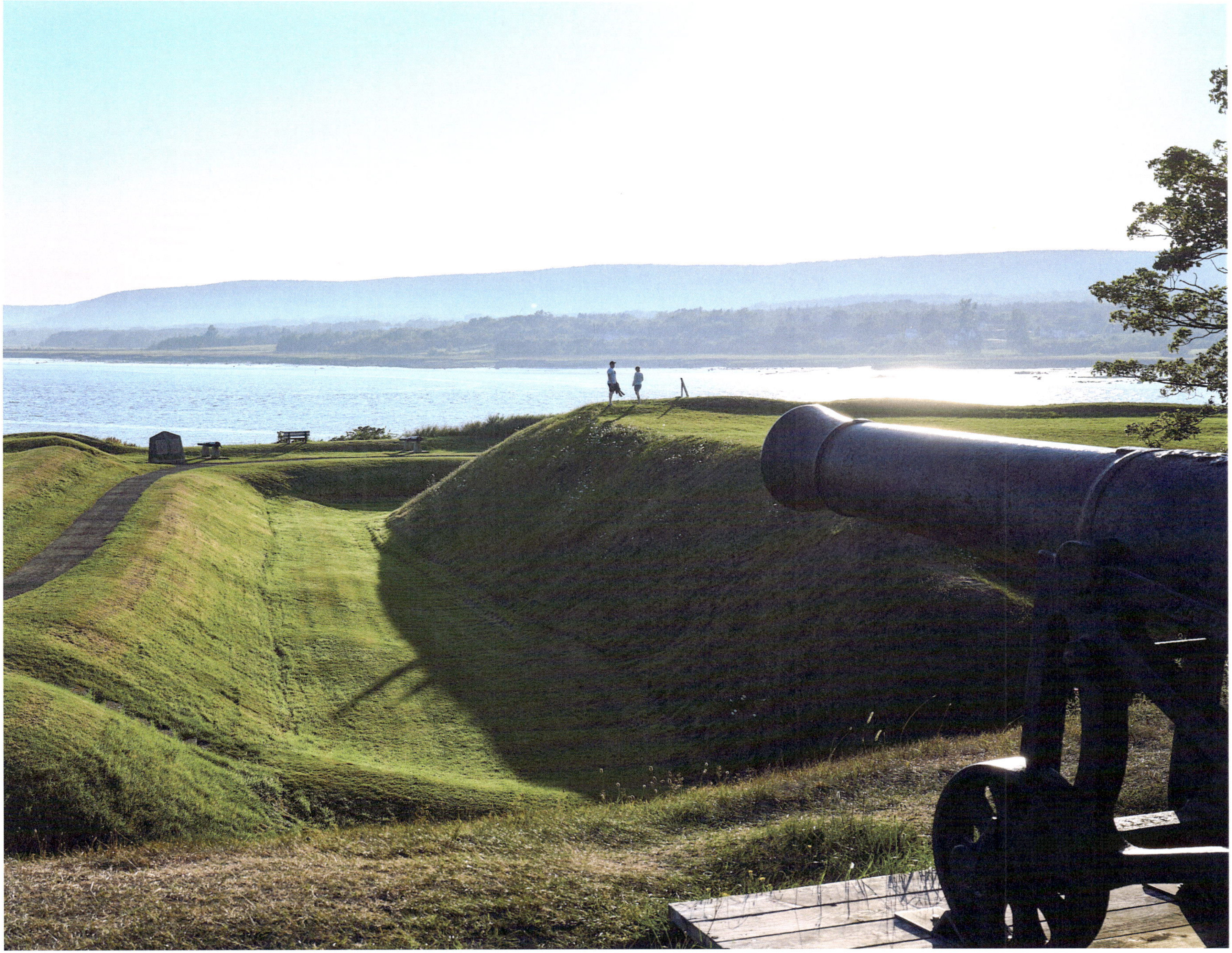

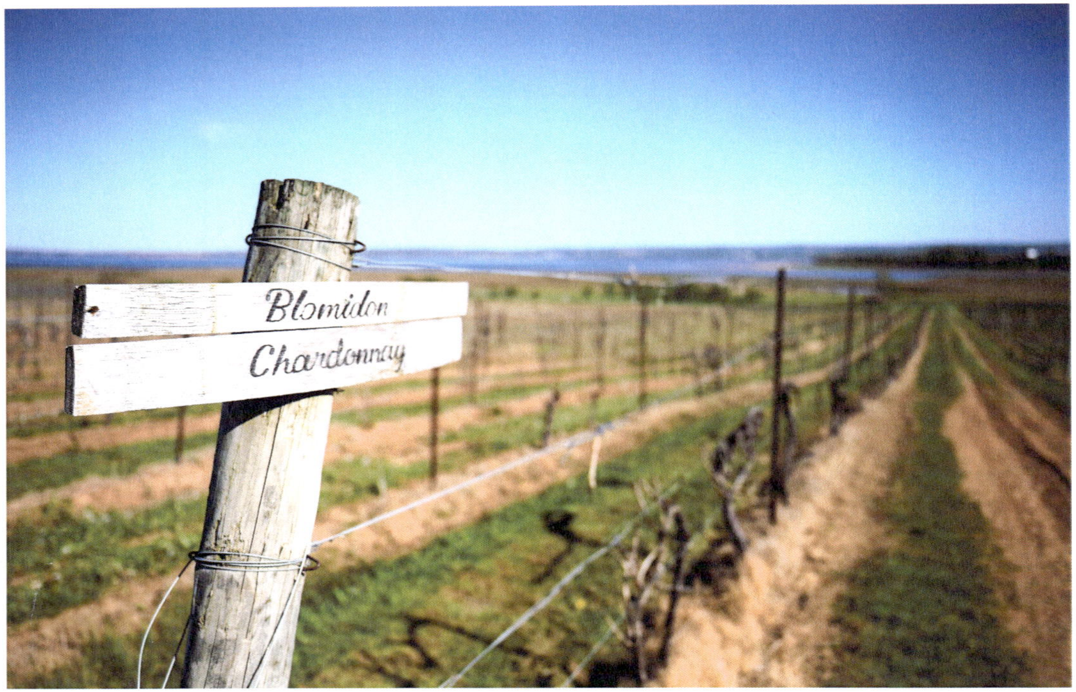

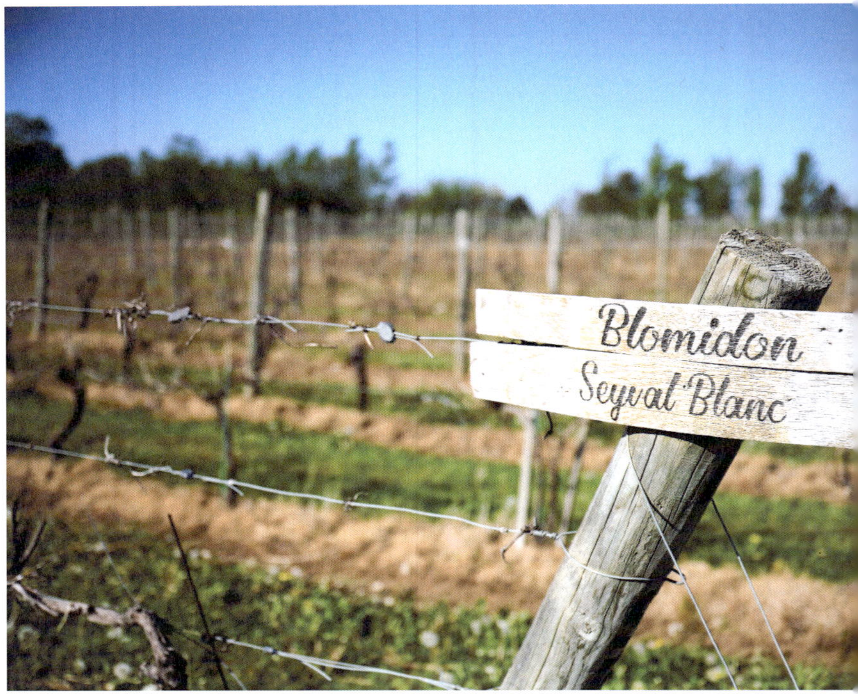

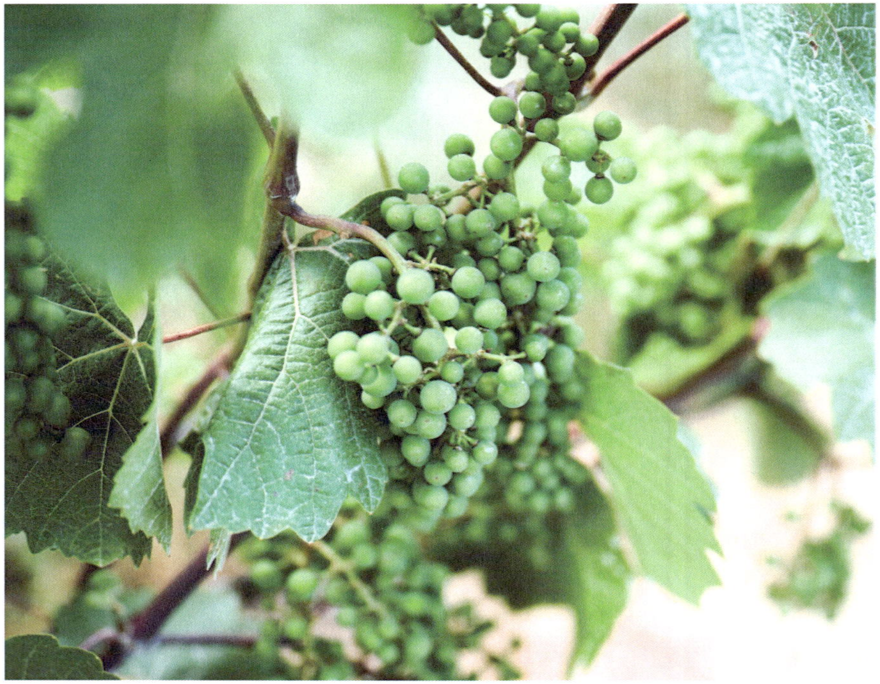

Blomidon Winery

Opposite page:
Luckett Vineyards
with Blomidon Provincial Park
on the horizon

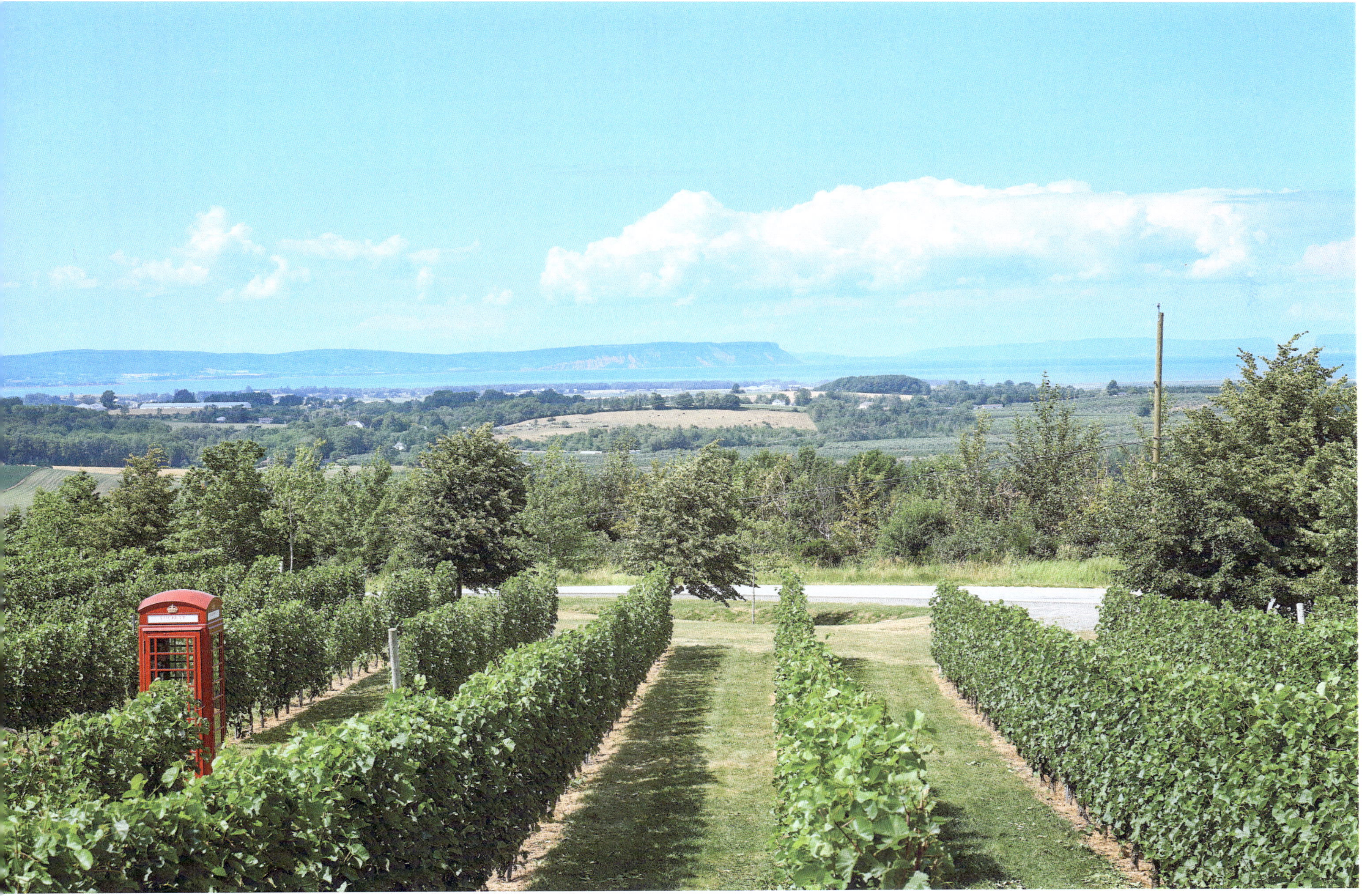

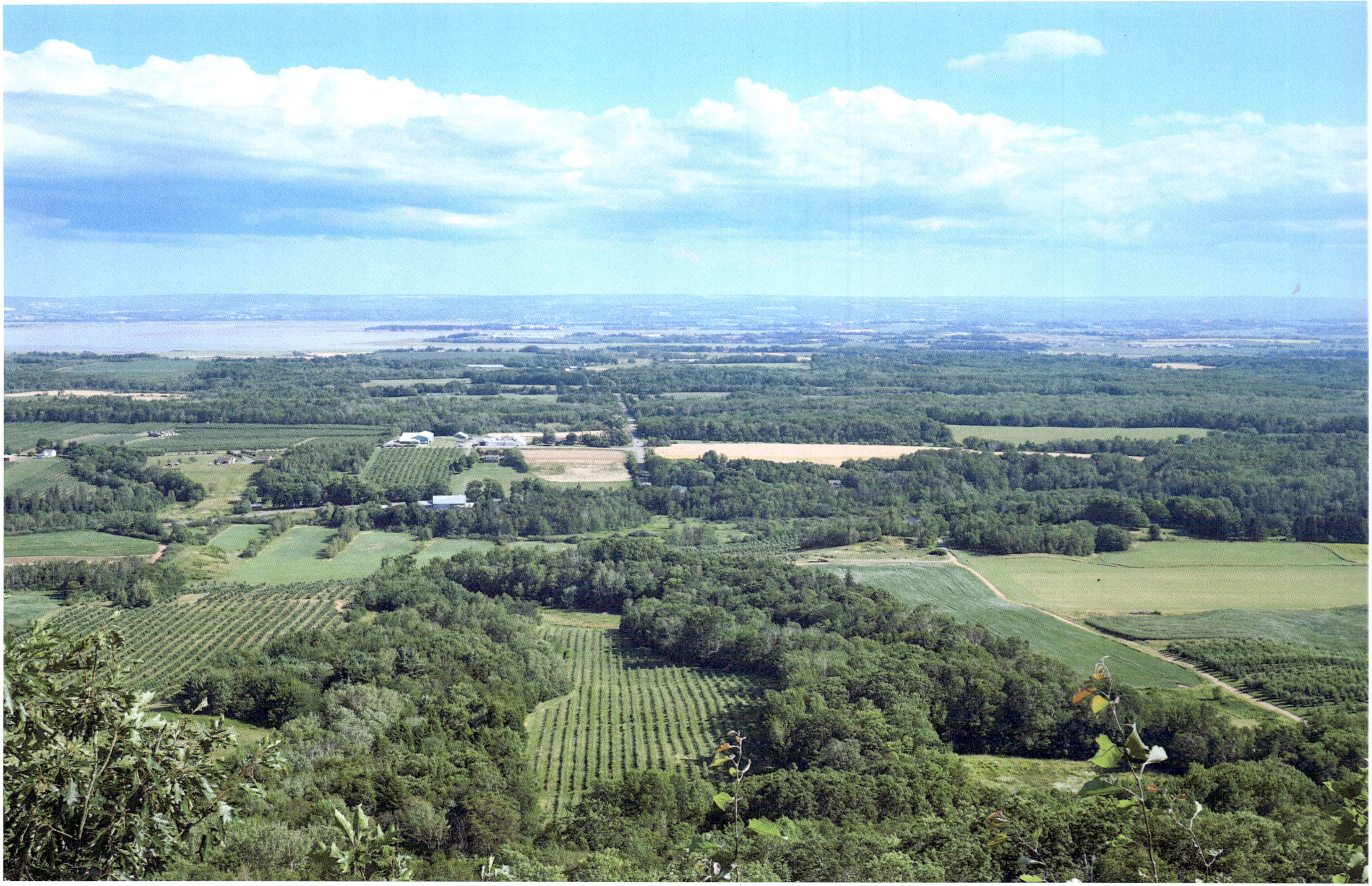

The rolling hills and windswept shores of the Annapolis Valley

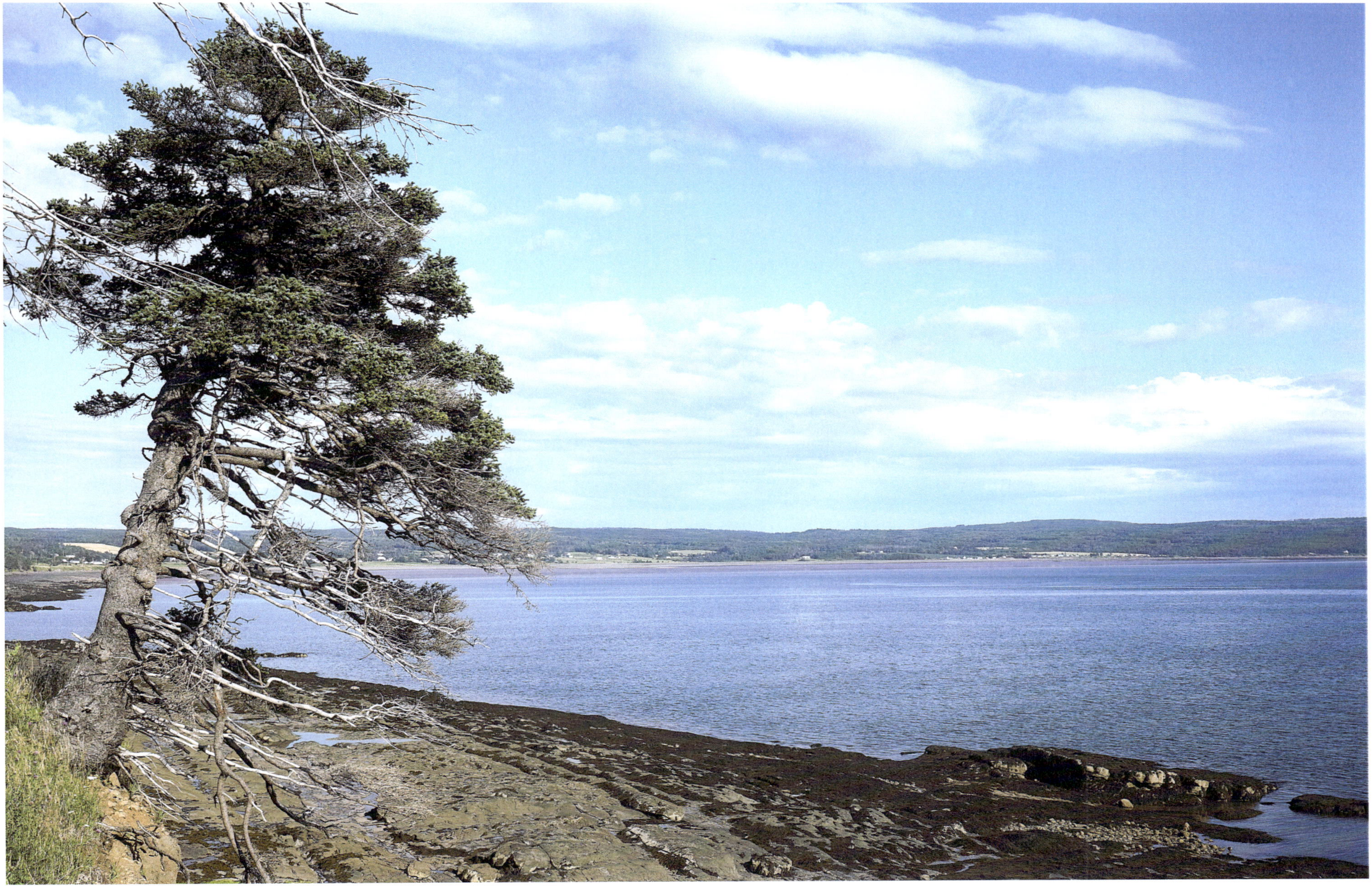

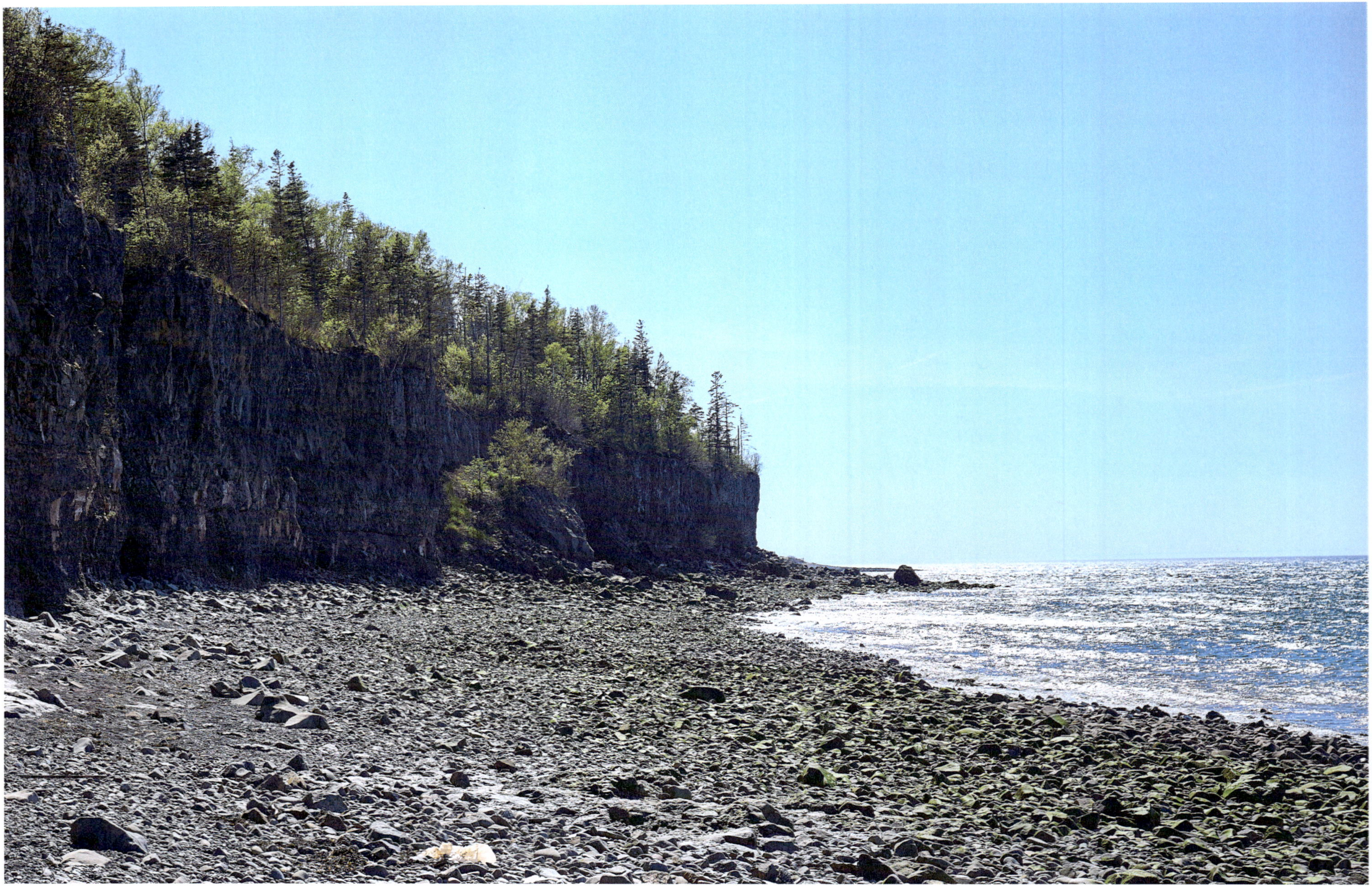

The shore and boat-launch of Hall's Harbour at low tide

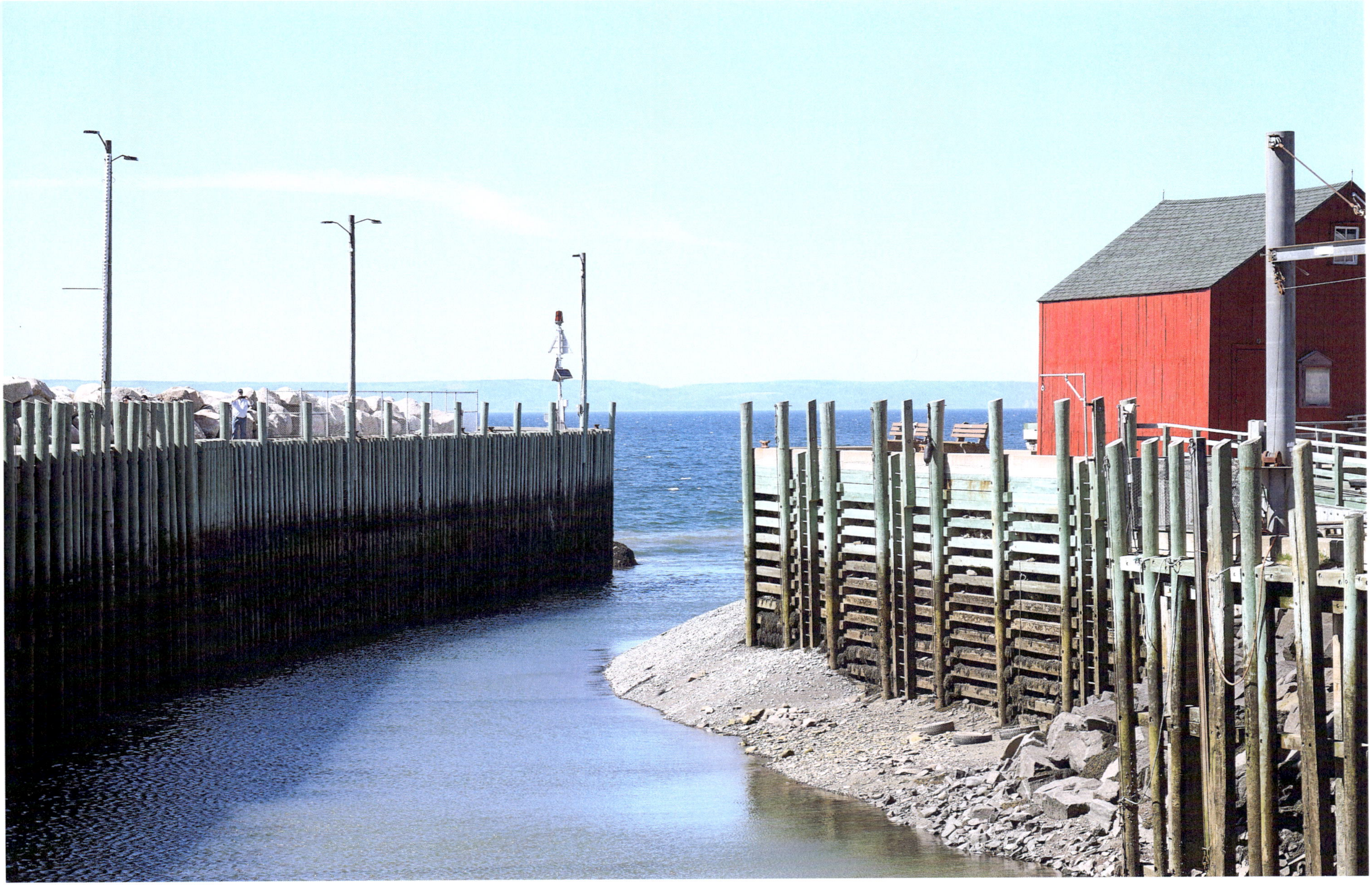

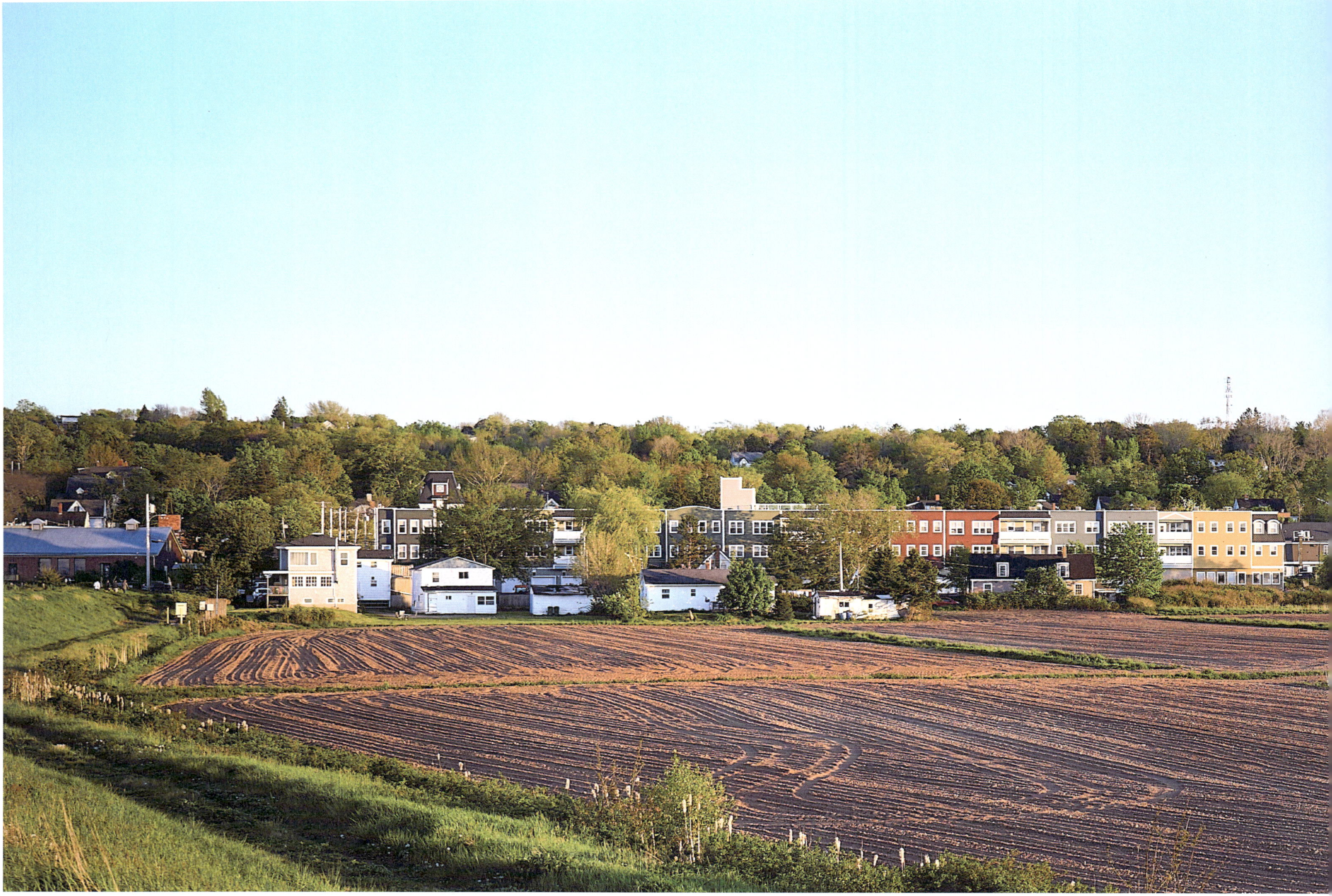

Wolfville and Acadia University

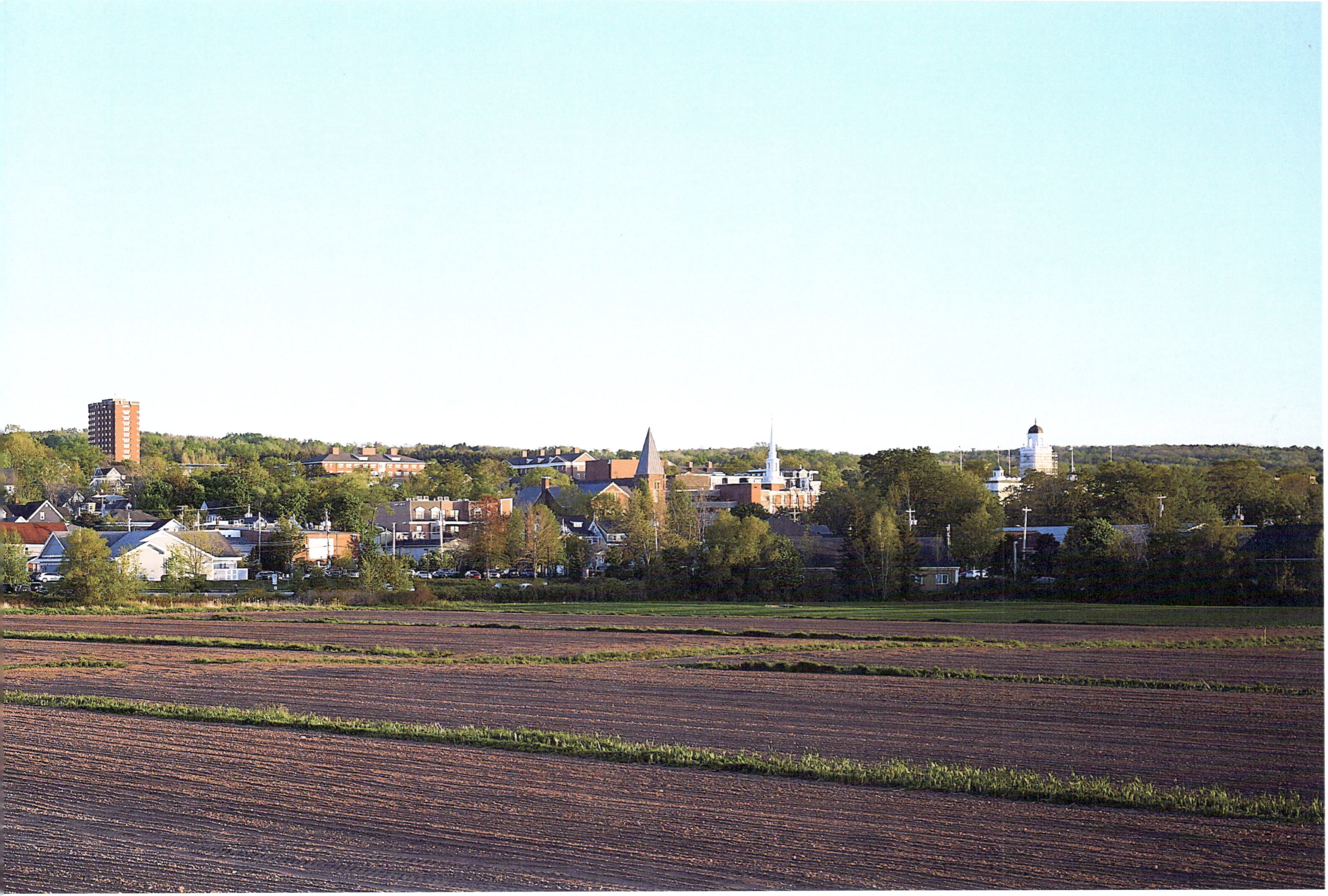

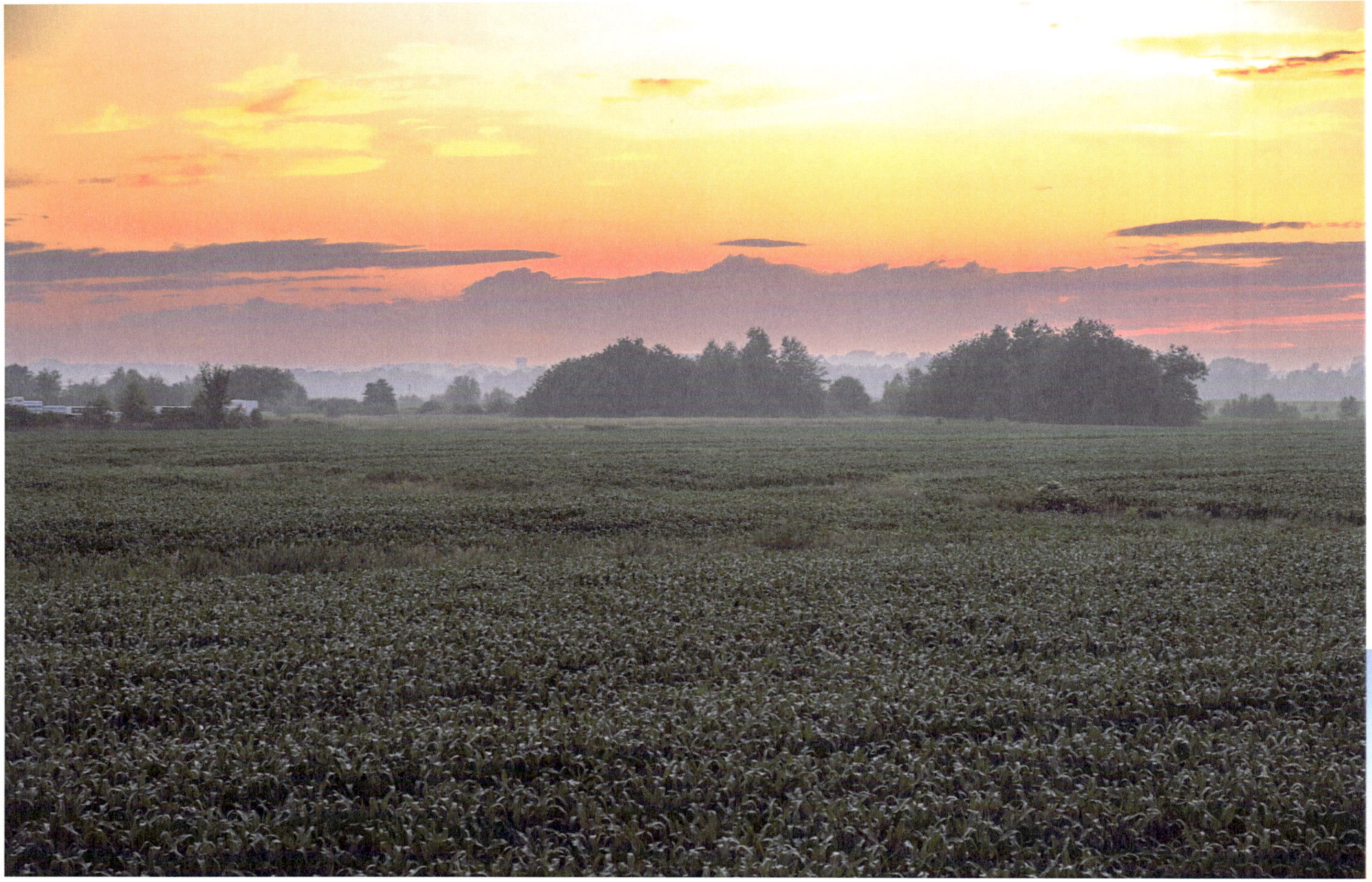

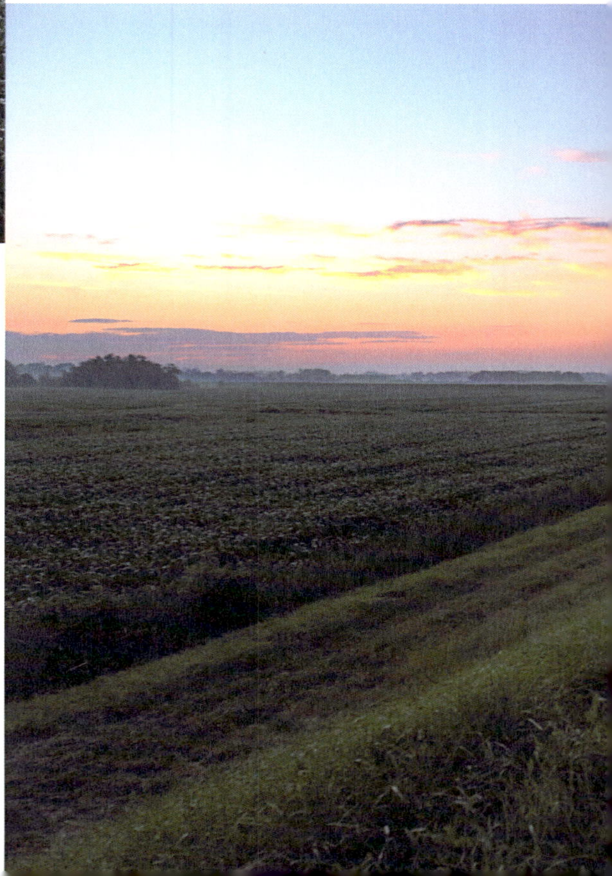

Sunset over Wolfville

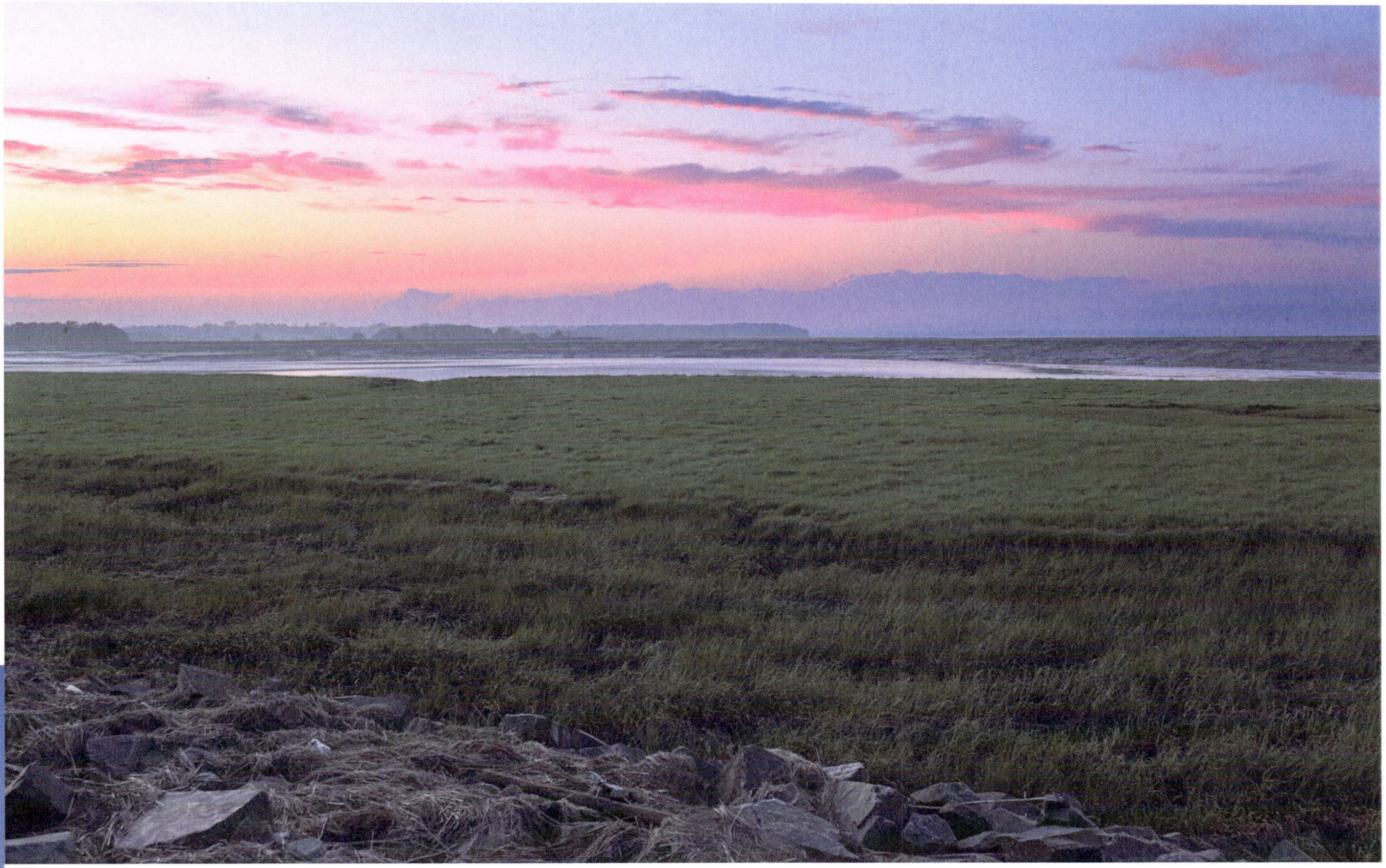

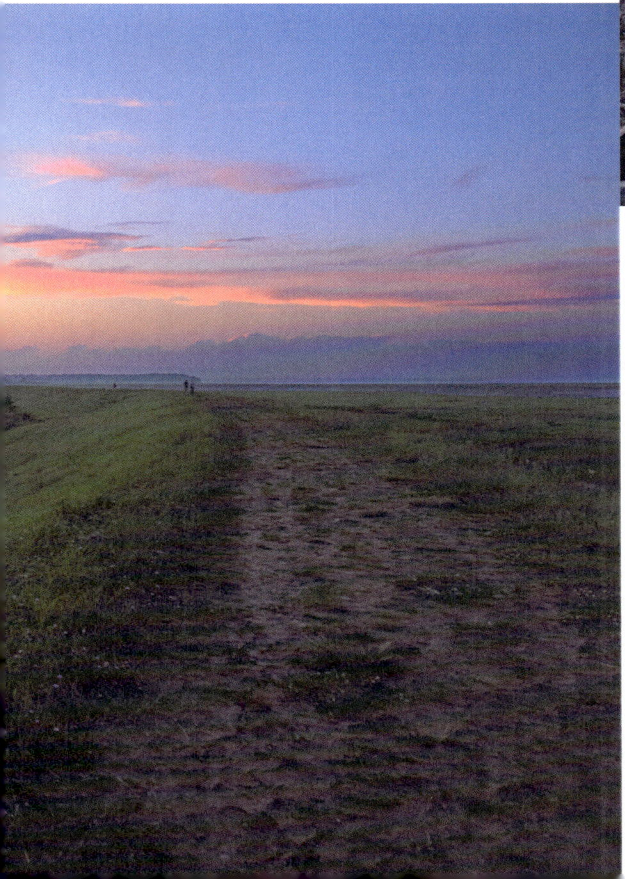

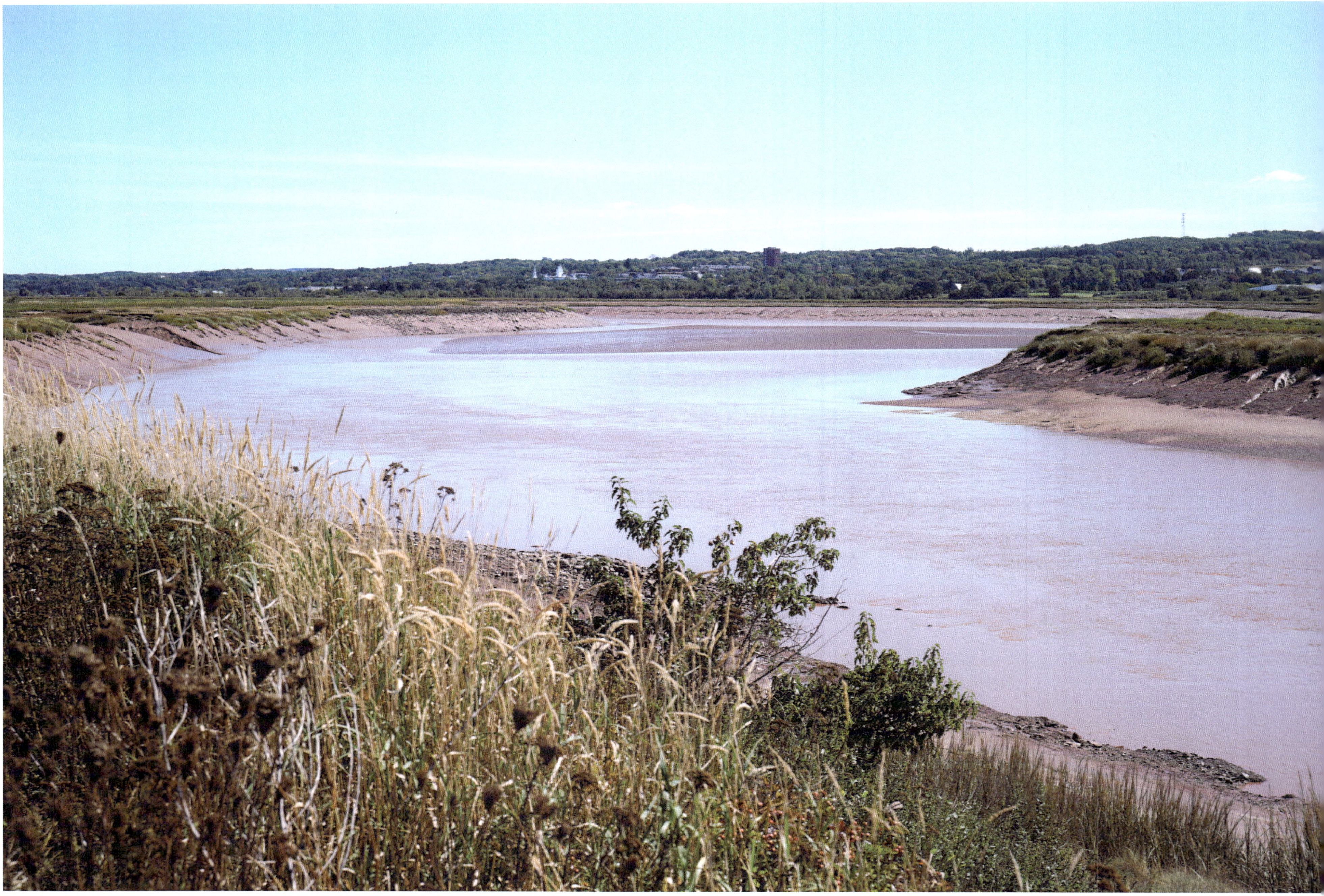

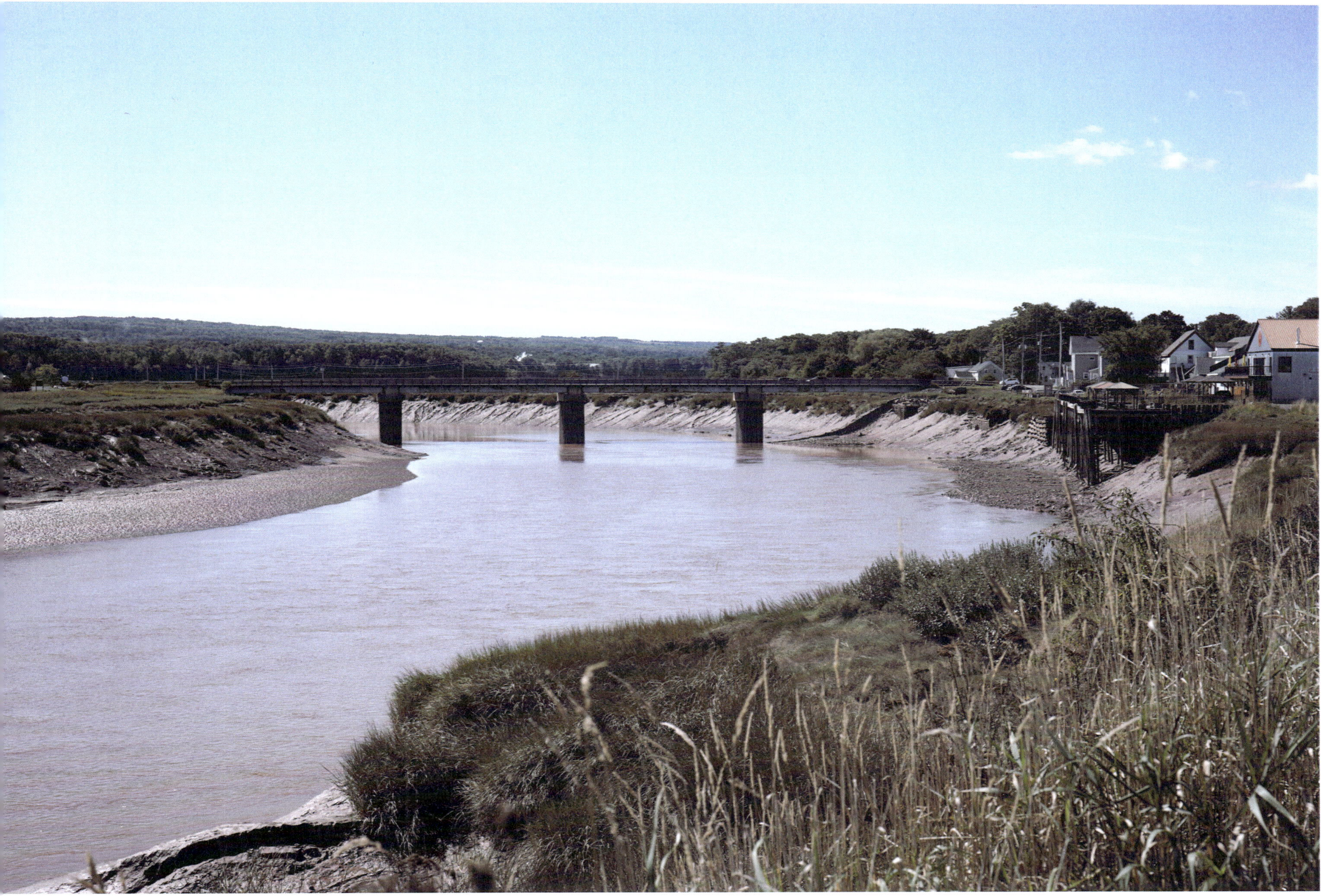

Tidal bore off the Minas Basin

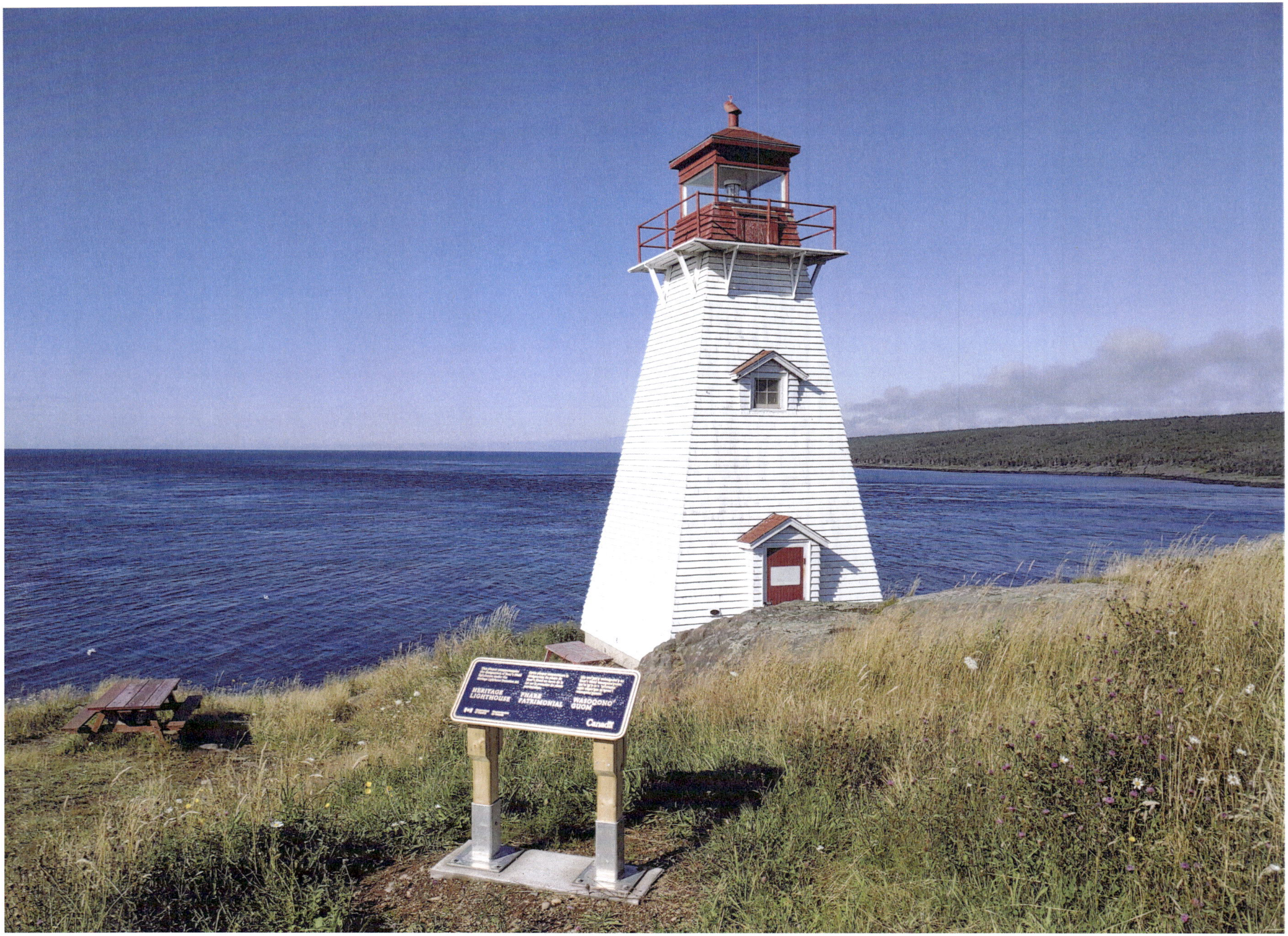

Boar's Head Lighthouse, Long Island, Digby

Chapter 6
Where the Wild Things Grow - Colchester and Cumberland Counties

Located on the shores of Cobequid Bay, Truro is the gateway to Nova Scotia's North Shore region. It's where the Trans-Canada Highway meets Highway 102, and where you'll find a rapidly growing city, not to mention the beautiful Victoria Park.

A little further north and west brings you to the wild blueberry capital of Canada, and eventually out to the New Brunswick border. With farms and fields as far as the eye can see, this region of the province has a lot to explore, including off-the-beaten-track gems like Ships' Company Theatre in Parsboro.
The shore of the Northumberland Straight boasts some of the warmest waters north of the Carolinas, so swimsuits are encouraged!

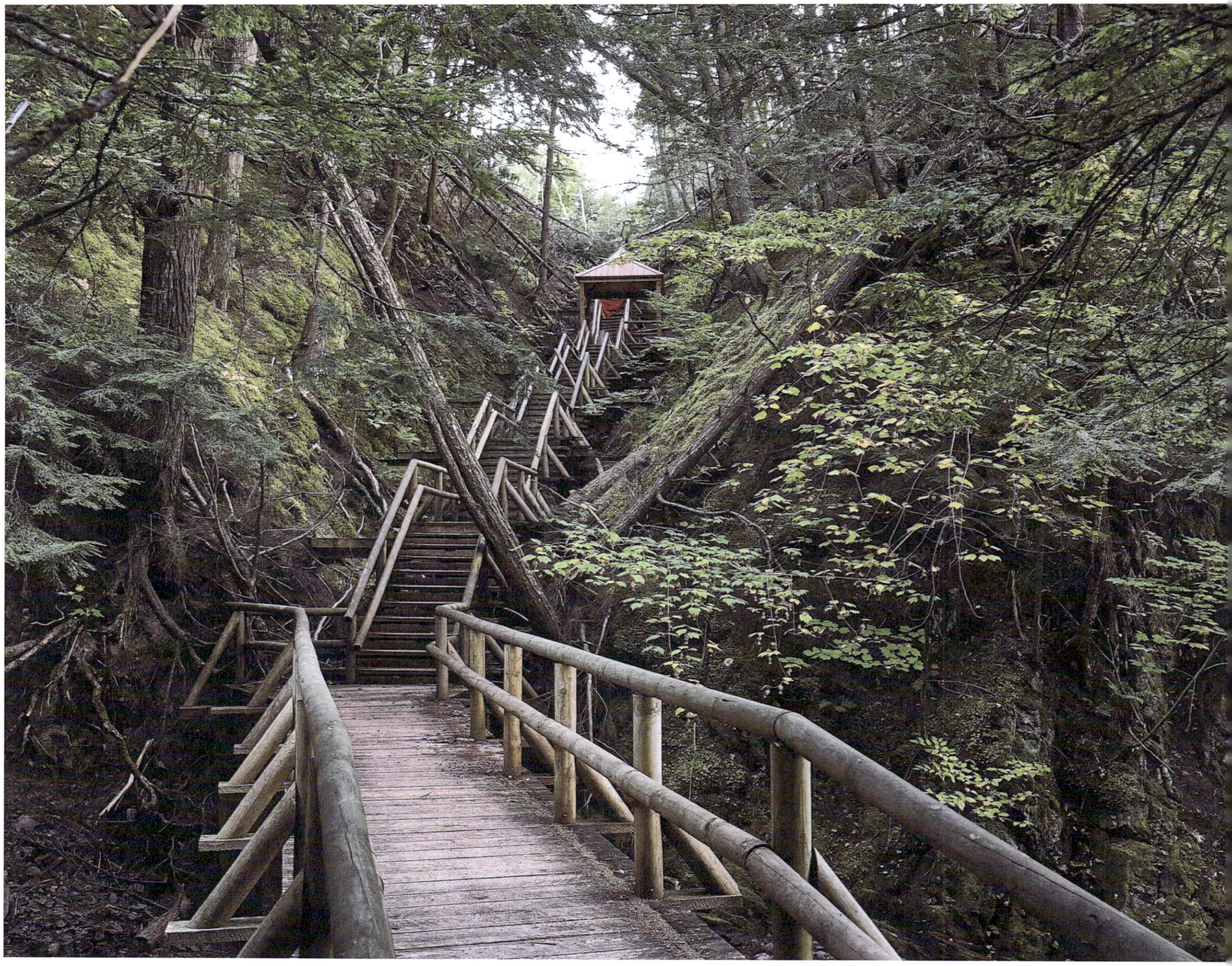

One of the many lookout points in Victoria Park

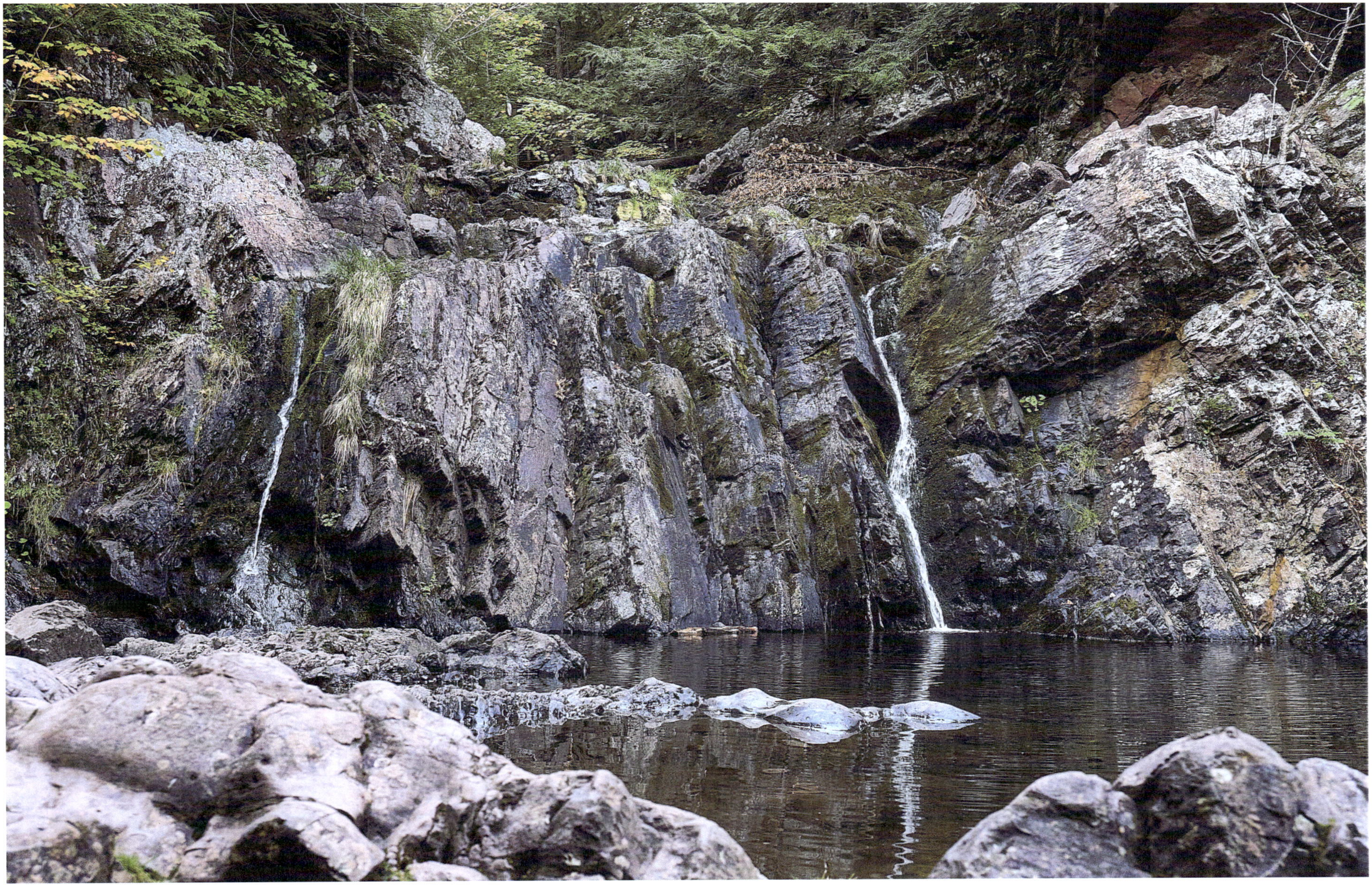

Victoria Park is home to several waterfalls including Joe Howe Falls

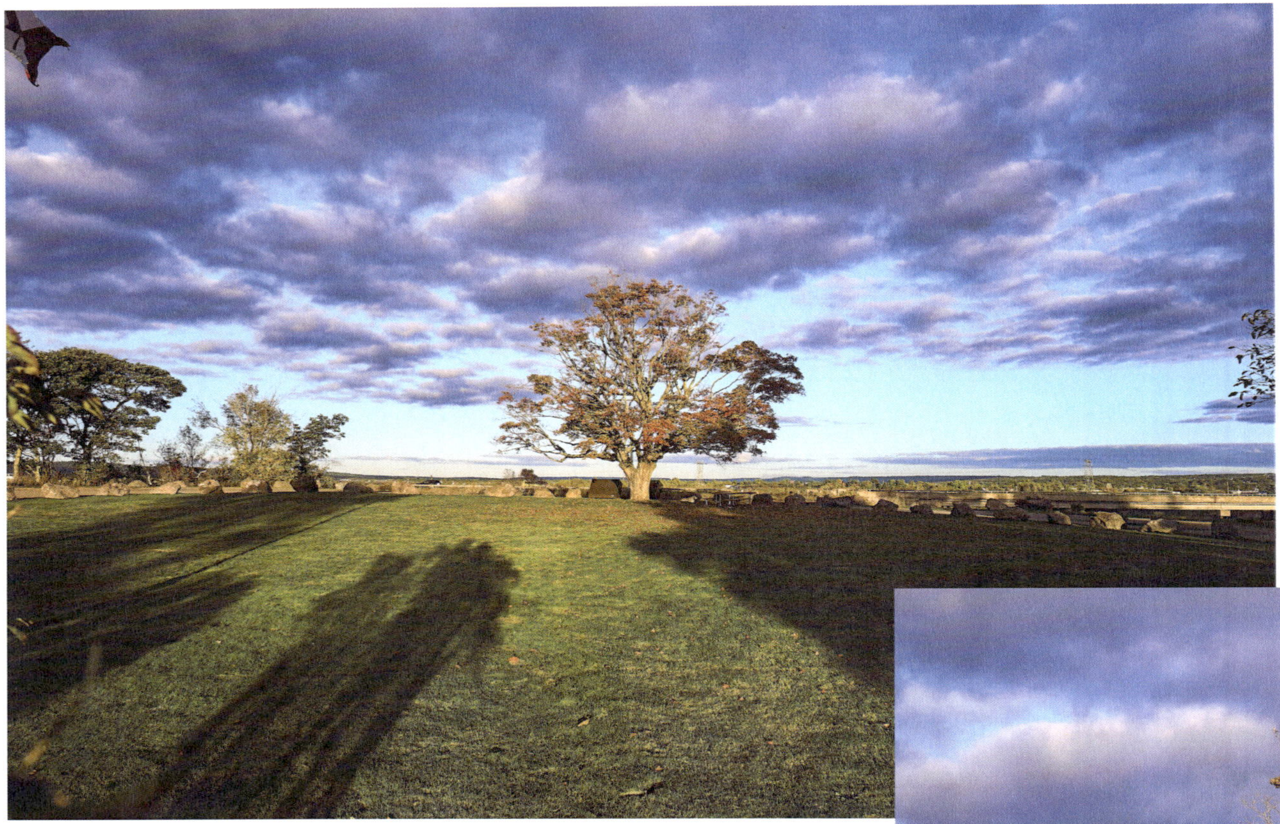

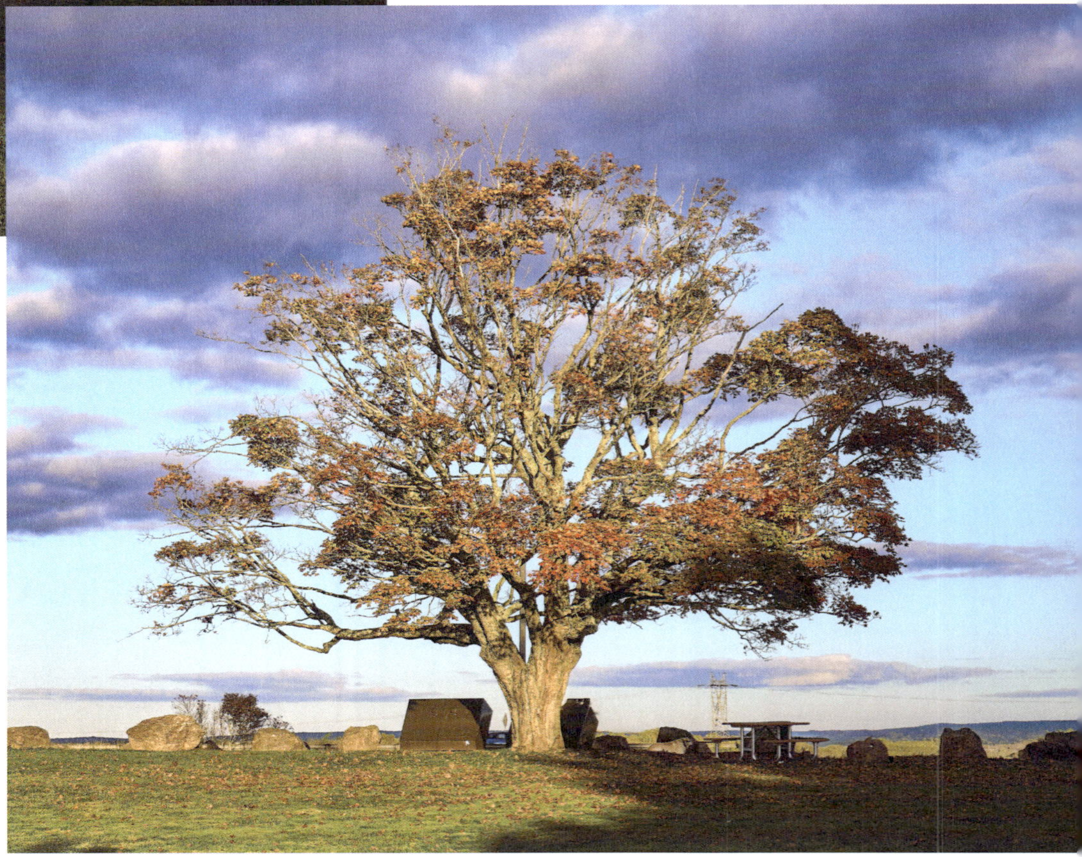

Autumn at the Fundy Discovery Site in Truro

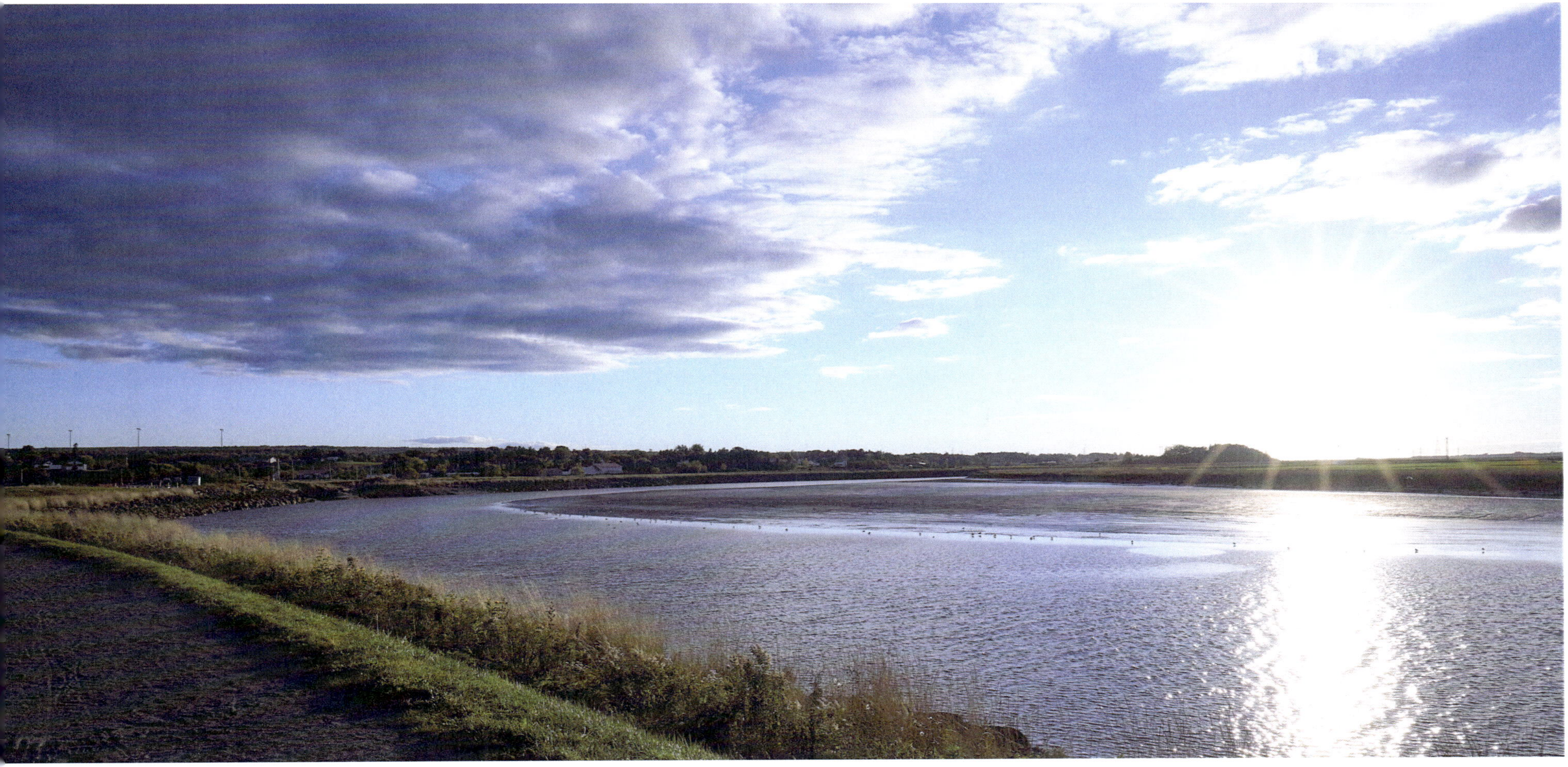

You can watch the Fundy tides come in or go out if you're here at the right time

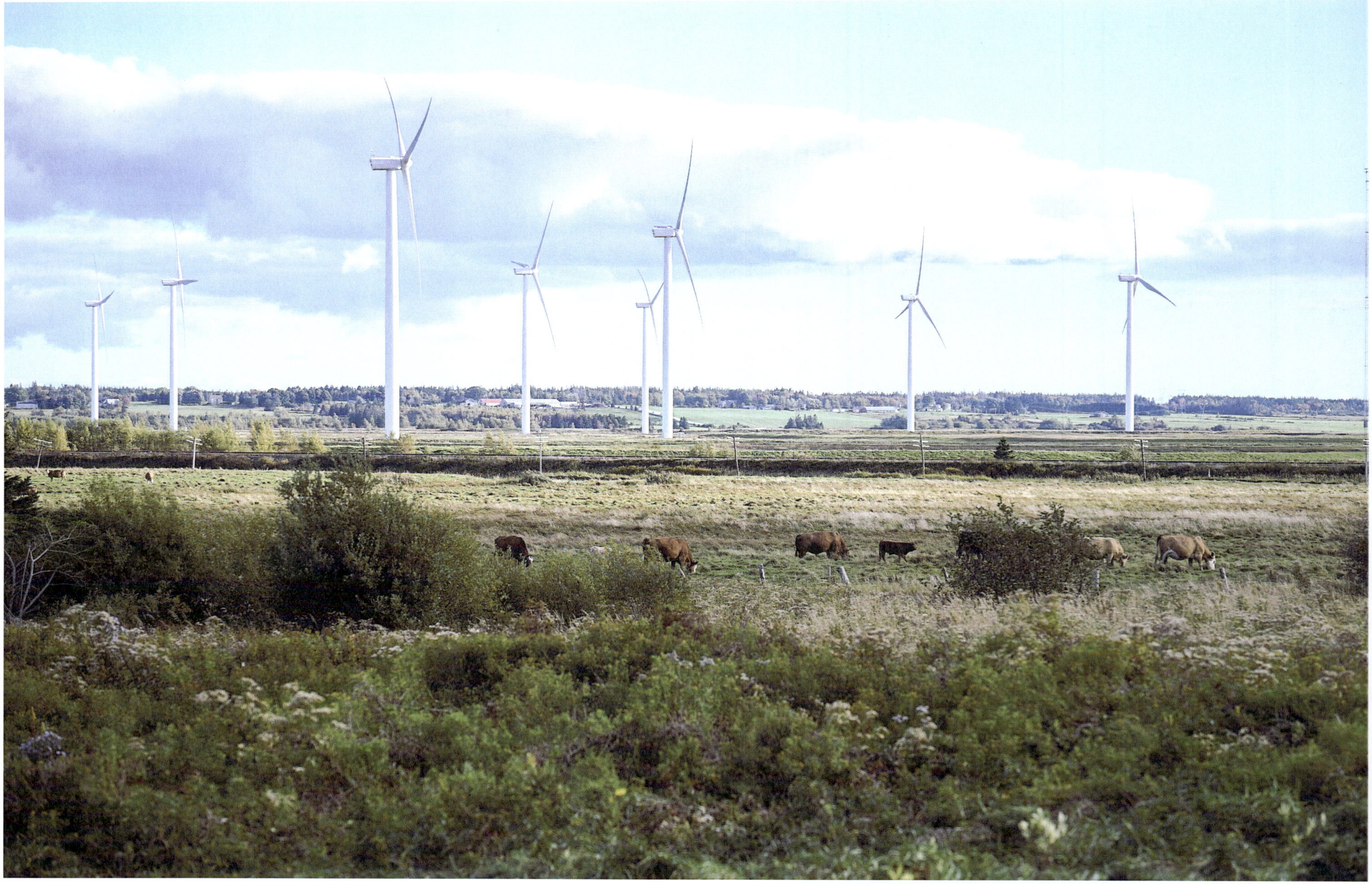

Farms of Cumberland County

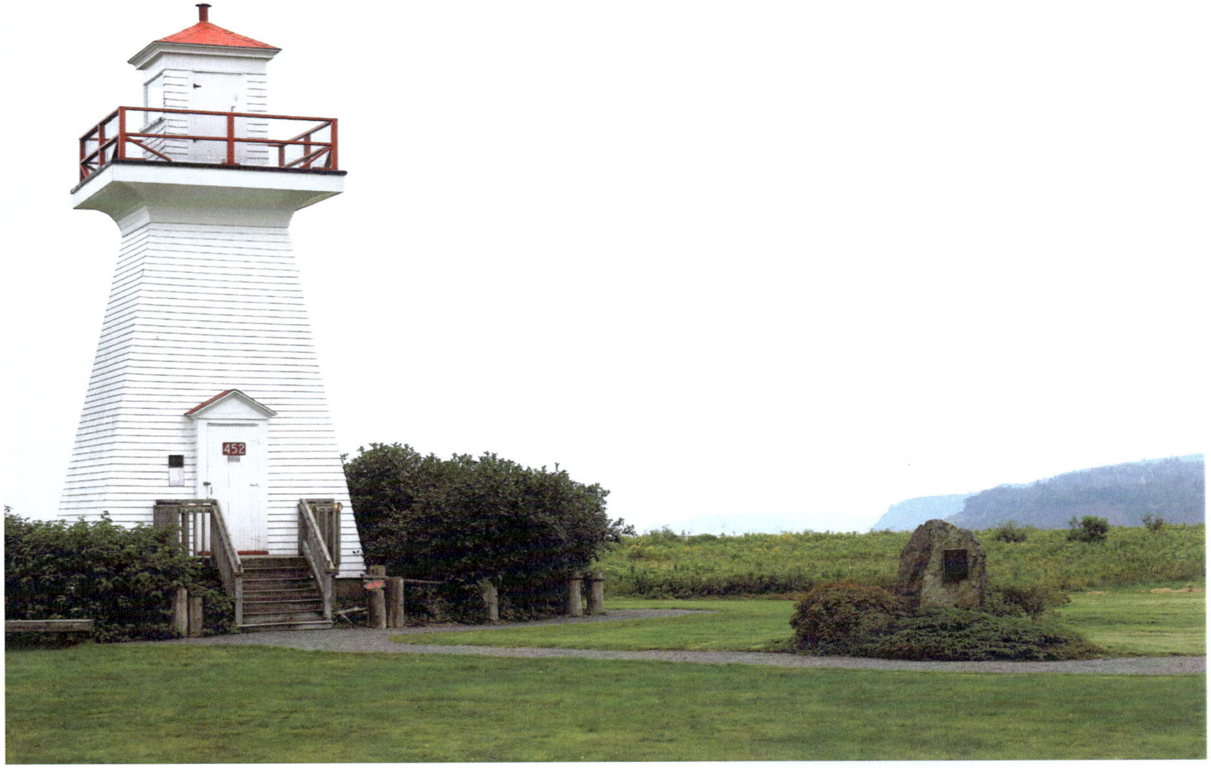

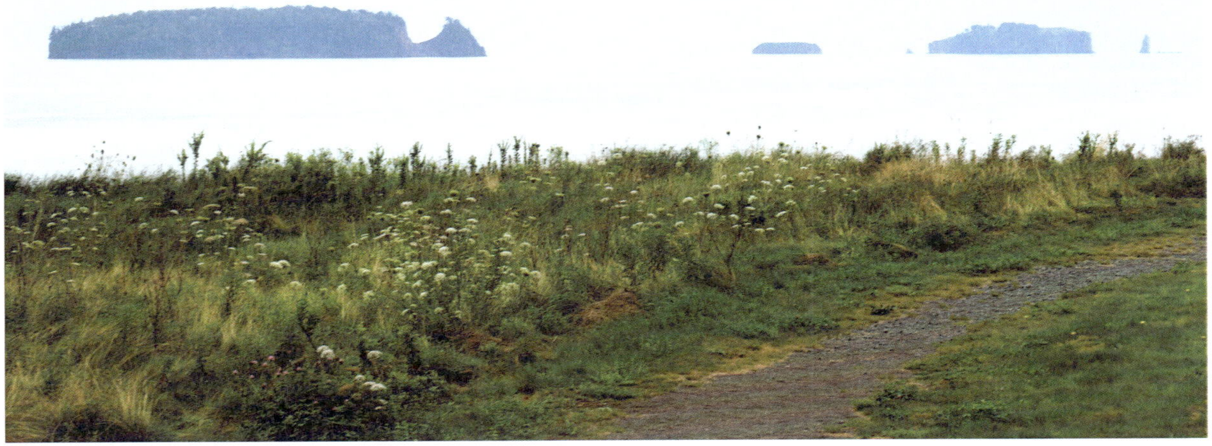

An overcast day at 5 Islands Park
Near Parsboro

Chapter 7
That “X” Factor - Antigonish County

The County of Antigonish makes up the northeastern most part of mainland Nova Scotia, and boasts some of its most scenic areas. Gaelic culture is alive and well in this part of the province, with neighbouring Pictou County being the birthplace of Scottish culture in Nova Scotia. Highland games have been celebrated there for over 150 years

The town of Antigonish is the home of St. Francis Xavier University (or "st efex" to the locals), which might just have the most dedicated and spirited alumni anywhere. Don't believe me? Just ask them about their rings....

Despite a local population of just over 5,000, this town is the hub city for this part of the province. The county and town work together to create a vibrant region, with a strong arts, culture, and music scene. Arisaig Provincial Park is a popular place for fossil hunters, and I've definitely spotted an eagle or two in the skies above.

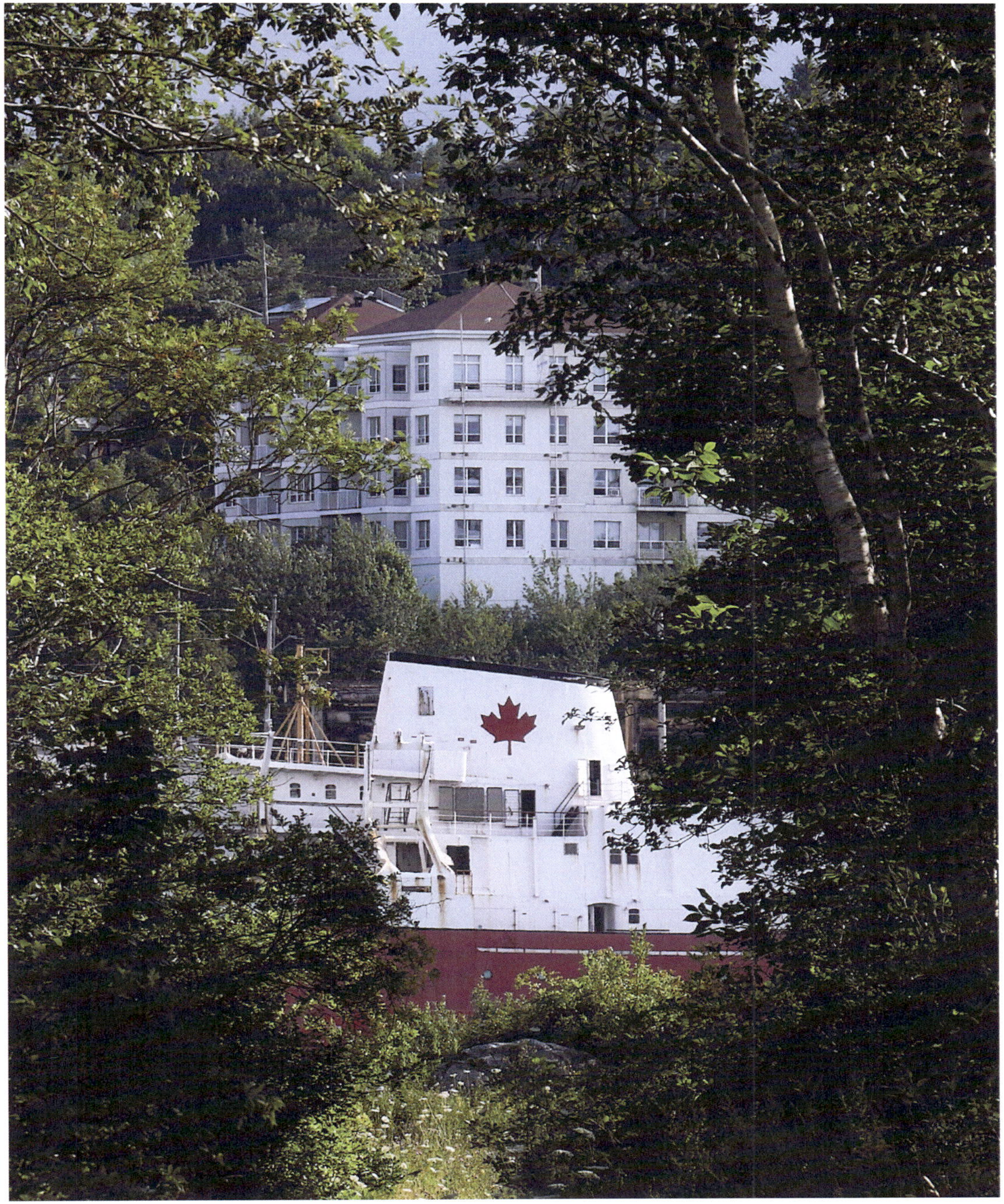

Coast Guard patrolling the waters near Antigonish

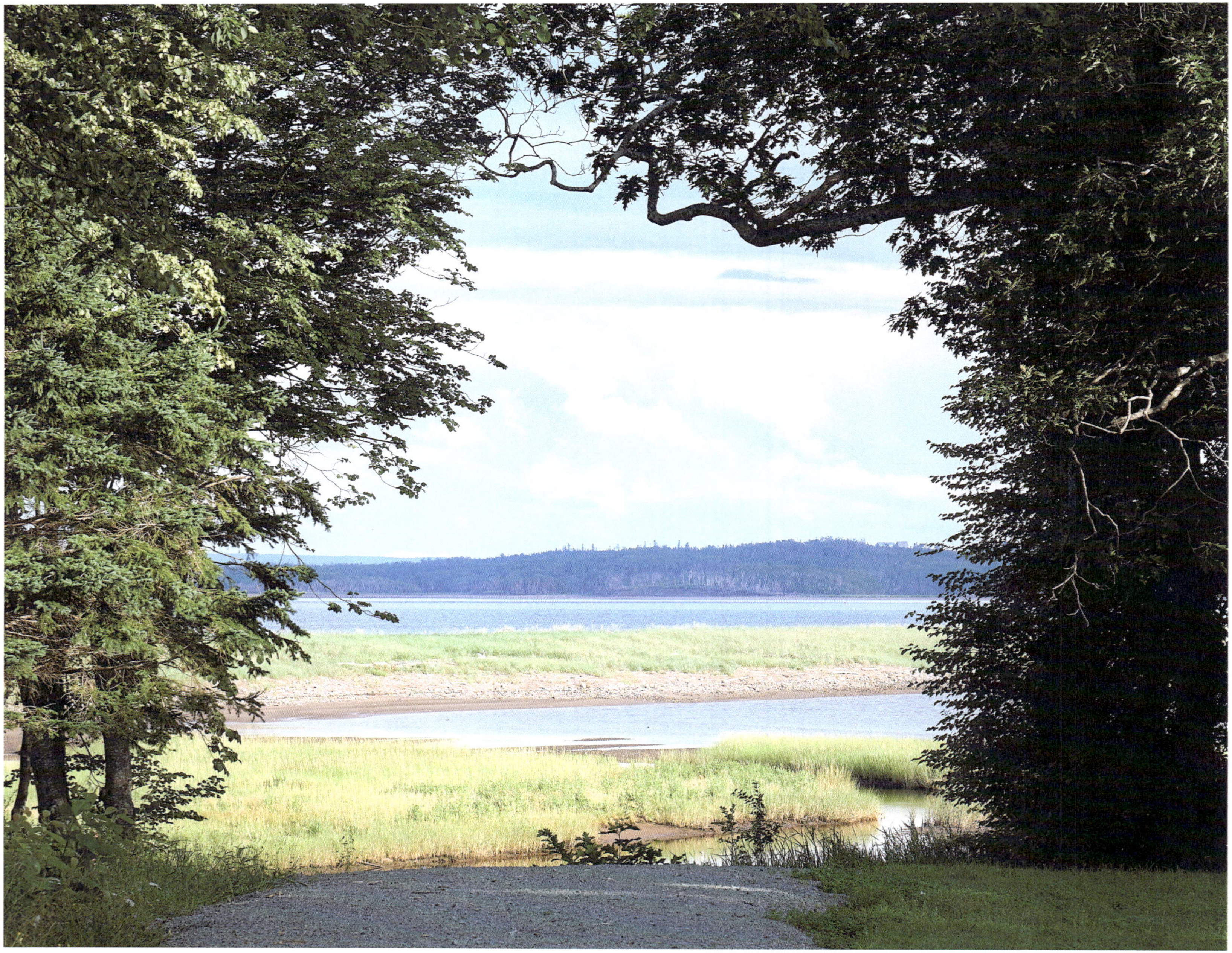

Crystal Cliffs - a popular wedding location owned by St F-X.
This ecologically significant land was gifted to the university for study and research

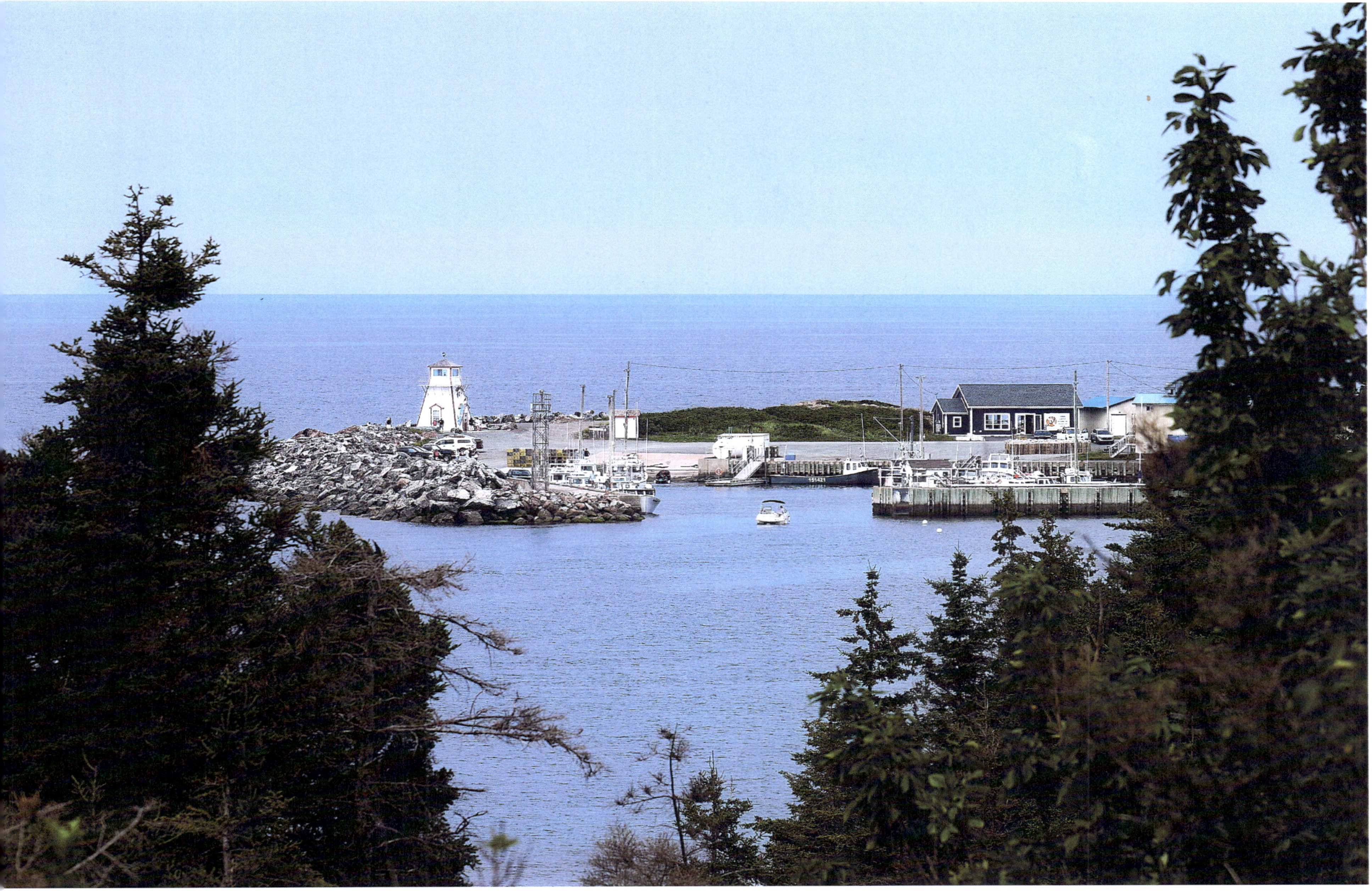

Arisaig lighthouse and marina

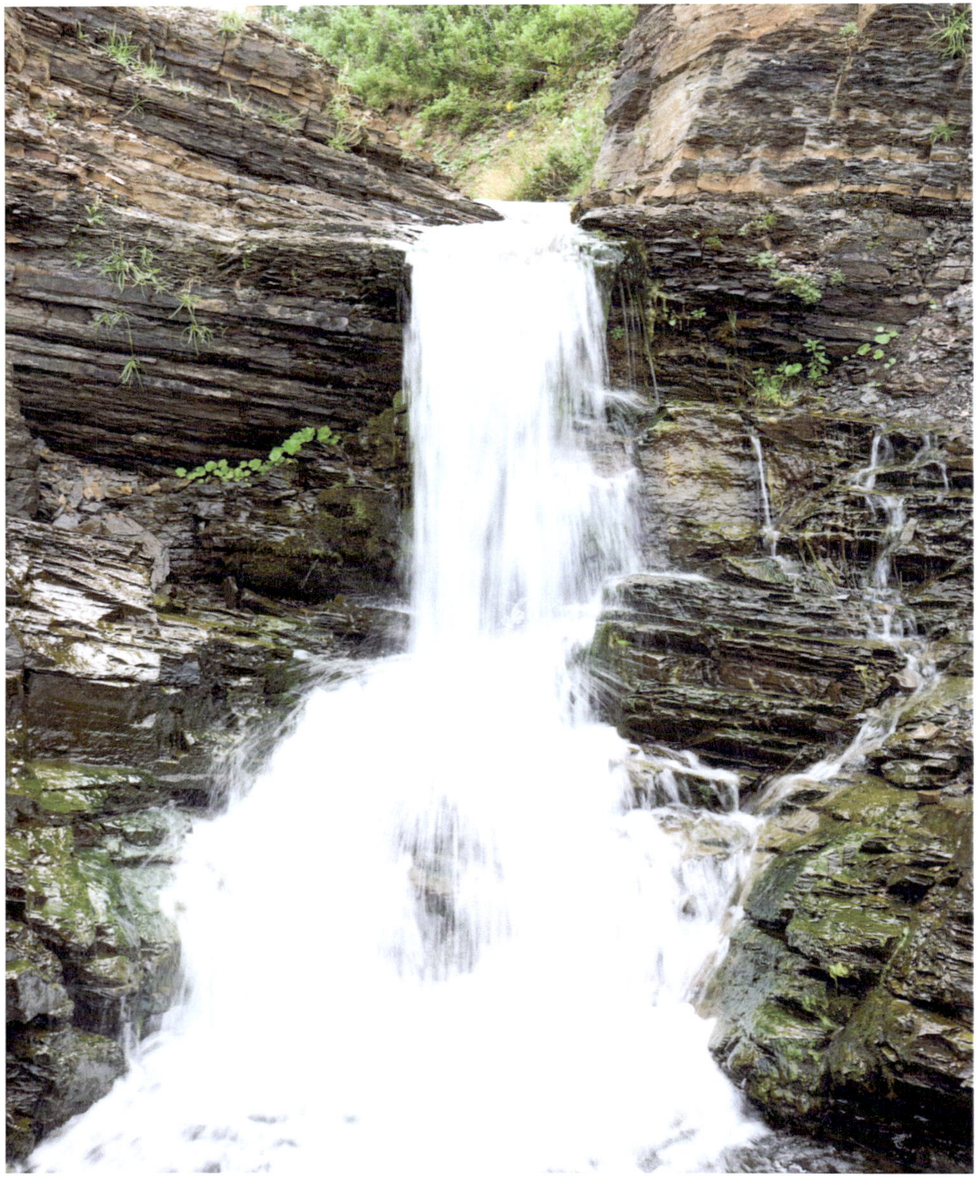

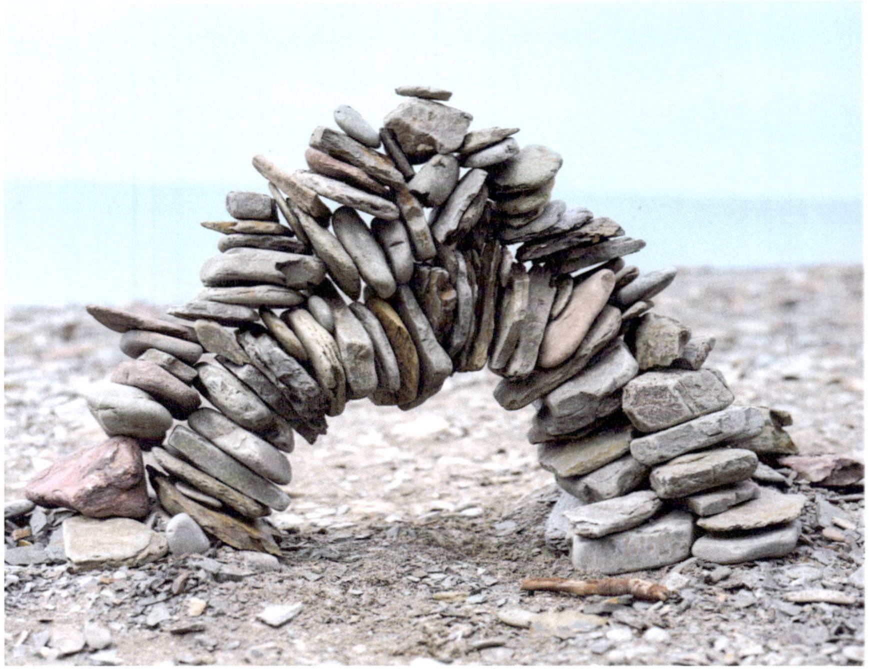

Waterfall leading down to the shore of
Arisaig Provincial Park

These stone structures can often be seen on
the beach, left by inspired visitors

Chapter 8
Your Heart Will Never Leave - Cape Breton

Cape Breton's slogan is pretty much on point. It is one of the most breathtaking places I've ever visited. Even the less nice parts of Cape Breton are nicer than a lot of other places. It's the kind of place that makes me want to pull over every 50 metres and take some more photos.

It's hard to know where to begin when talking about Cape Breton. The eastern part of the island will take you out to it's largest city, Sydney, and out to historic Fort Louisbourg, where you can enjoy immersive historical experiences, and along the shores of beautiful Bras D'Or Lake. The western part of the island takes you along the Celtic Shore, and up to the world famous Cabot Trail and Cape Breton Highlands.

Between the natural beauty, the vibrant Celtic, Acadian, and Indigenous culture, and historic places of interest, it feels like there's never enough time to see everything you want to see in this majestic part of the province, and the 300,000 people who visit each year would most likely agree with that!

And if you're still looking for more to see, there's Cape Breton University, amazing golf, and North American's first single malt distillery.

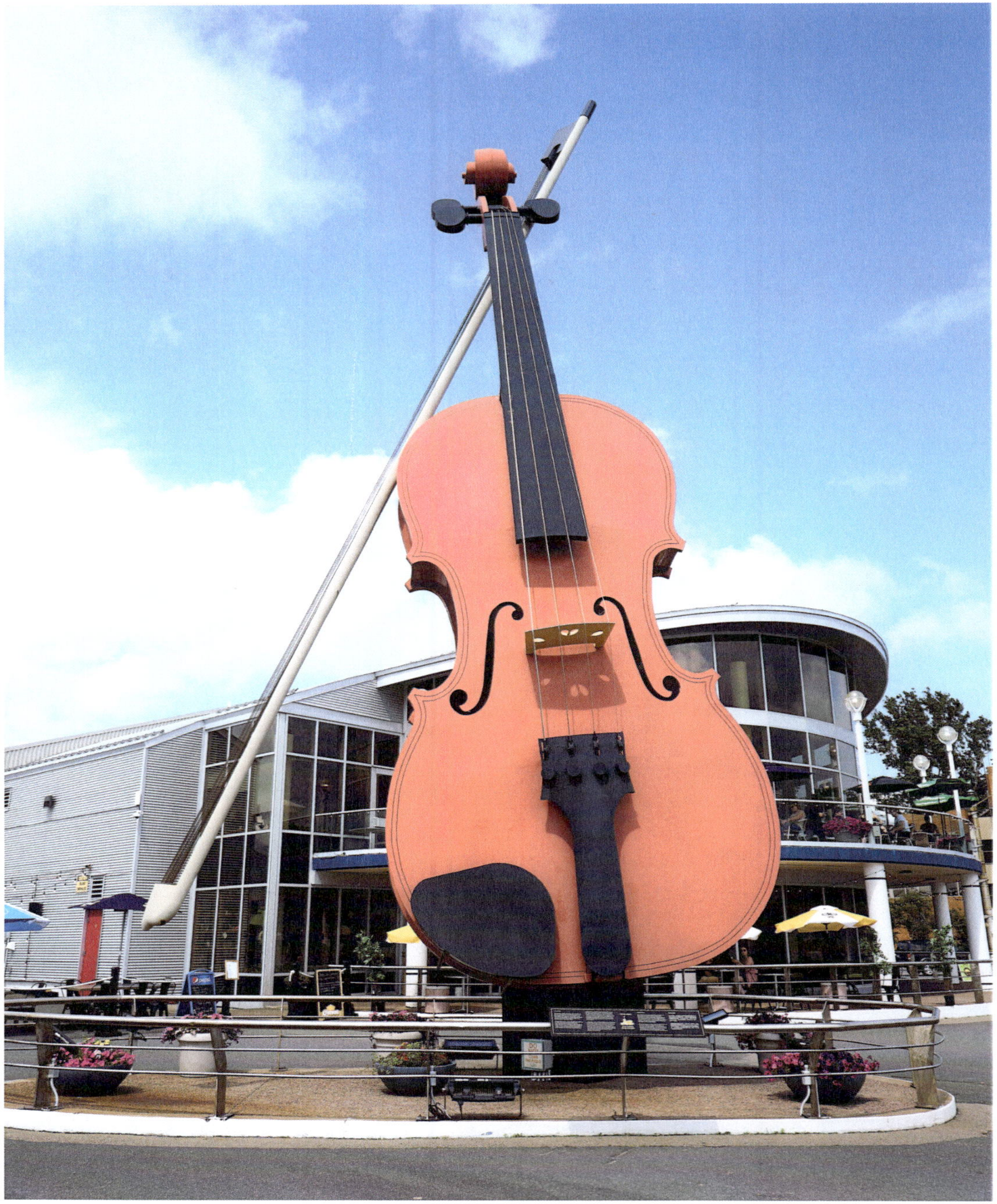

Sydney's famous Big Fiddle, celebrating local music

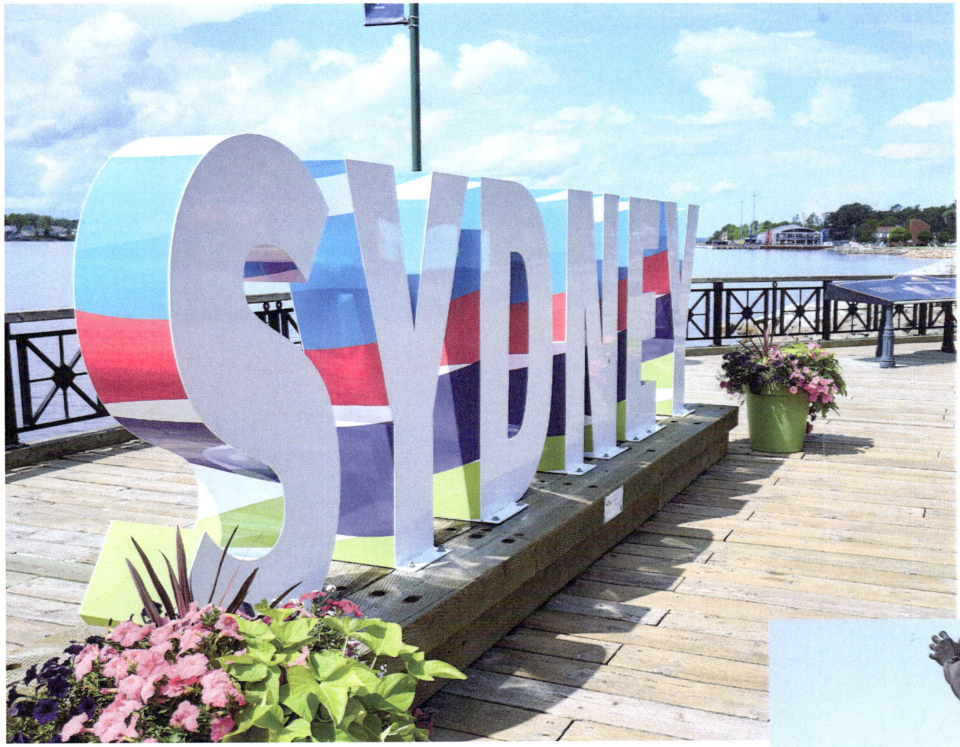

The big sign kicks off the walk along the waterfront where you can see statues like this that tell the history of the area

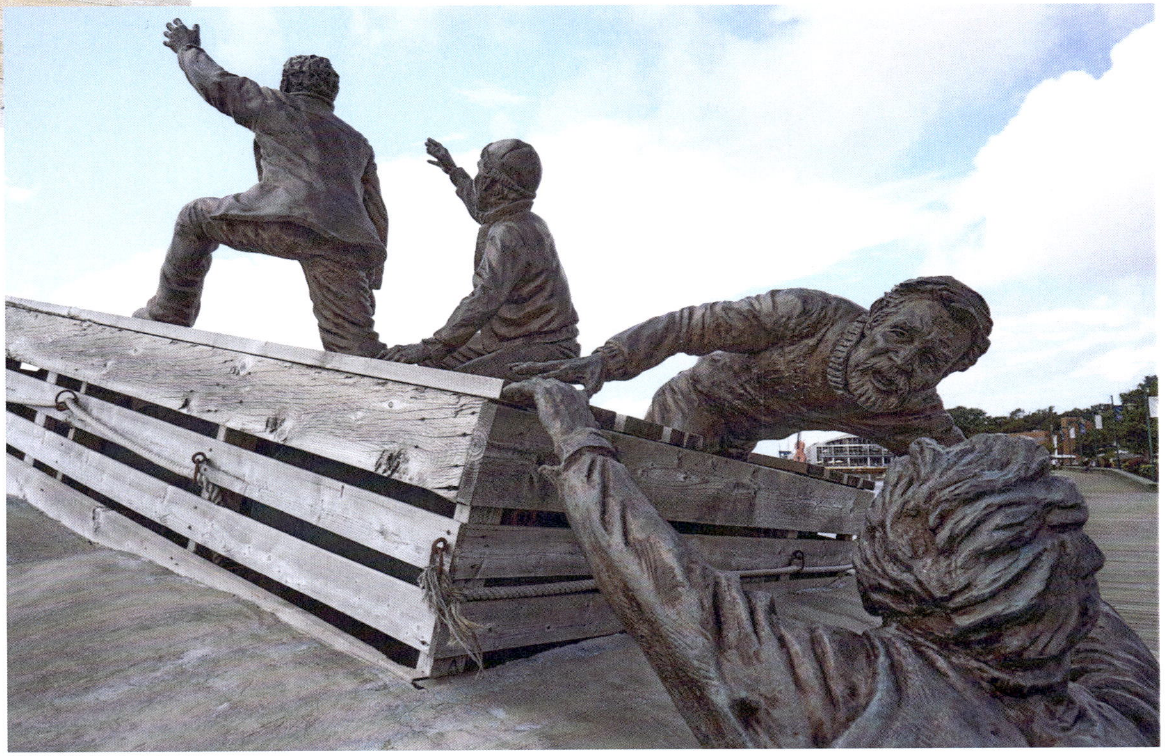

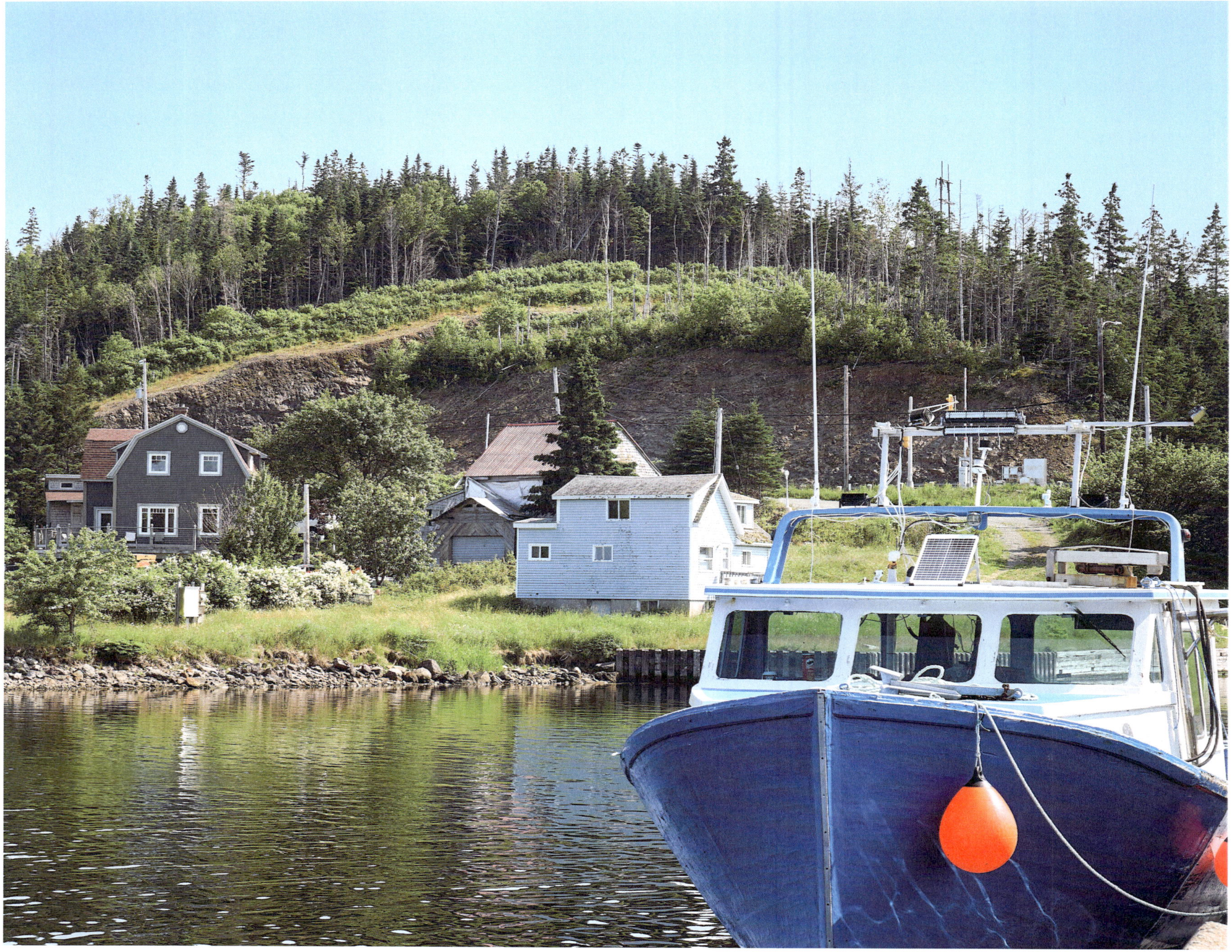

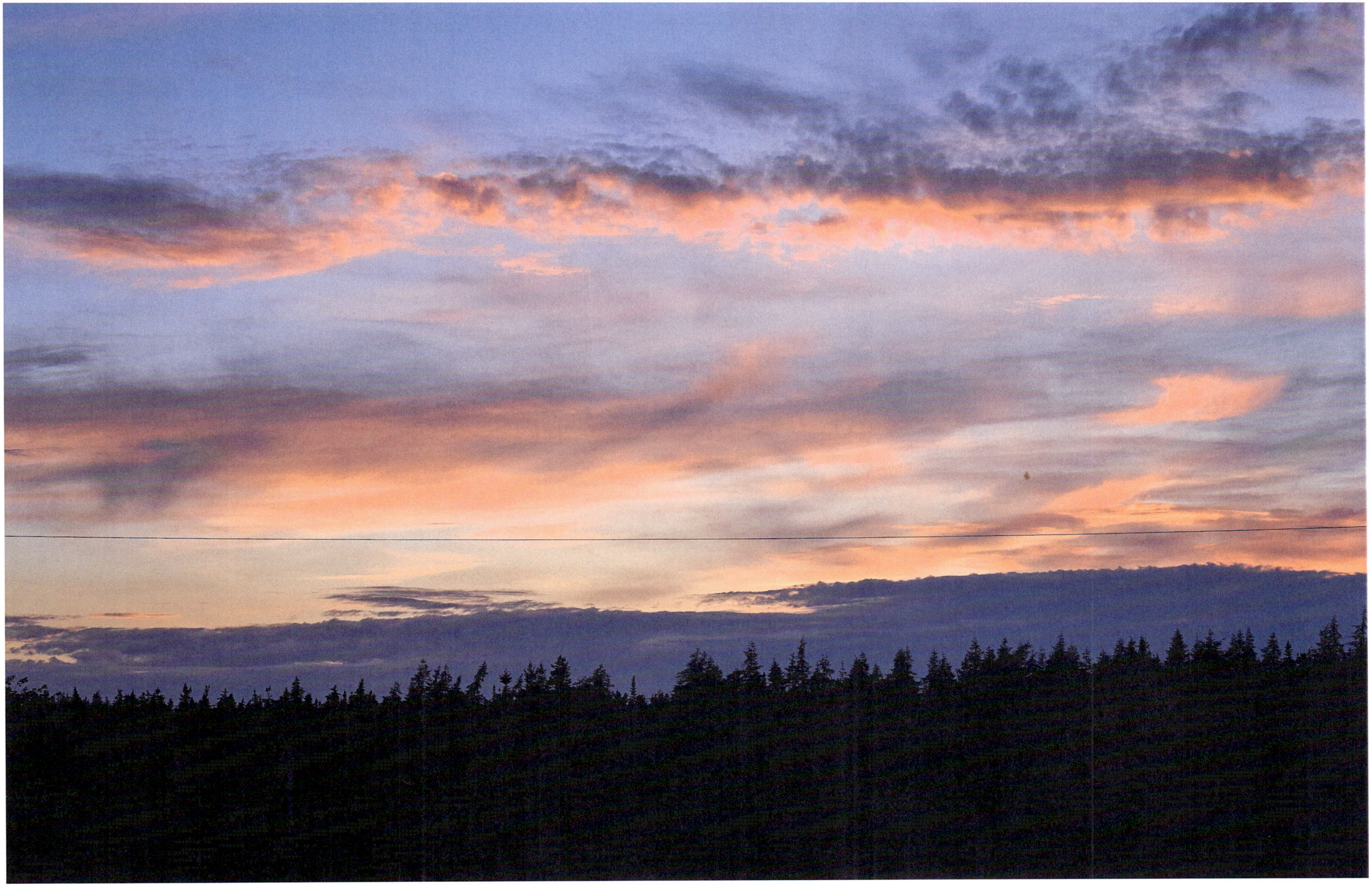

Sunset near River Bourgois
Opposite page: Boat in the St. Peters Canal

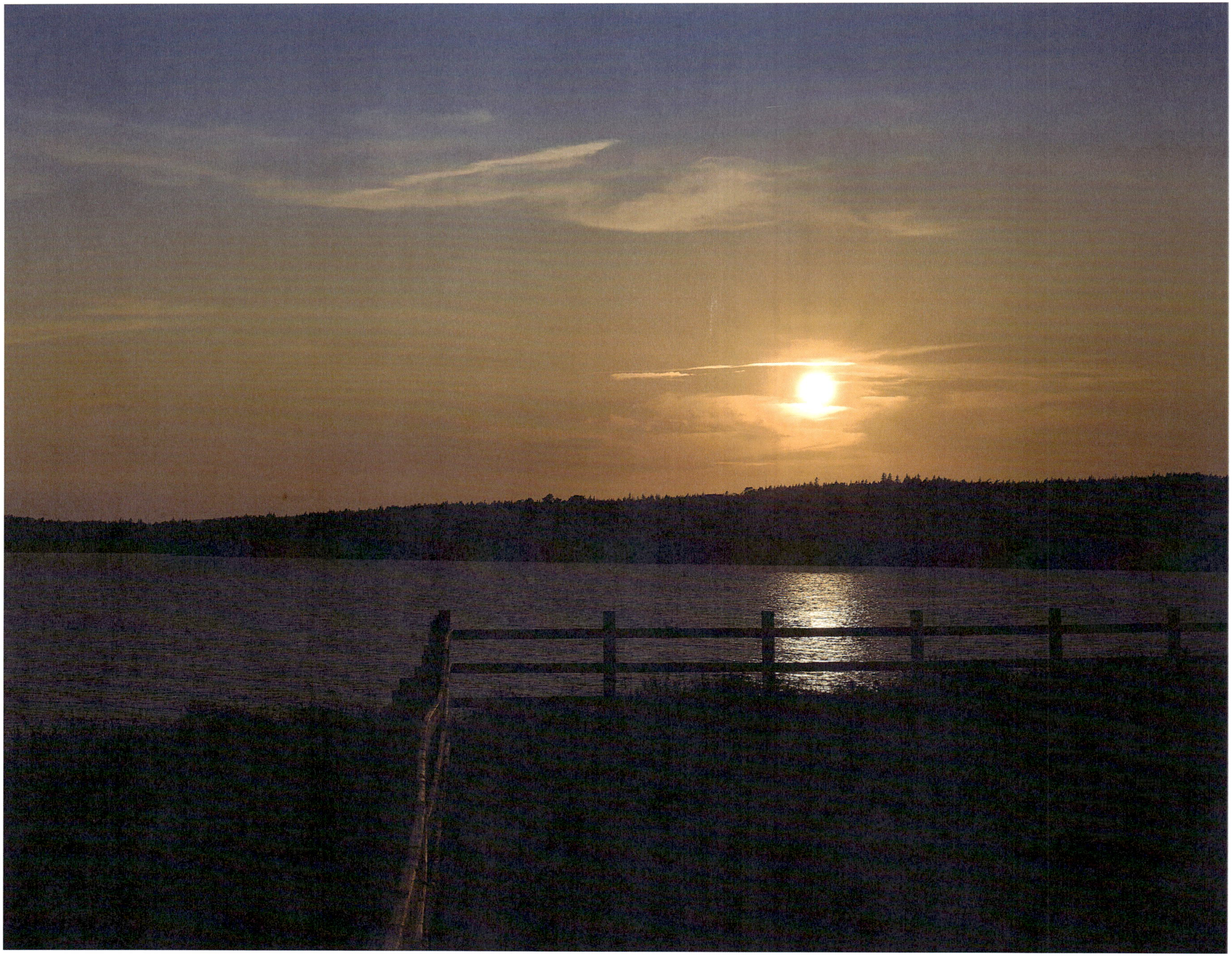

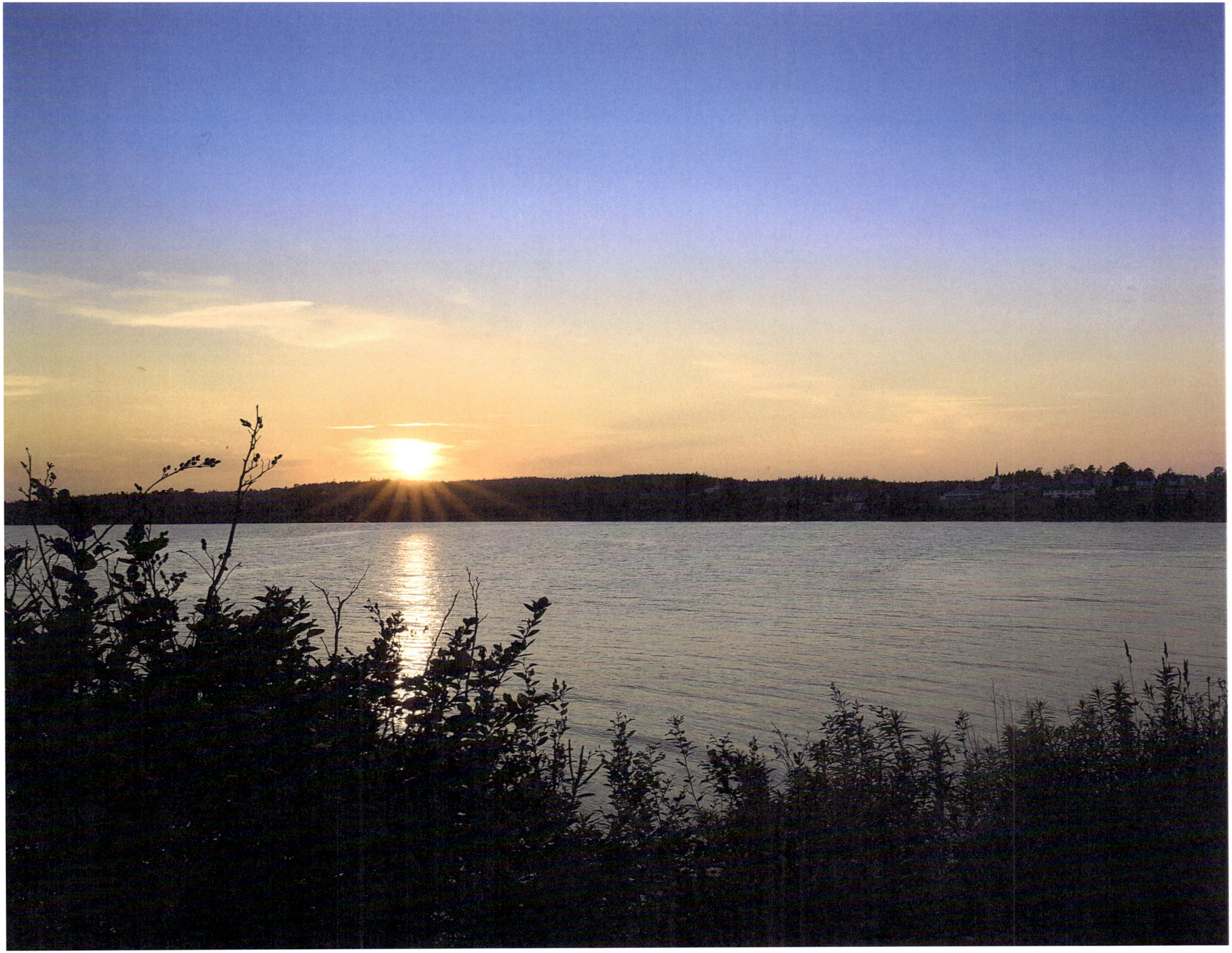

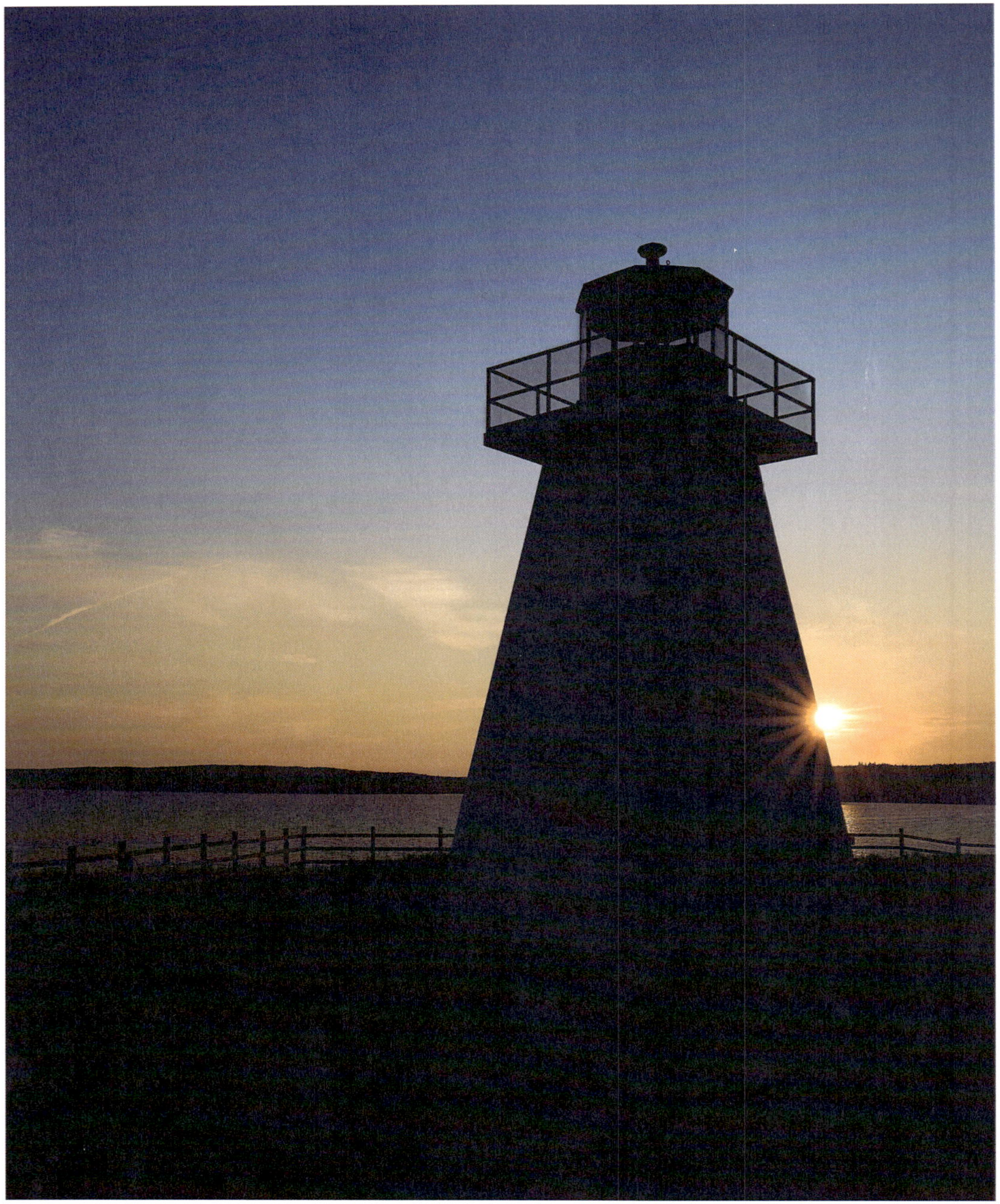

Jerome Point Lighthouse
In Battery Provincial Park

Previous pages:

Sunset at Battery Park

Sunrise over Meat Cove

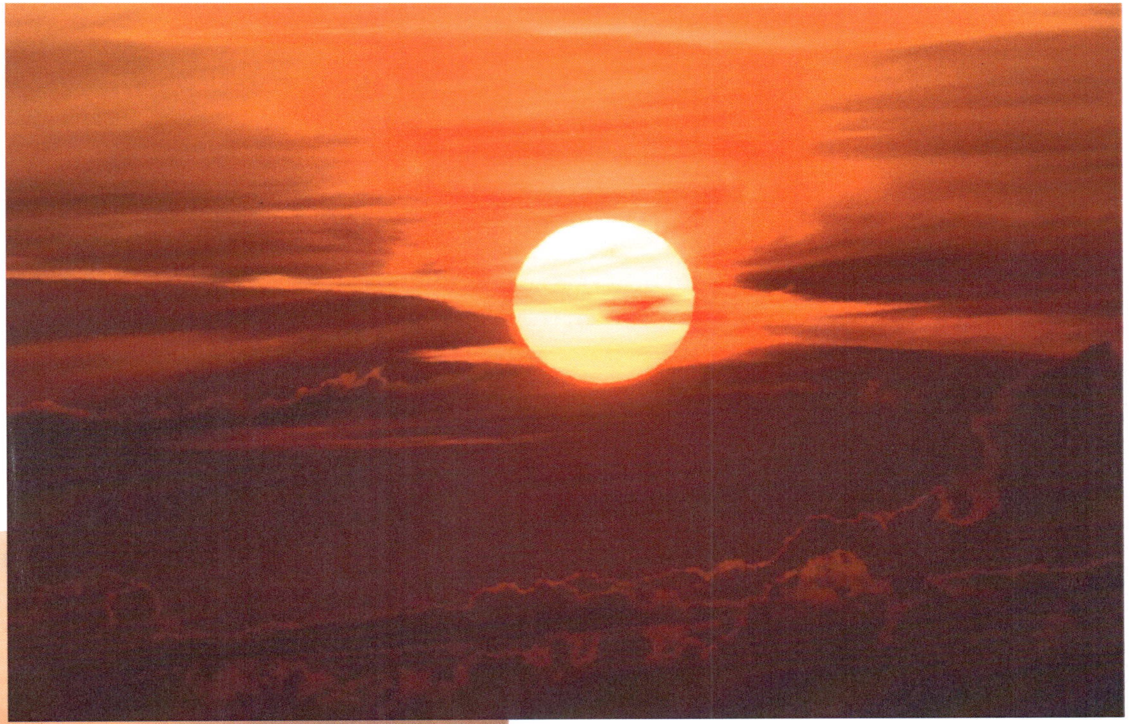

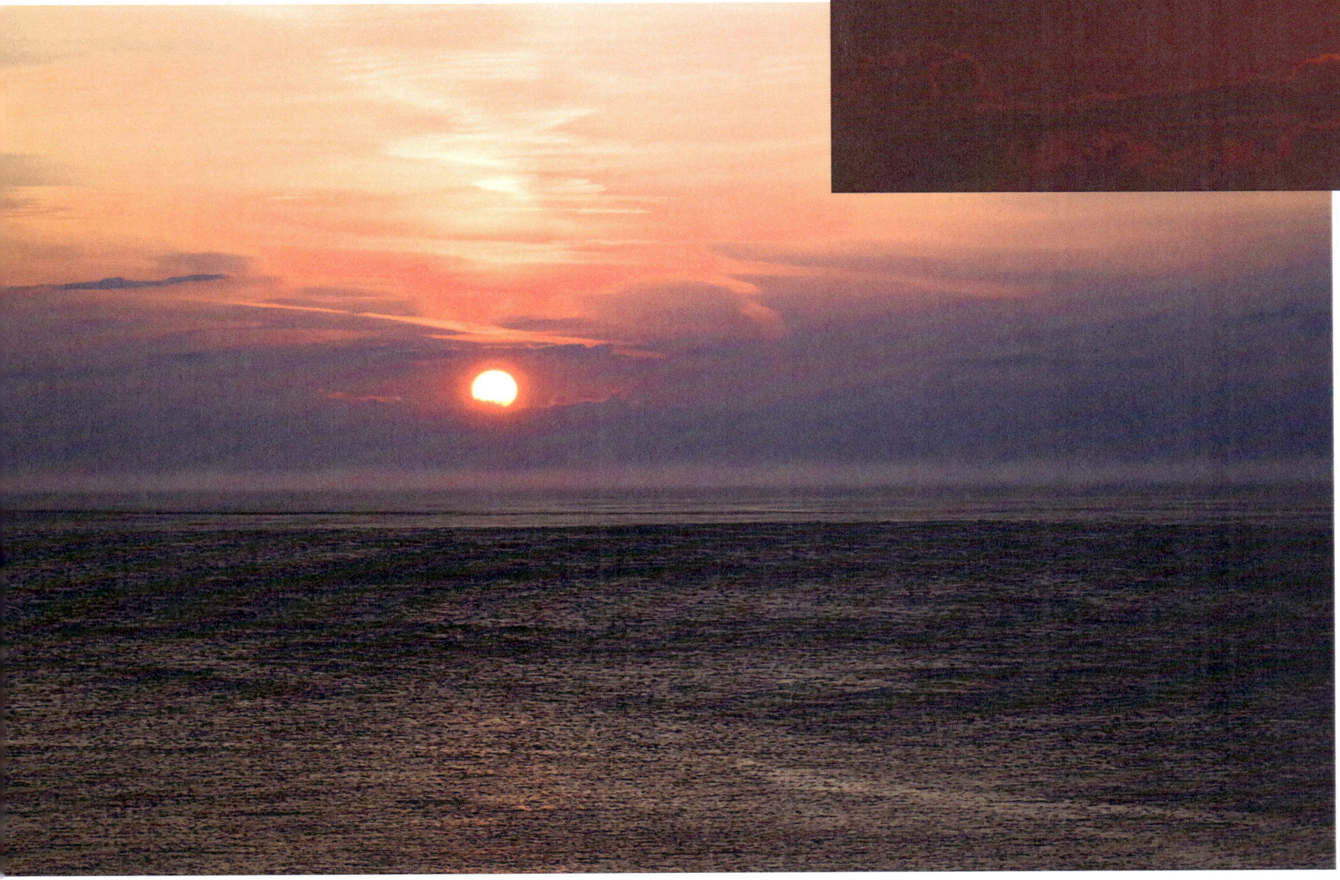

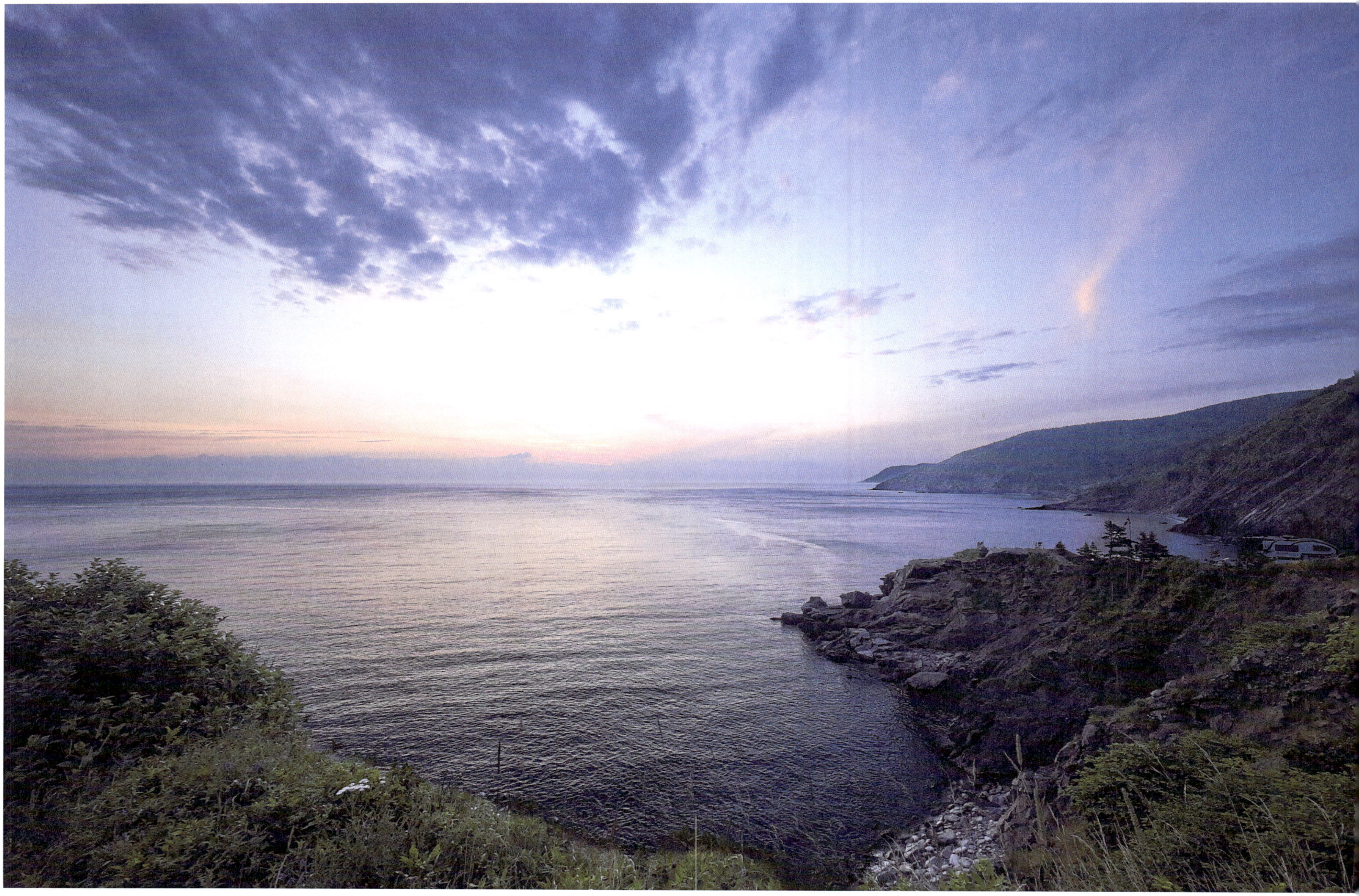

Sunrise over Meat Cove, at the northern tip of Nova Scotia

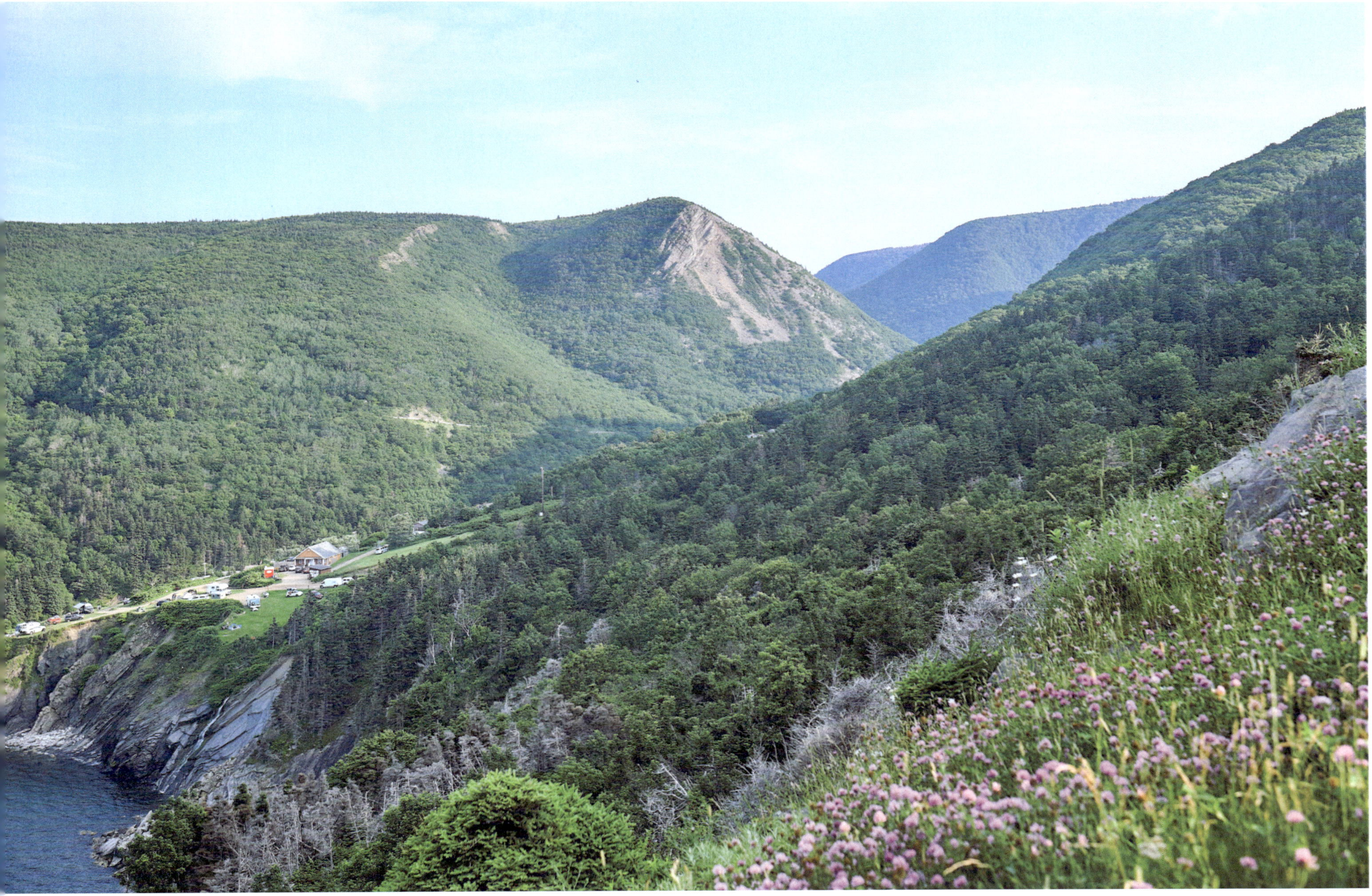

Overlooking Meat Cove Campground and the Highlands

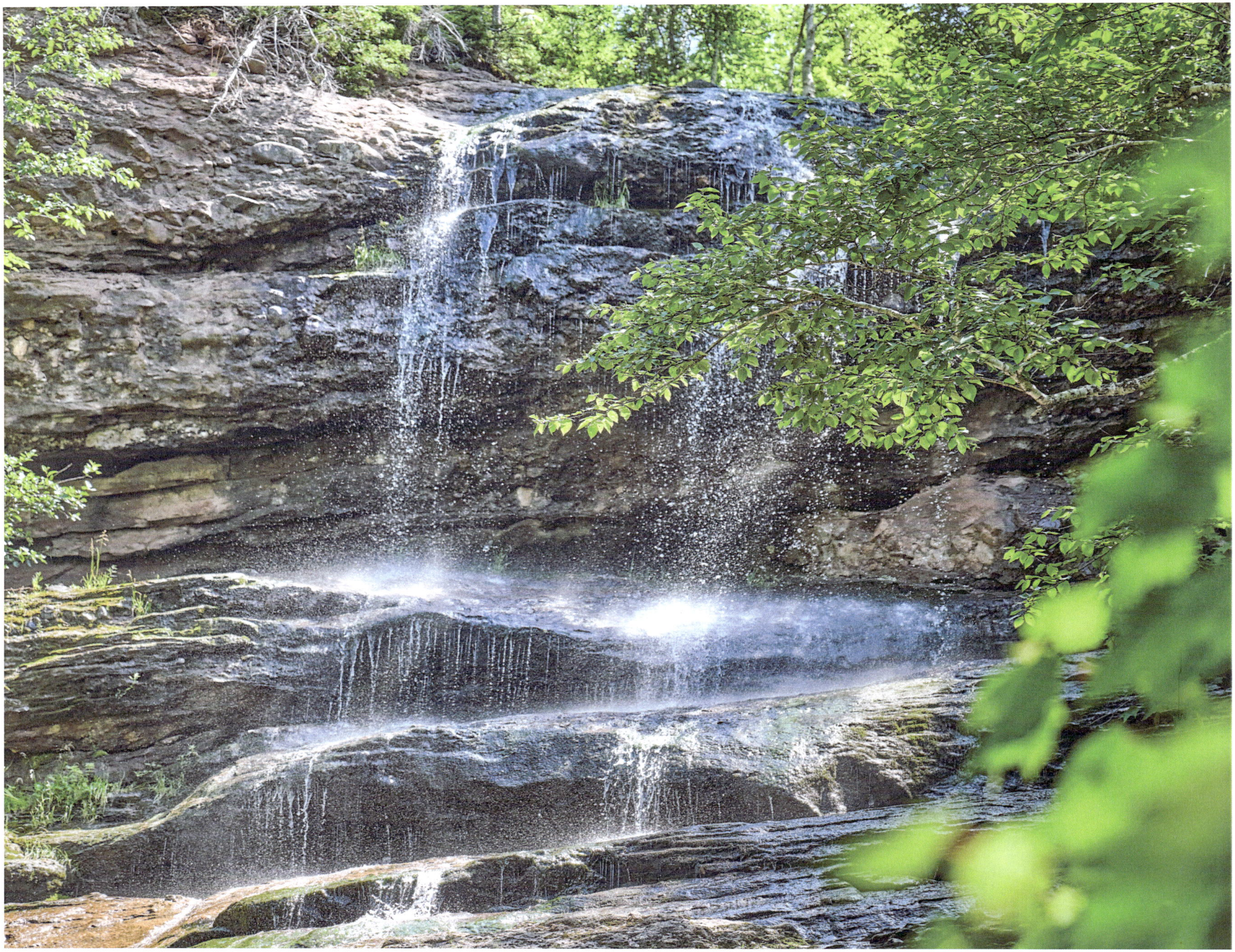

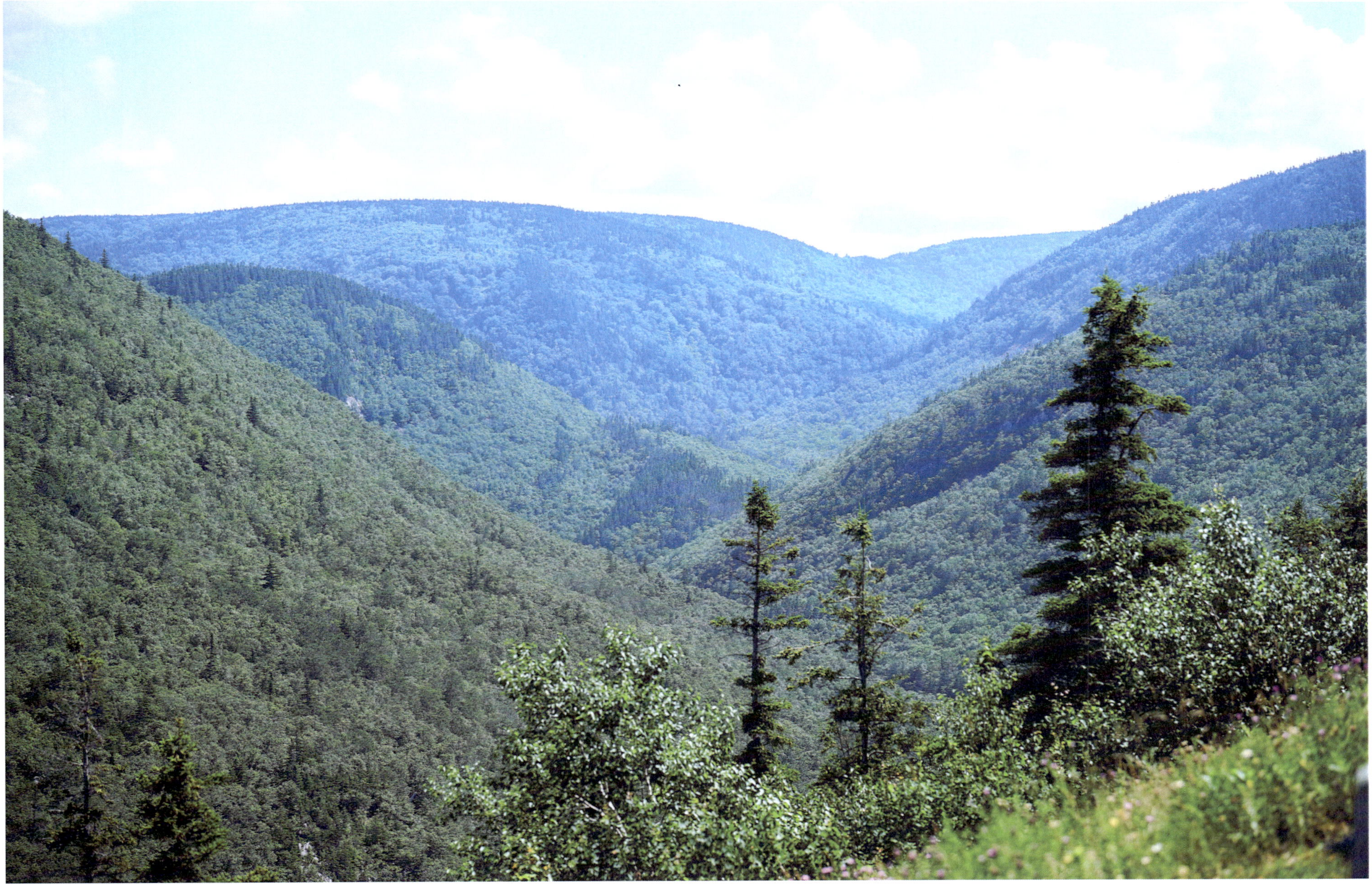

The Aspy Fault extends 40 km out to the ocean
Opposite page: Beulach Ban Falls

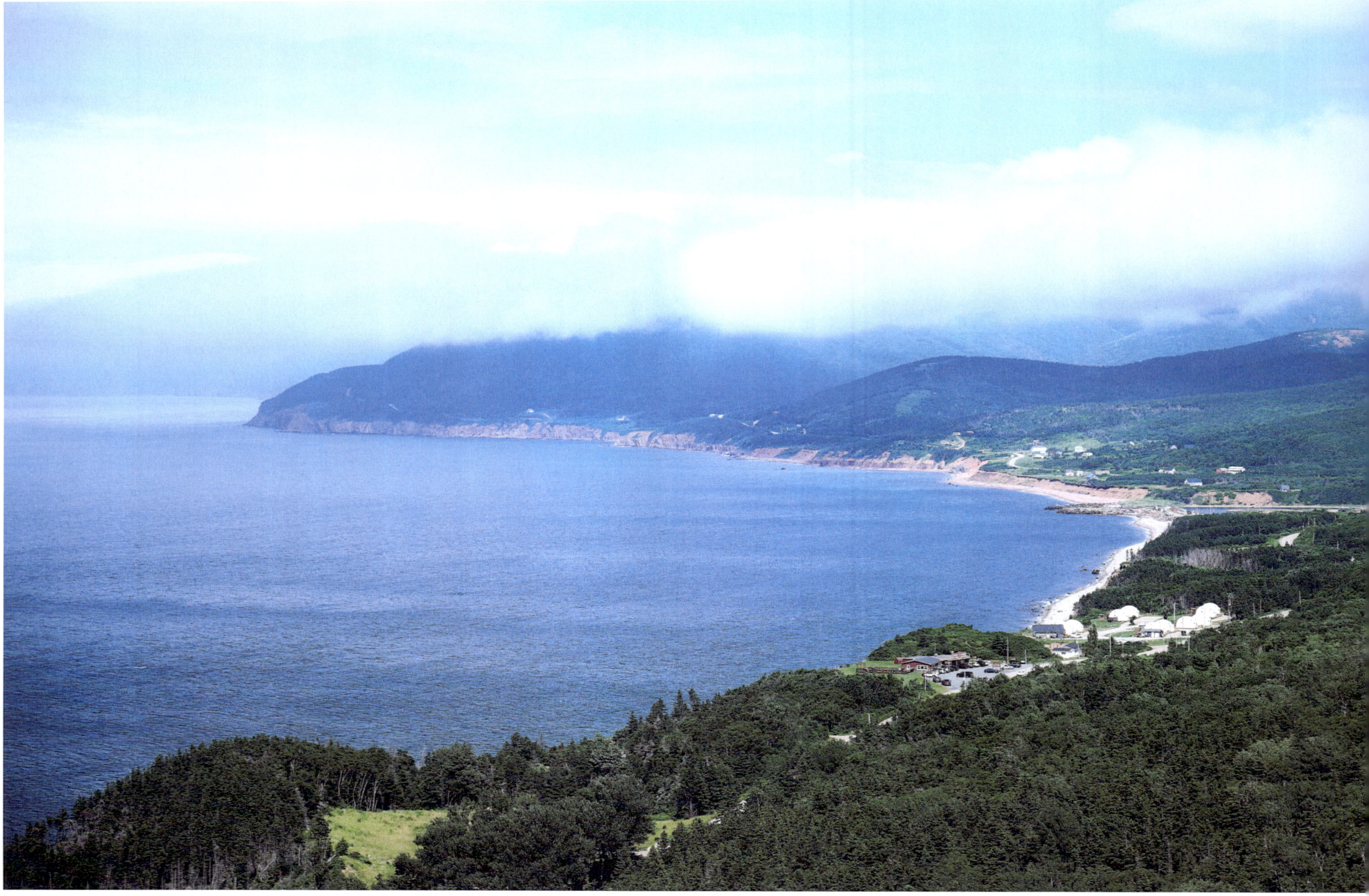

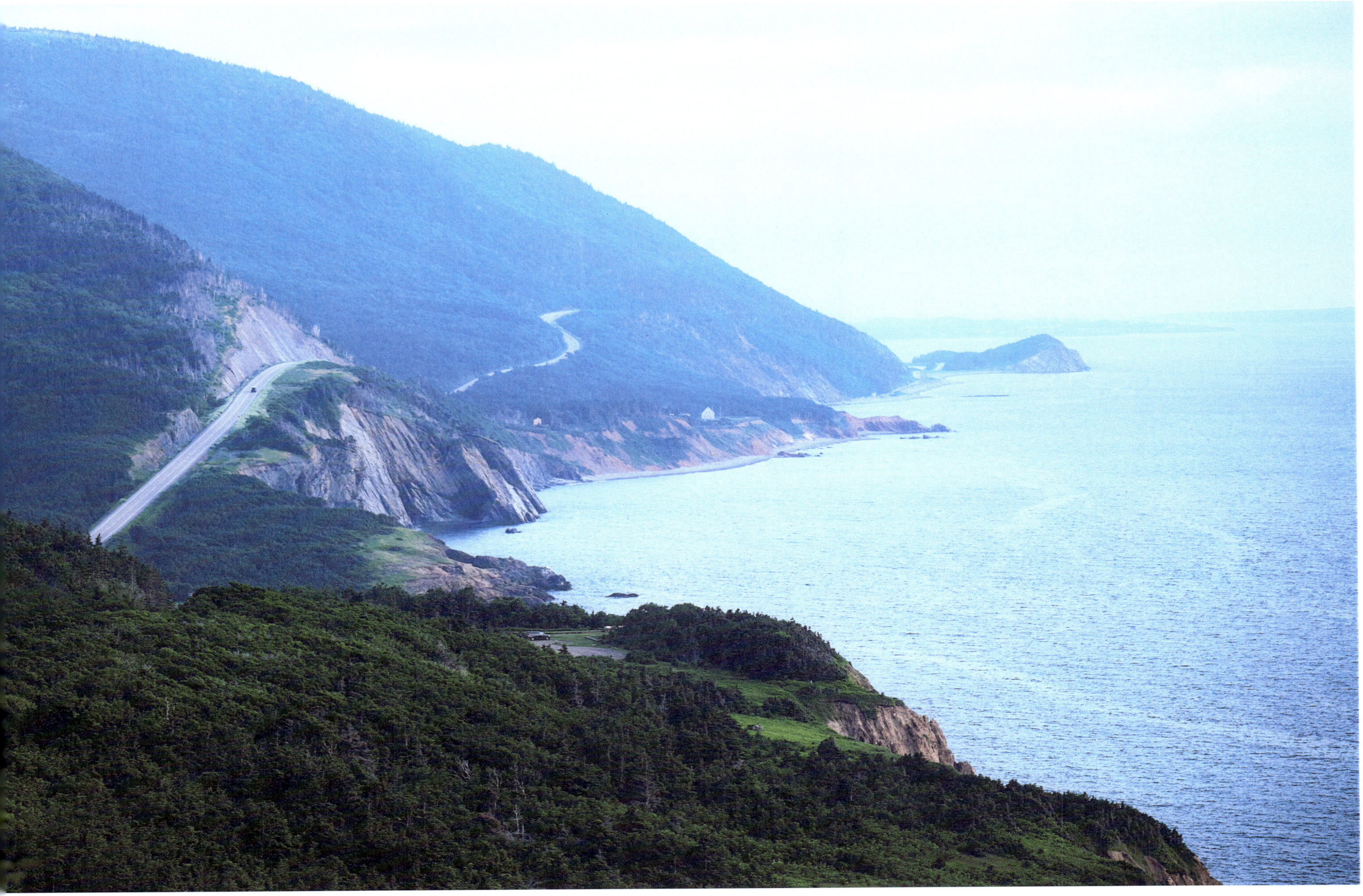

The Cabot Trail and a small lake near Cheticamp

Previous pages:

The Cabot Trail overlooking the majestic western coastline of Cape Breton

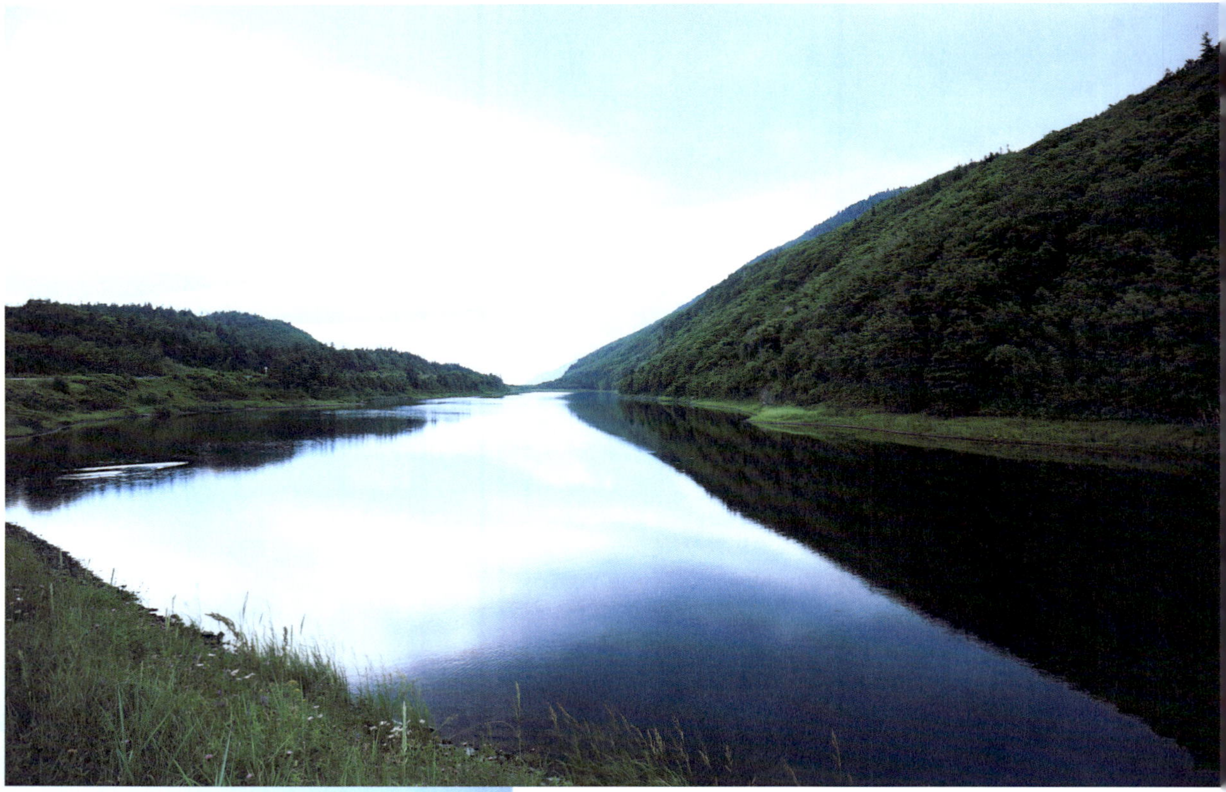

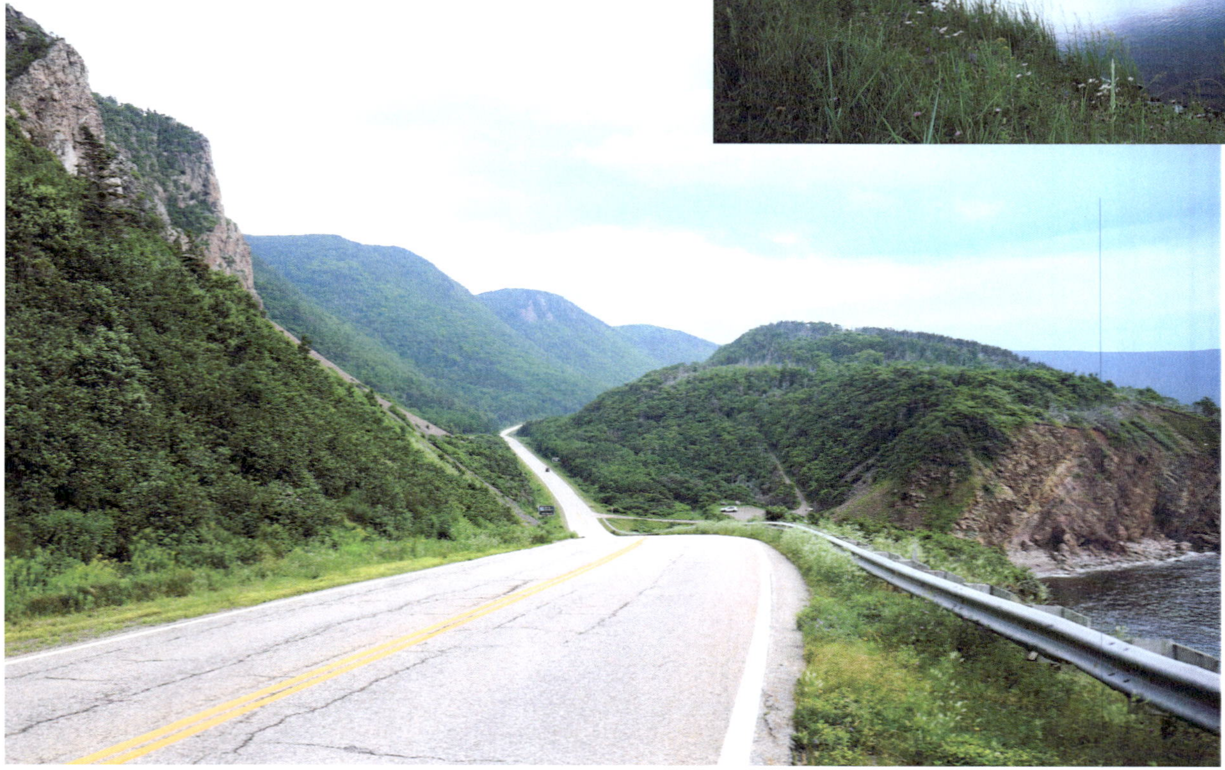

Opposite page:

The Keltic Lodge in Ingonish

Glenora, North America's first single malt distillery
Between Inverness and Mabou

St. Mary's Church peeking through the leaves and
Some of the beautiful countryside in Mabou

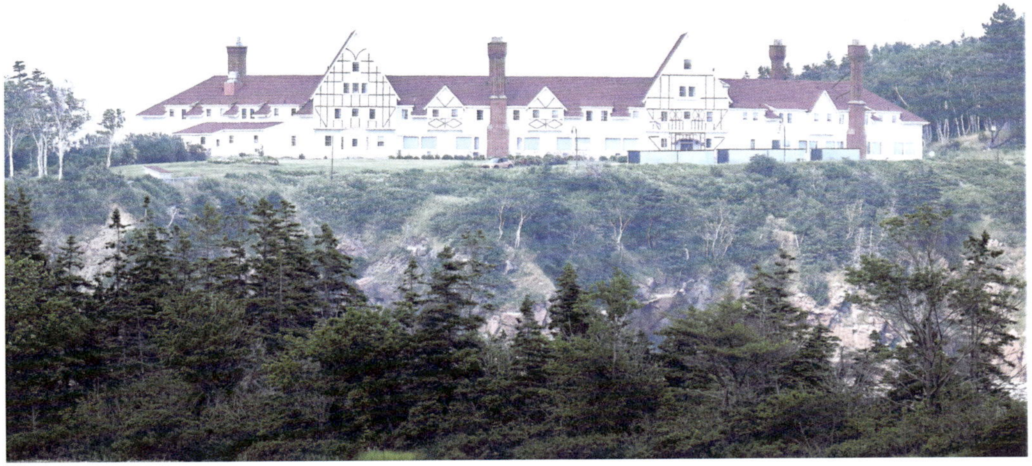

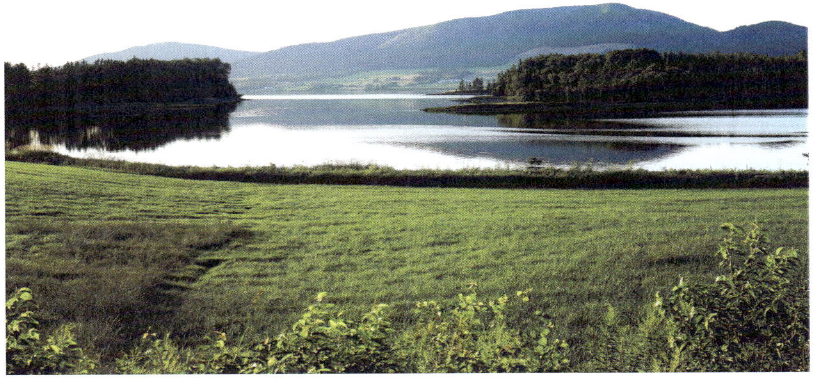

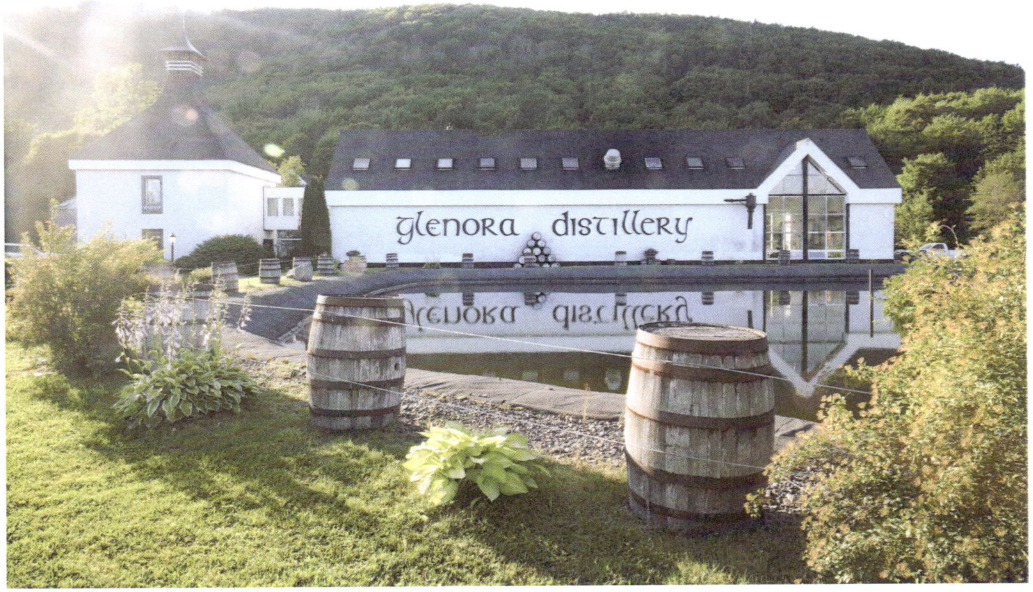
glenora distillery

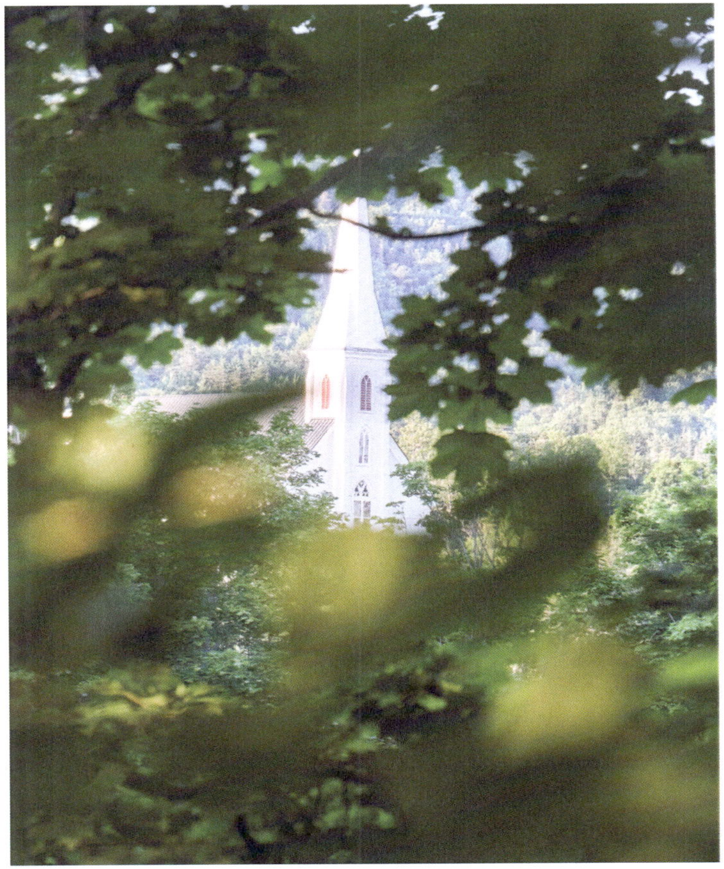

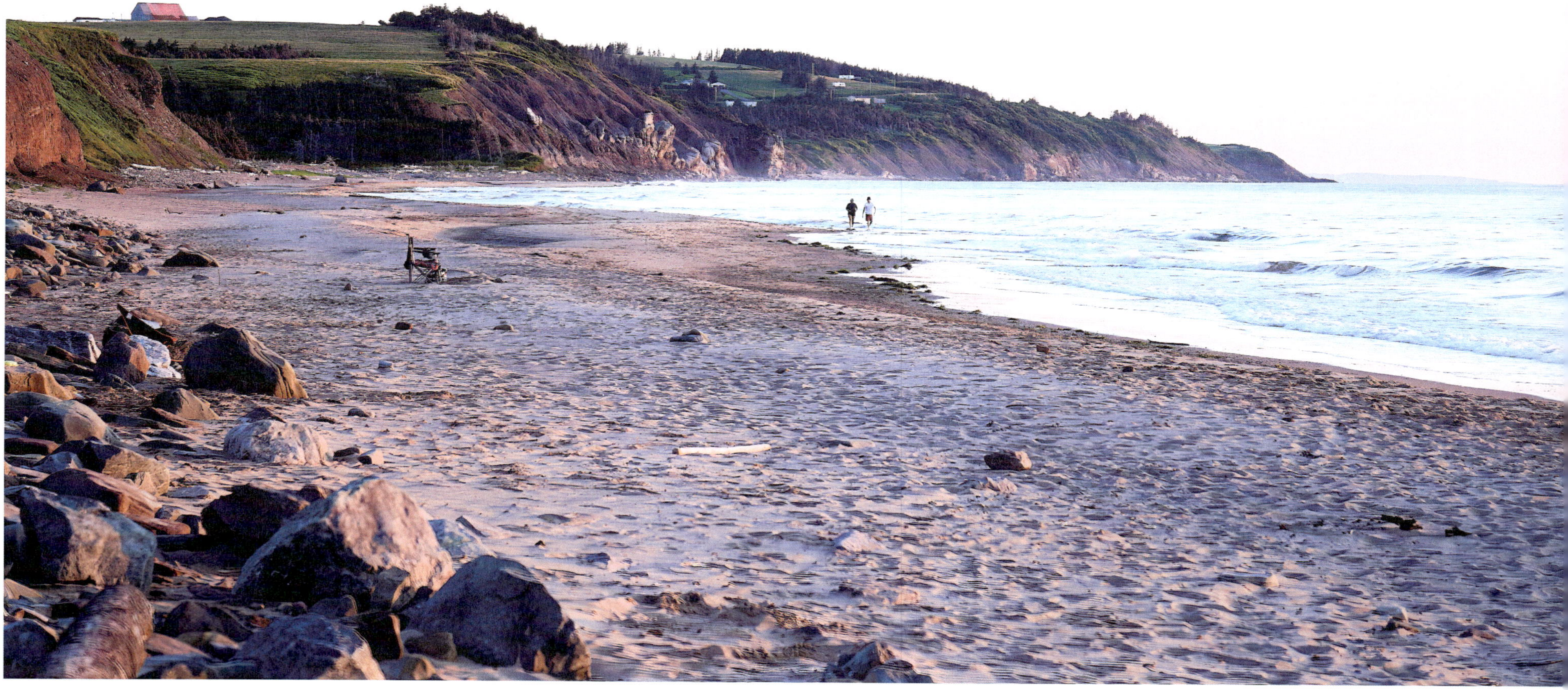

This and opposite page: Sunset over West Mabou Beach Provincial Park

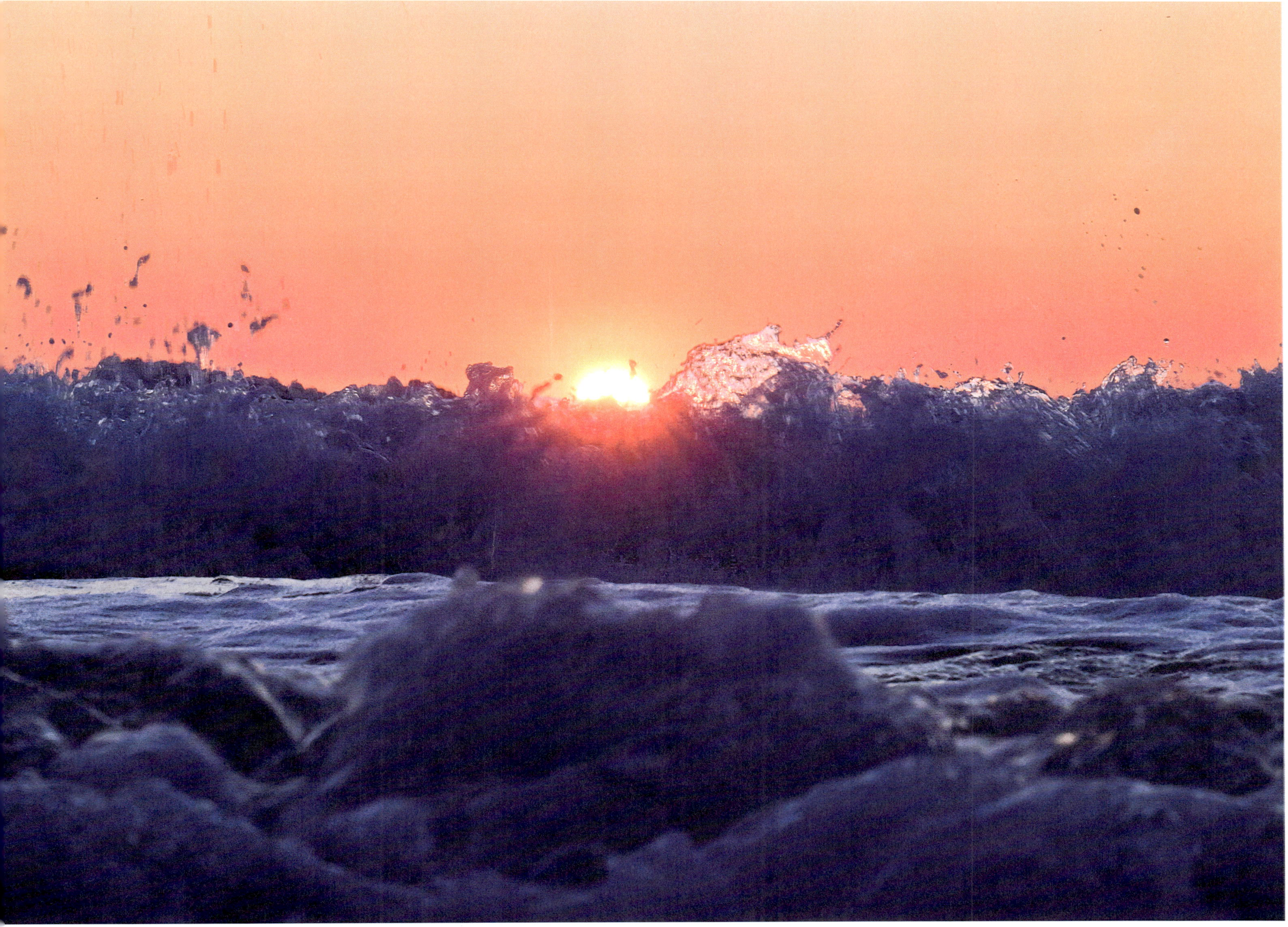

Chapter 9
And All The Rest -
Birds, Animals, and the Night Sky

Believe it or not, before moving to Nova Scotia, I had never given much thought to landscape photography. Sure, I would take my camera on trips or camping, but little inspired me on a daily basis the way just being here does.

Along the way, I found a couple new ways to explore the world around me - animal and astro photography.

The photos in this chapter are from all over the province, and while I could have added them to the previous chapters, I felt they deserved a home of their own. So I'll start right in my own backyard, and follow the path from there.

Maybe, if I get good enough, a whole edition of their own? Probably too early to say. So for now, I hope you enjoy my latest passions.

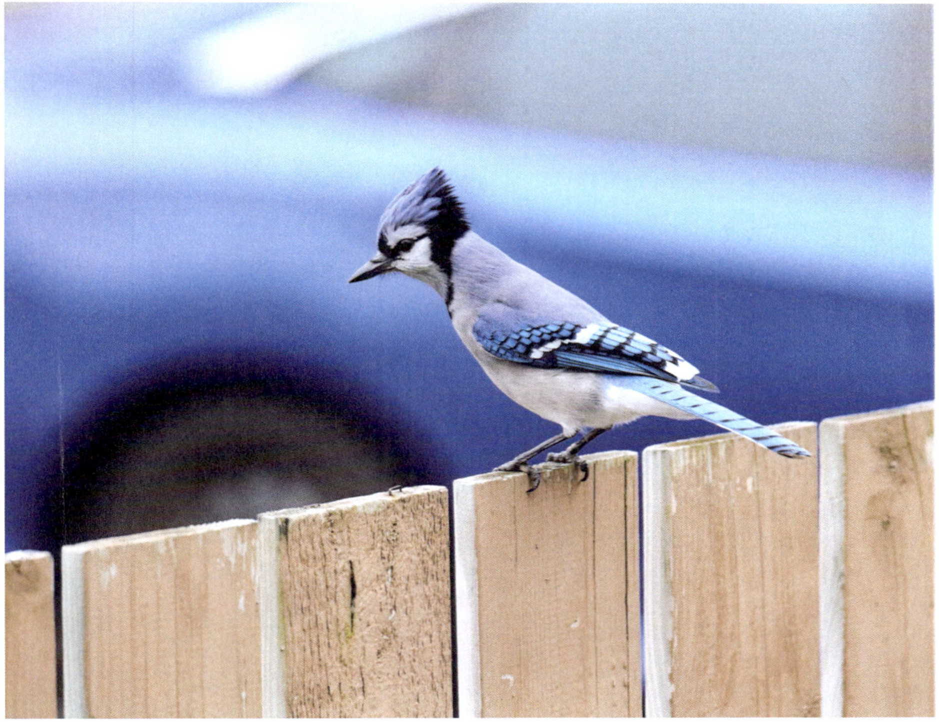

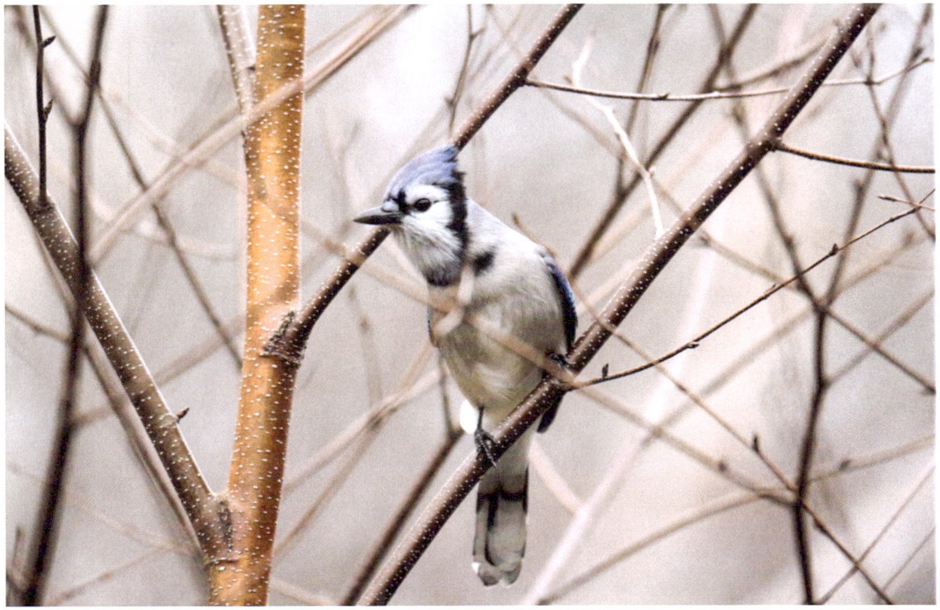

Toronto may have the baseball team but if you really want to see blue jays you have to come to Nova Scotia!

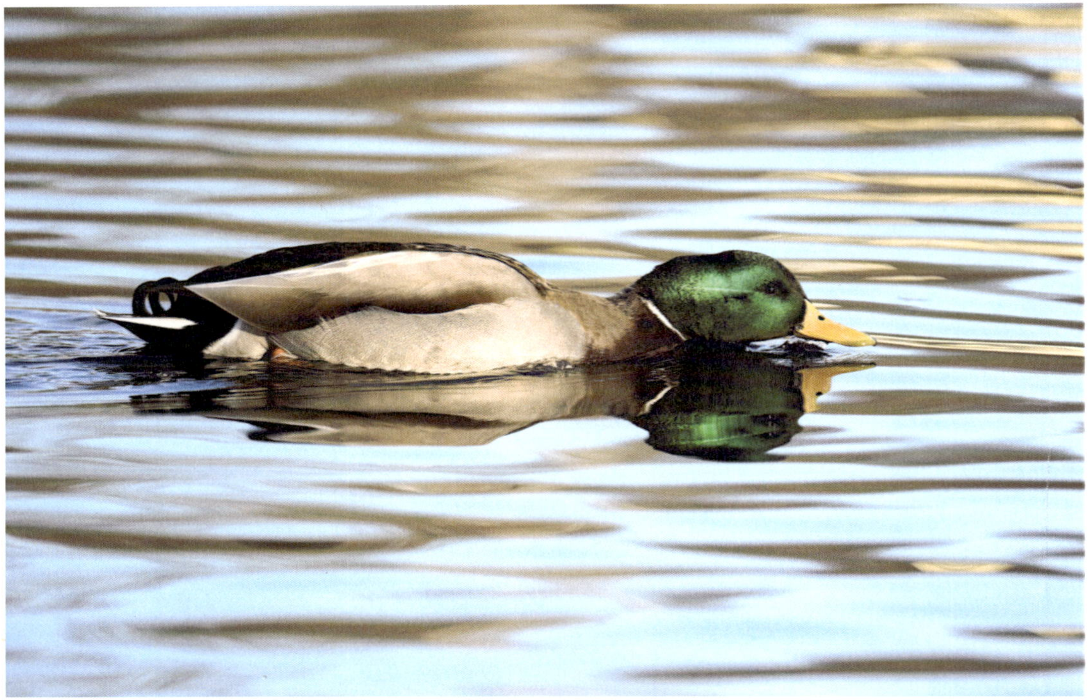

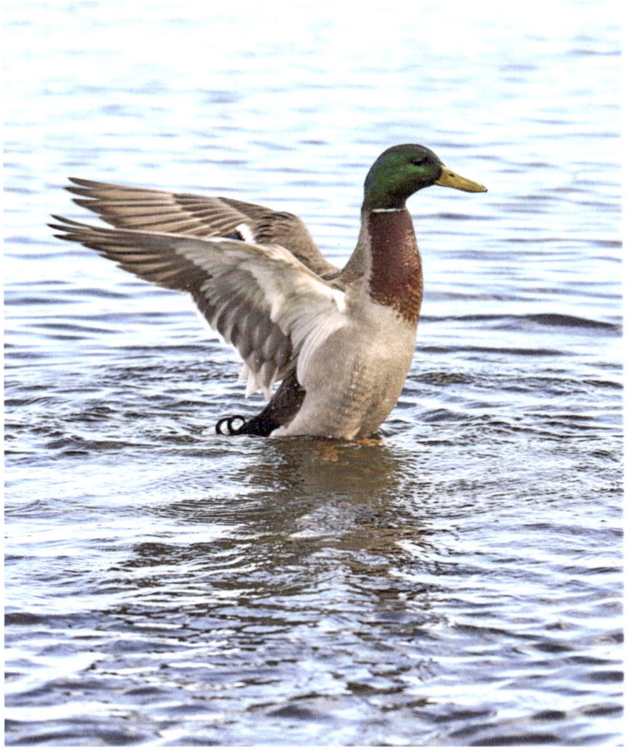

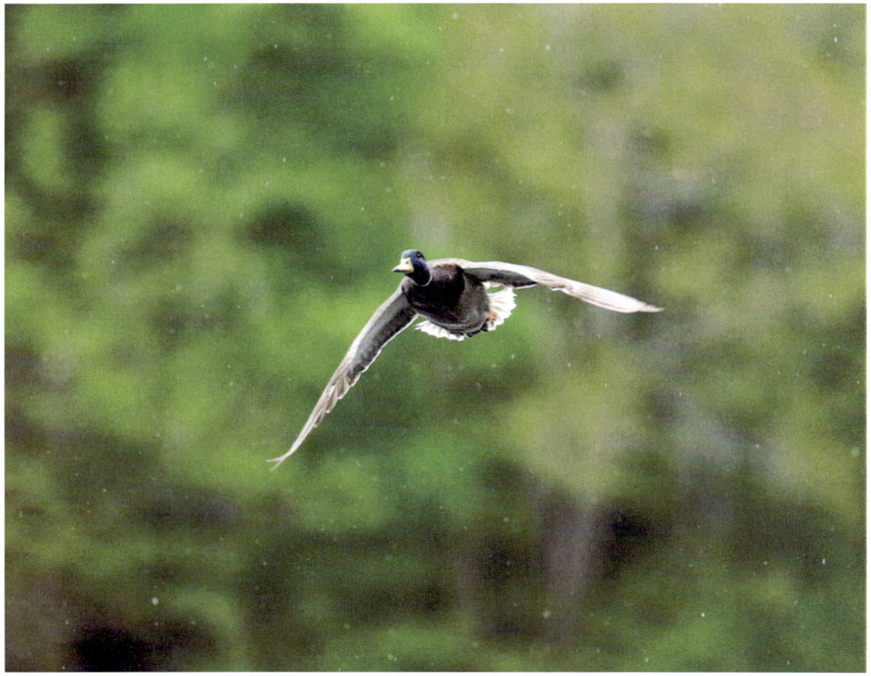

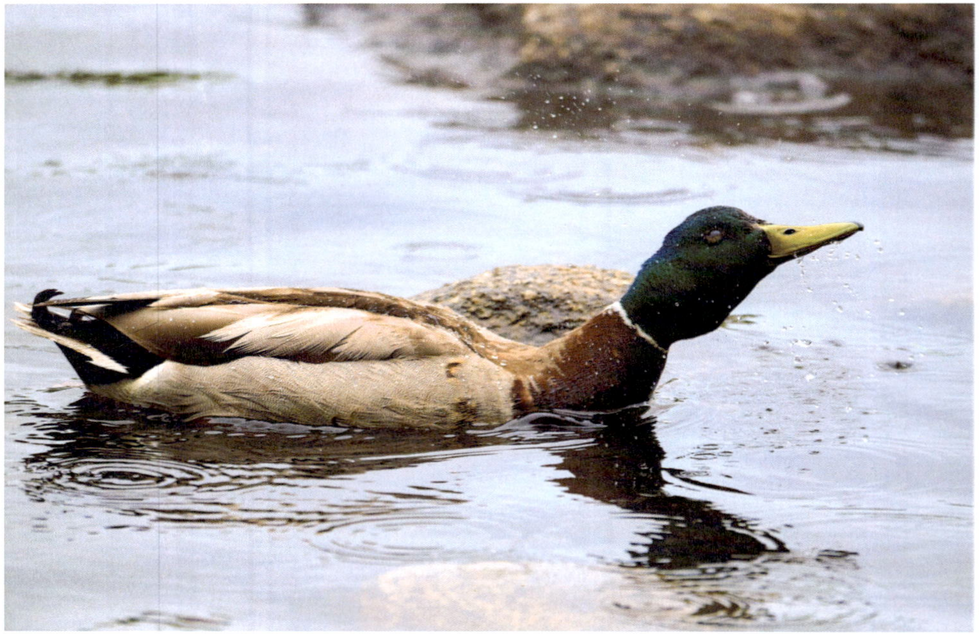

No shortage of ducks or eagles either!

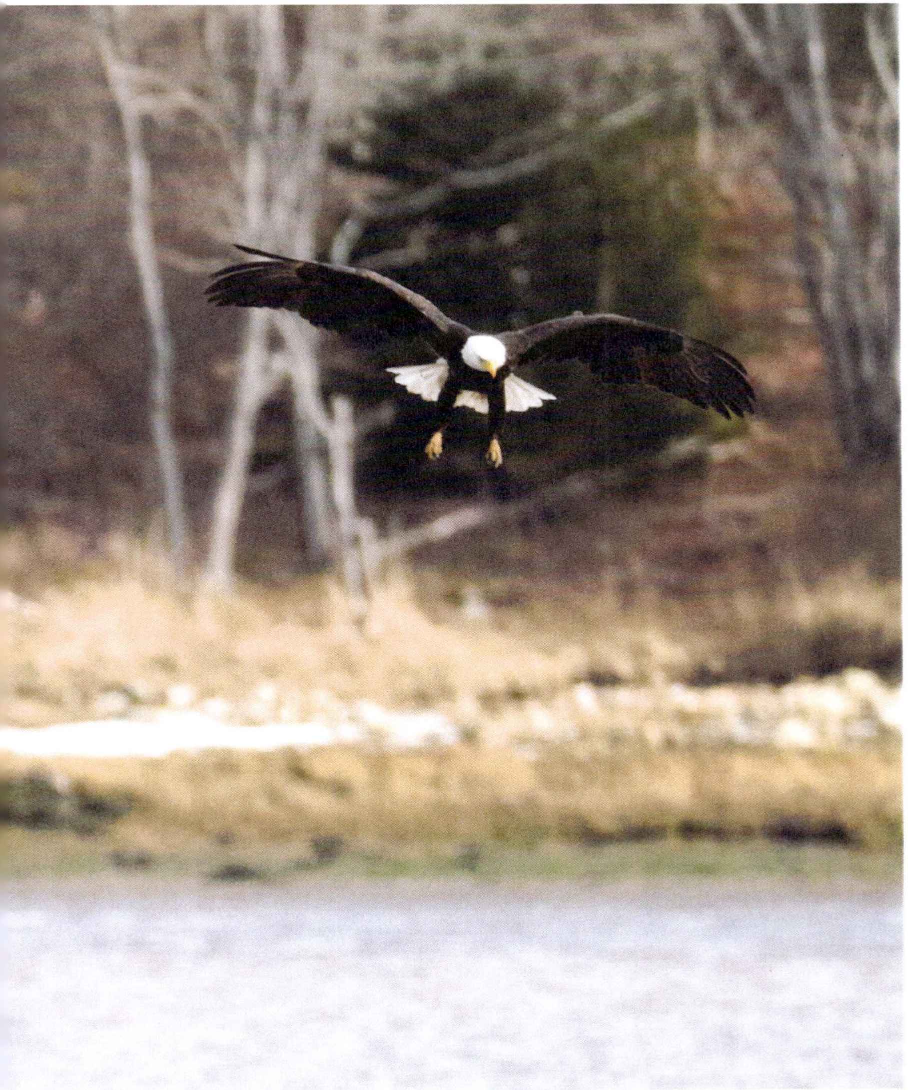

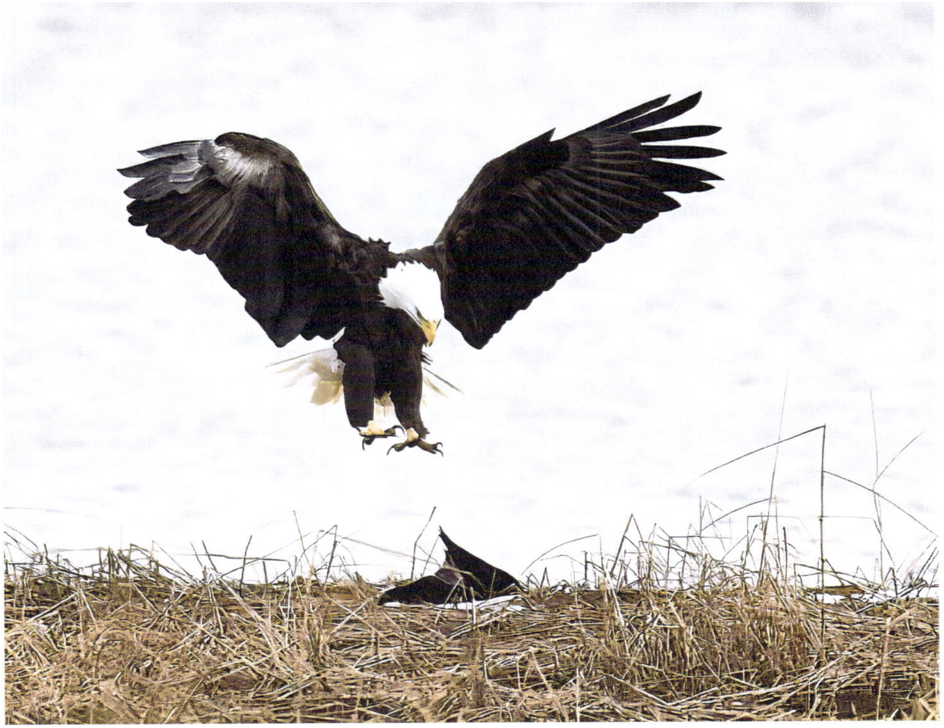

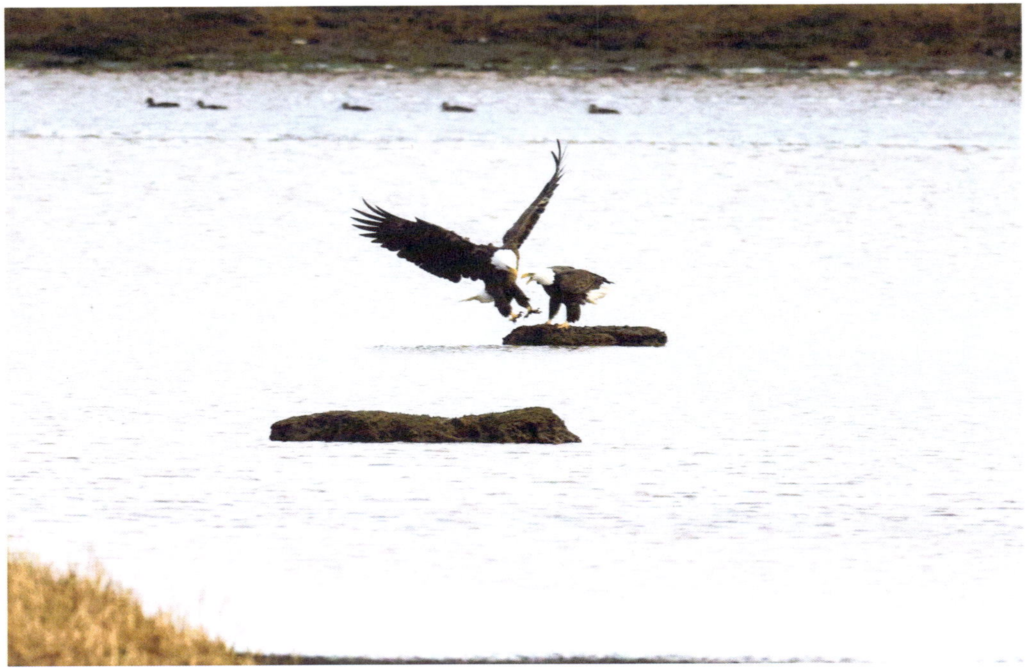

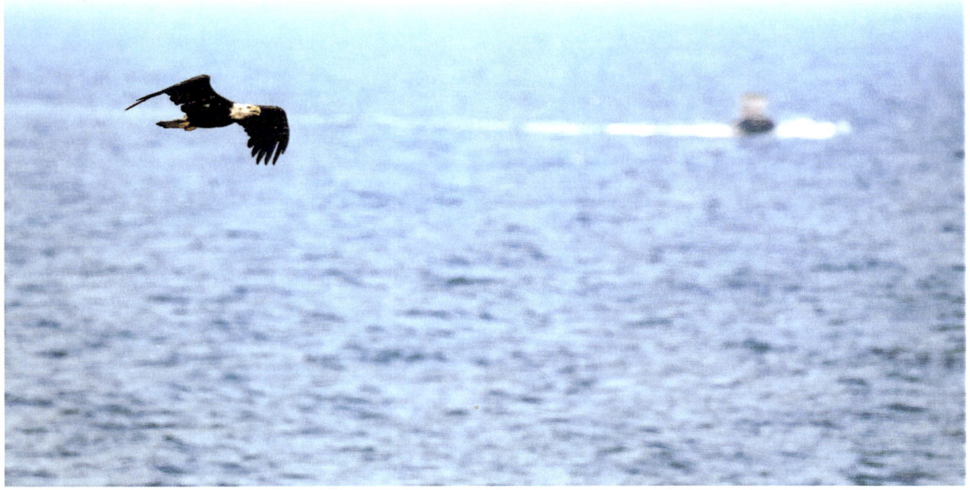

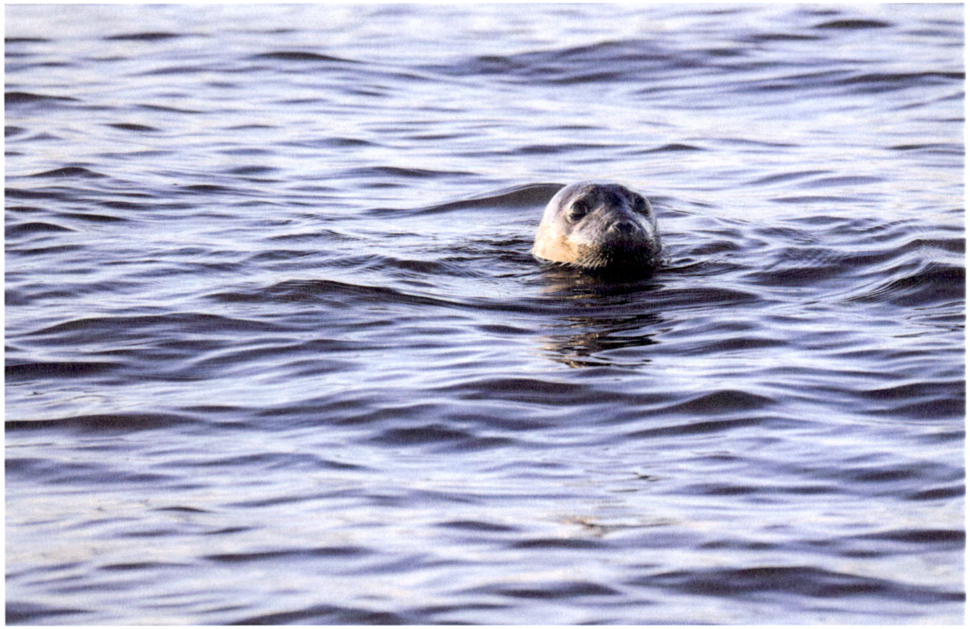

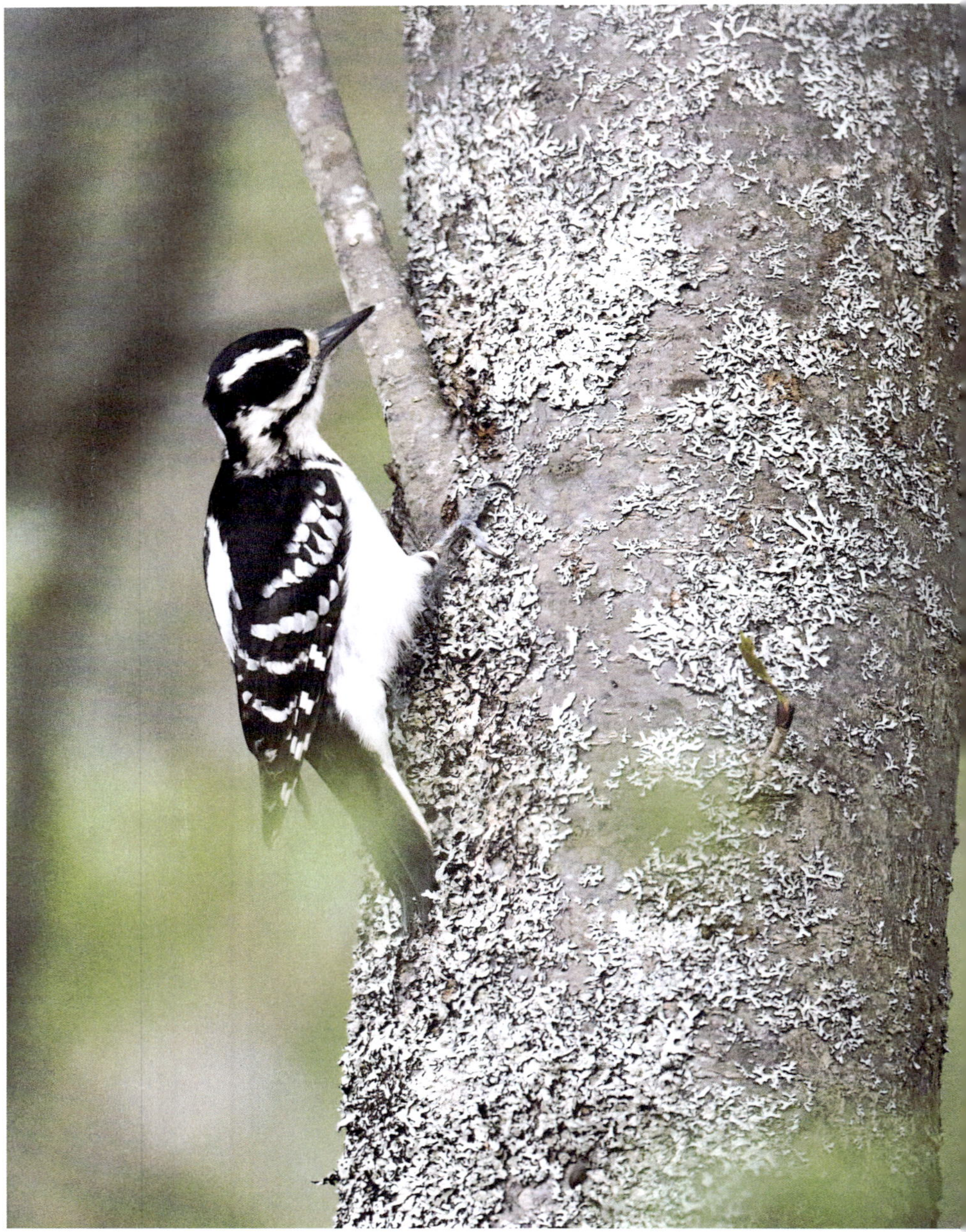

I was tracking the boat in the distance when this eagle flew into fra
I don't think I'd ever seen so many wild seals before moving h

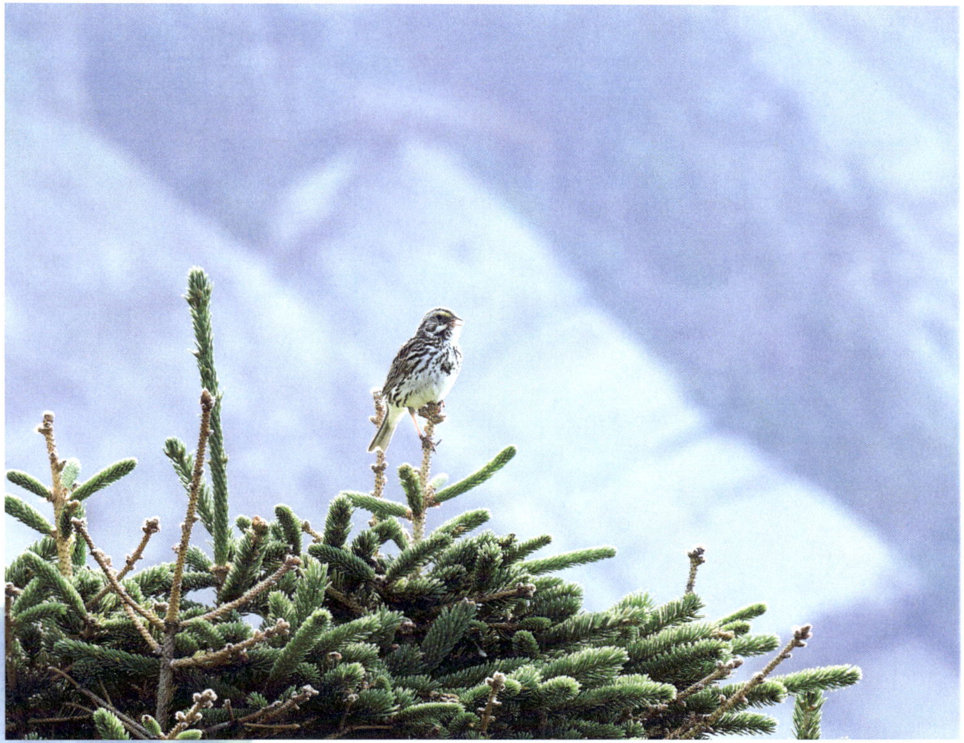

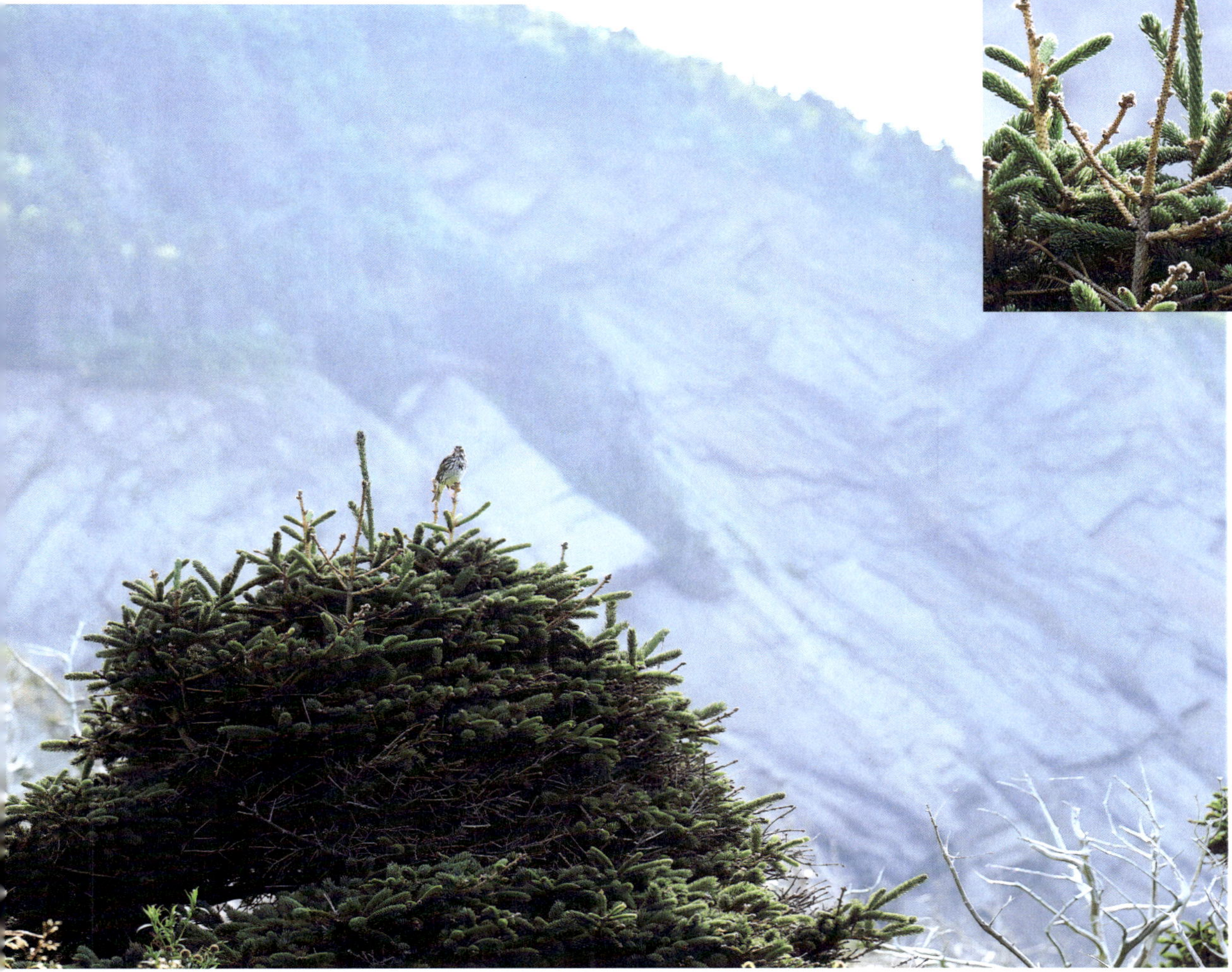

This sparrow was kind enough to wait until I got a couple photos before flying away

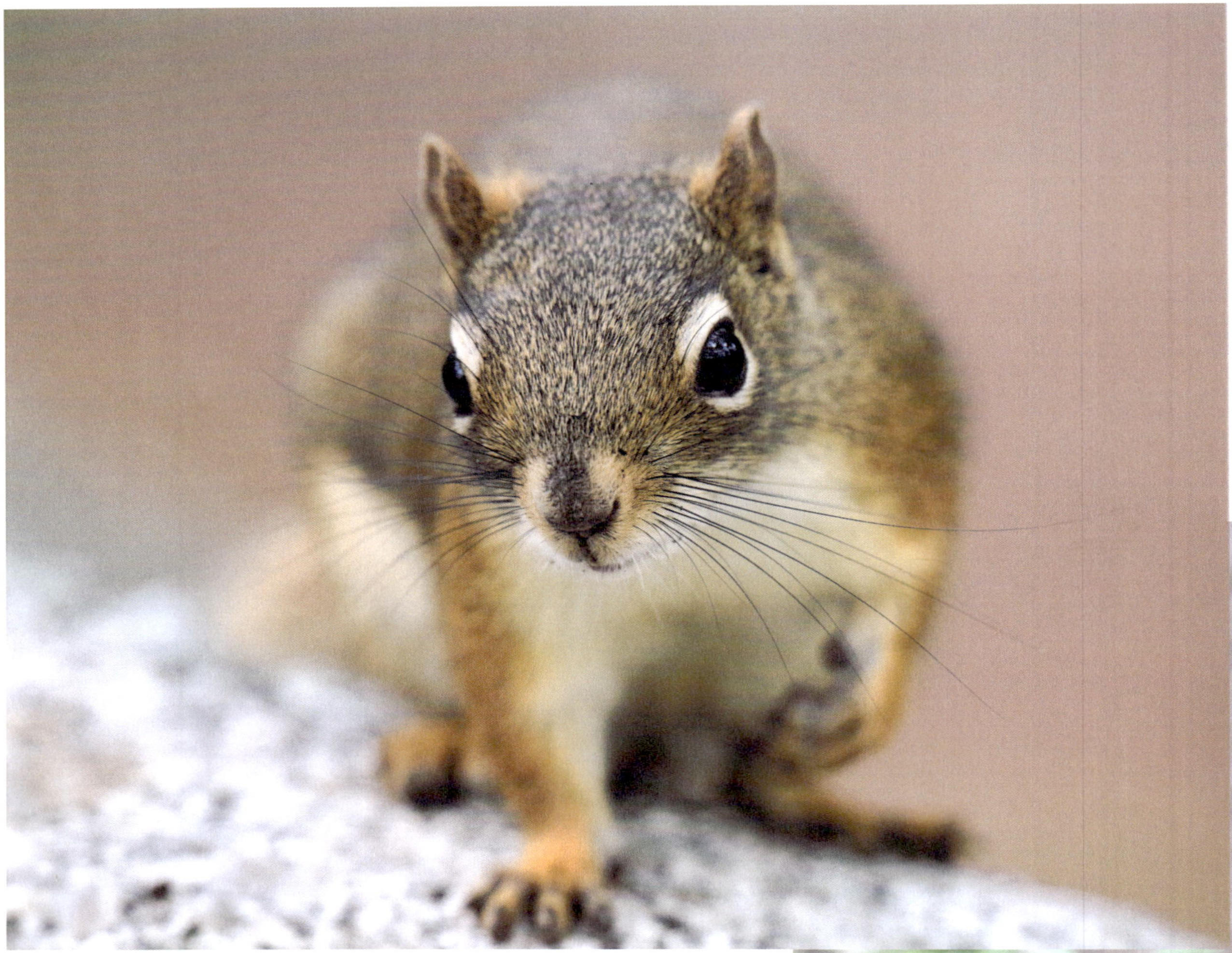

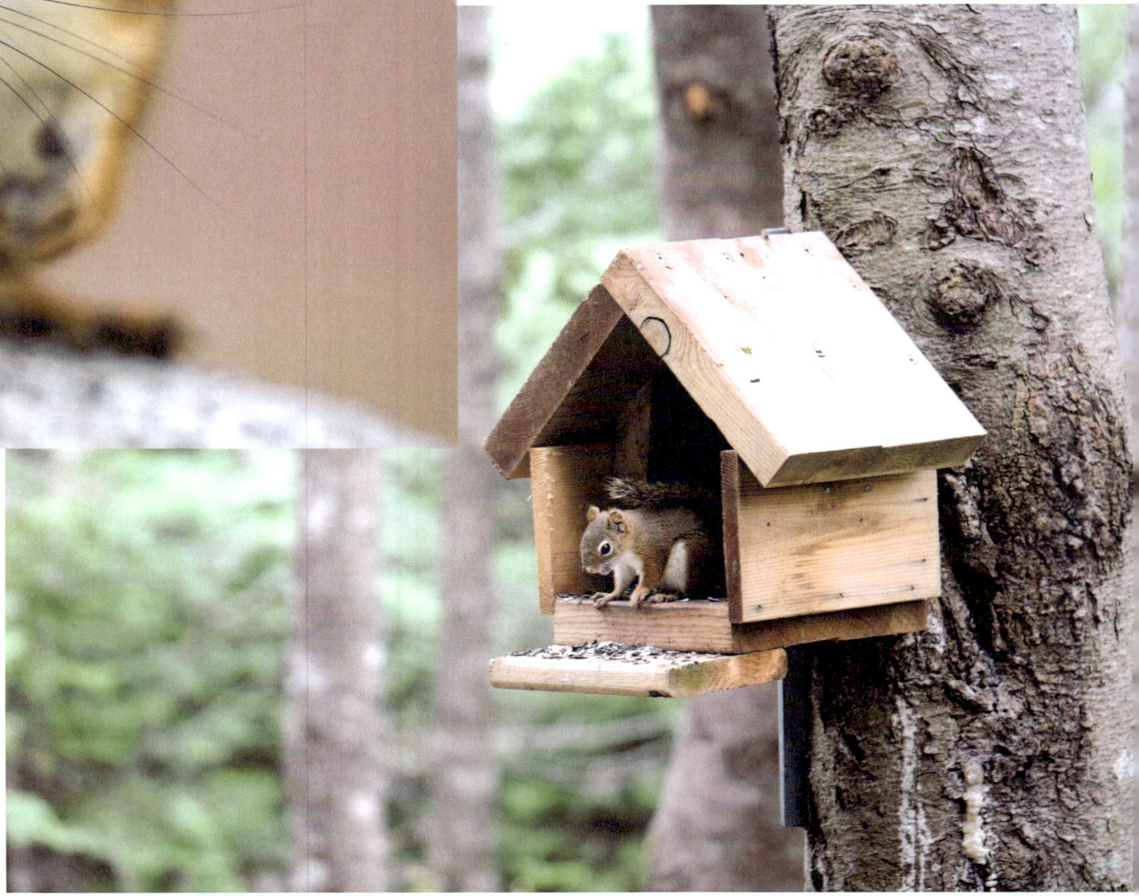

Red squirrels just have so much personality!

Opposite page:

This hunting heron's reflection was just too good to pass up

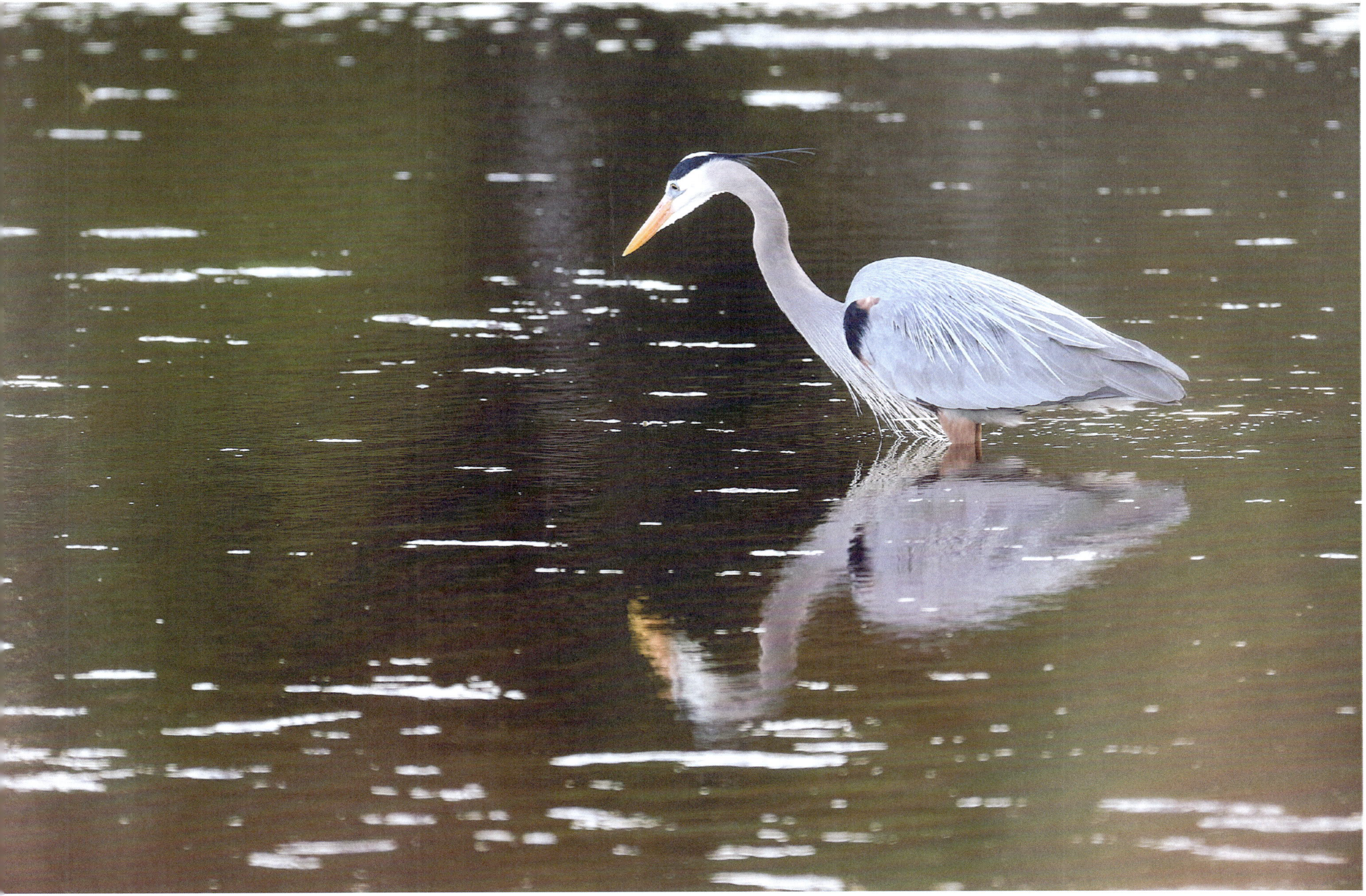

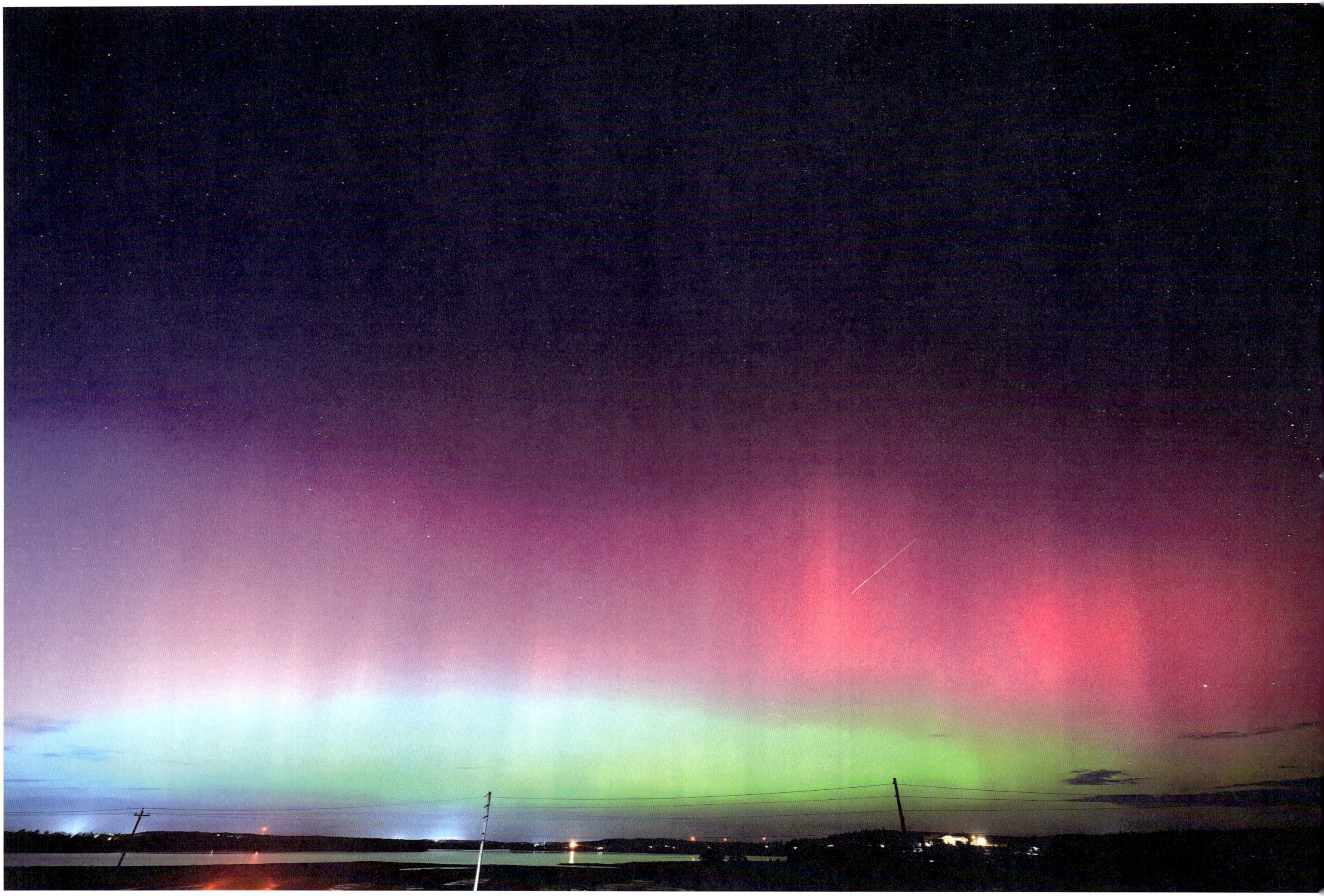

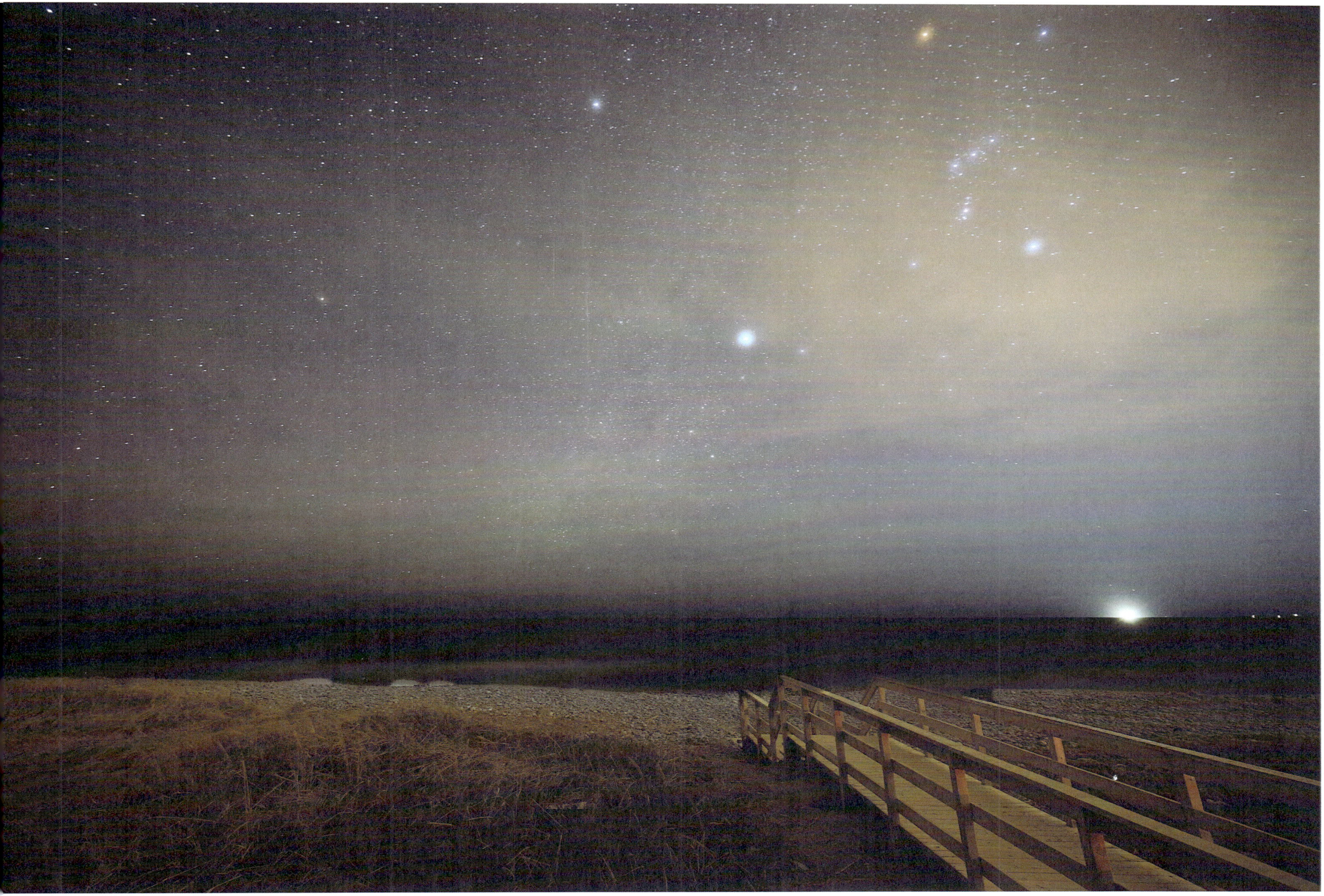

Milky Way
Shooting Stars
Aurora Borealis
Constellations

I don't think I'll ever get tired of photographing the night sky...

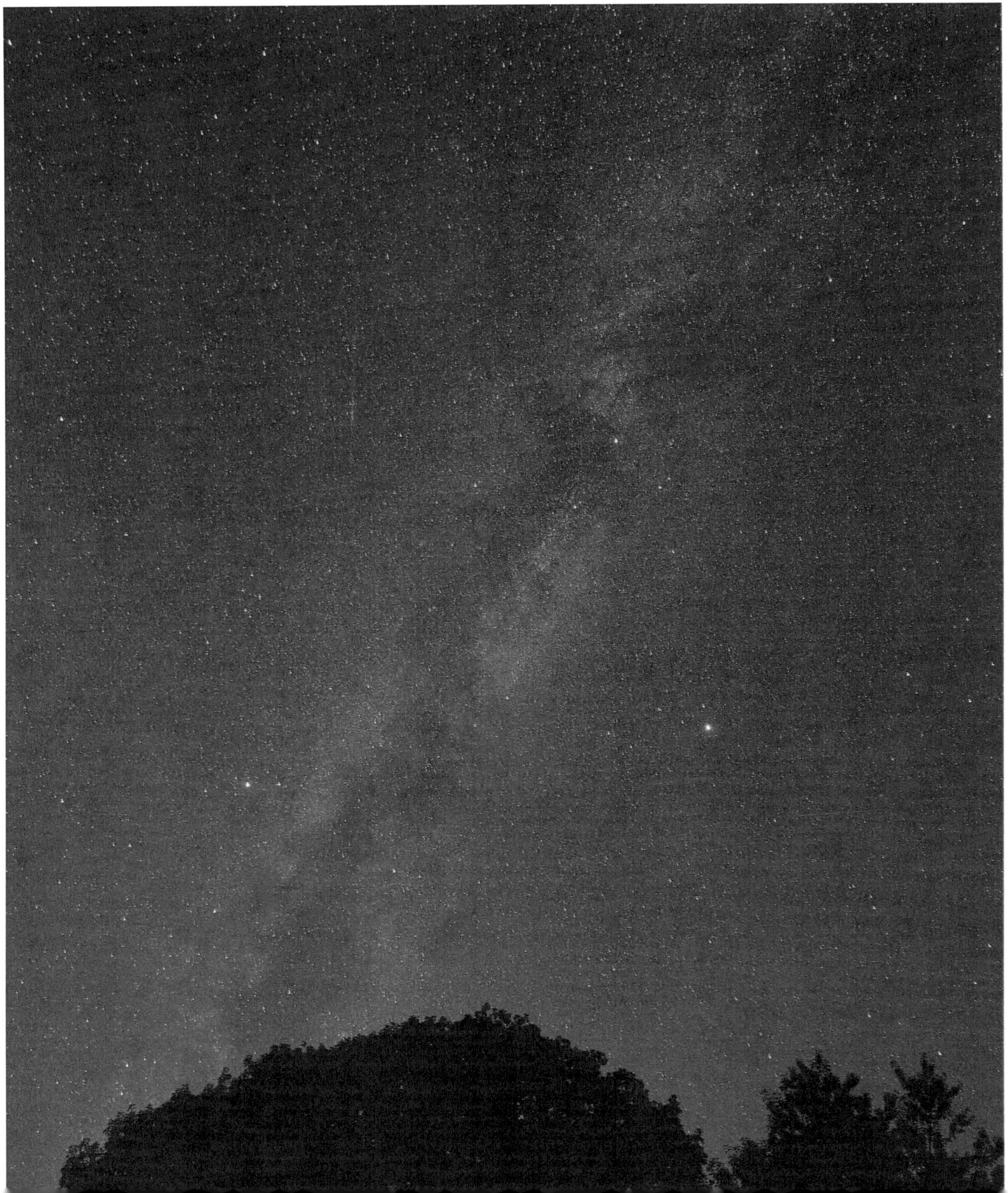

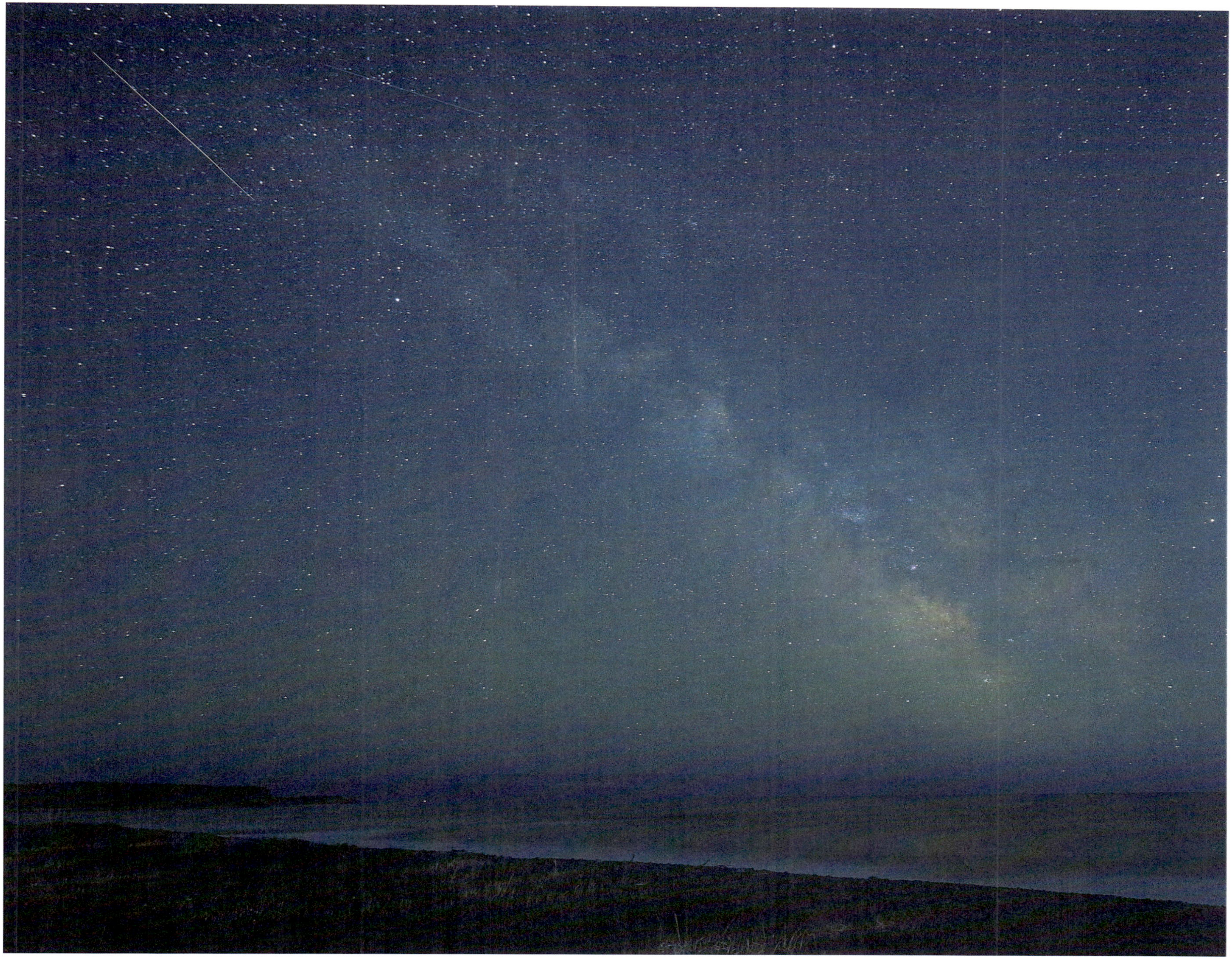

Outro:
The Journey So Far

Four years in Nova Scotia have been a roller coaster. When we got here, the world was in the grips of a pandemic, masks and distancing were the norm, almost all communication was happening online, and what in the world was I thinking starting a photography business in all of this? But I'm the type who looks for community wherever I am, and Nova Scotia has responded in kind, in the biggest way.

There's so much to explore here, and my travels are taking me increasingly to New Brunswick and Prince Edward Island. No Newfoundland yet, but I've been wanting to see 'the rock' for years now, so it's just a matter of time (maybe there will be a volume two... eventually....). In four years here I've seen and explored more of Atlantic Canada than I ever did my previous home of 40 years. A lot of it has actually been for work, but a lot has also been for pleasure - for the sake of exploring. I can't wait to see where the next four years takes us as we continue on our adventure in our new home.

If you'd have told me 5 years ago that I would be living in Nova Scotia, with a thriving photography business, and writing a book about my landscape photography, I'd have asked what you were smoking. But here I am - the universe is funny that way.

And onward we go - thanks for joining the ride!

Jay Fisher, Oct 2024

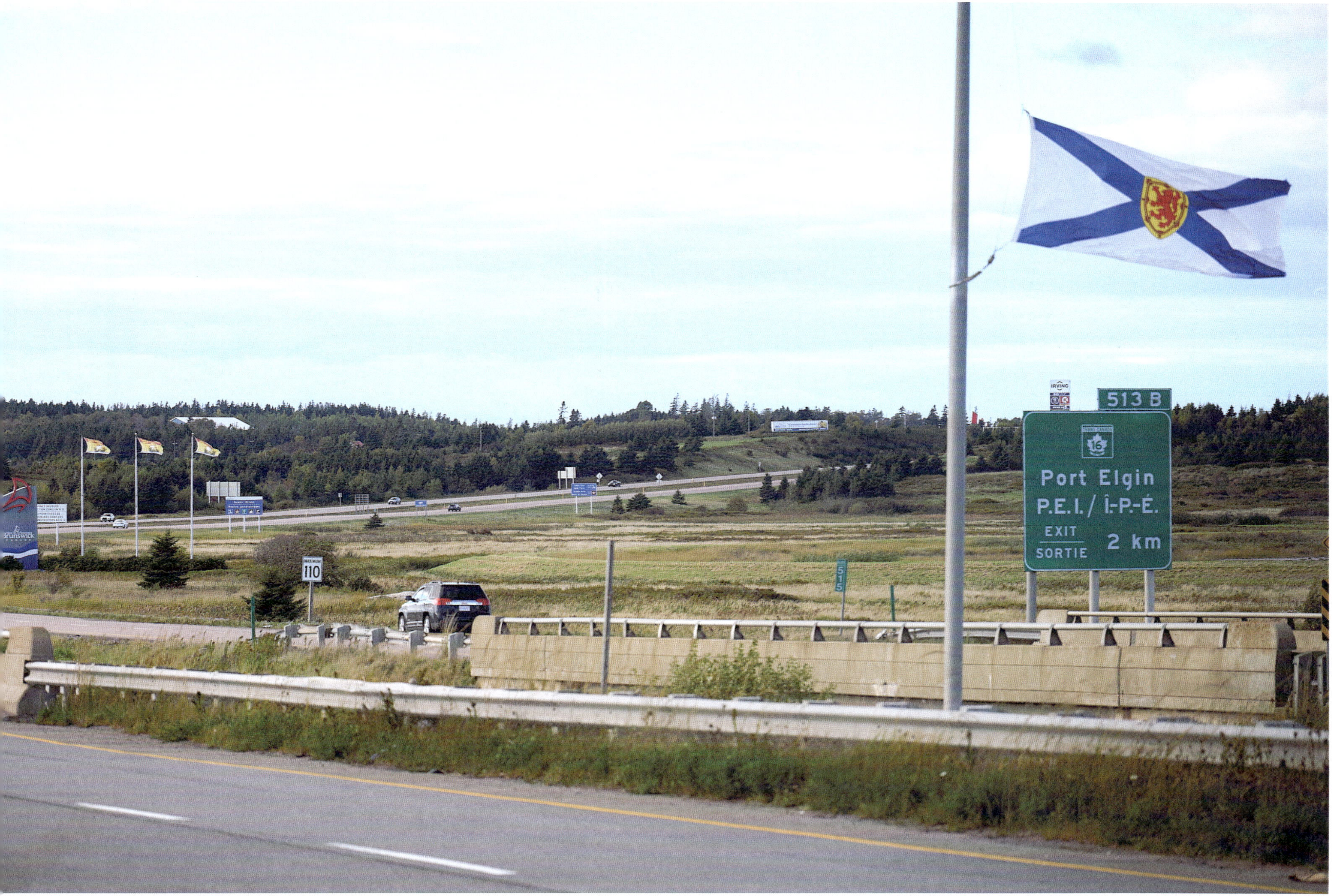
513 B
16
Port Elgin
P.E.I. / Î.-P.-É.
EXIT
SORTIE
2 km
MAXIMUM
110

About the Author

Jay Fisher has been living in Dartmouth, Nova Scotia since 2020, with his partner Ashley, and their dog Bleu. He's had the pleasure of studying with many different amazing teachers from many different artistic disciplines.

Jay's love of photography started when he was a kid, with disposable and point-and-shoot film cameras. He's gotten a bit better since then. He is the owner and photographer at Capture It Photography, specializing in headshots for people who hate having their photo taken. Armed with his technical skill, and an arsenal of 'Dad jokes', Jay photographs individuals, corporate teams, events, and more.

When not behind the camera (or in front of the computer), Jay enjoys cooking, music, sci-fi, and generally geeking out.

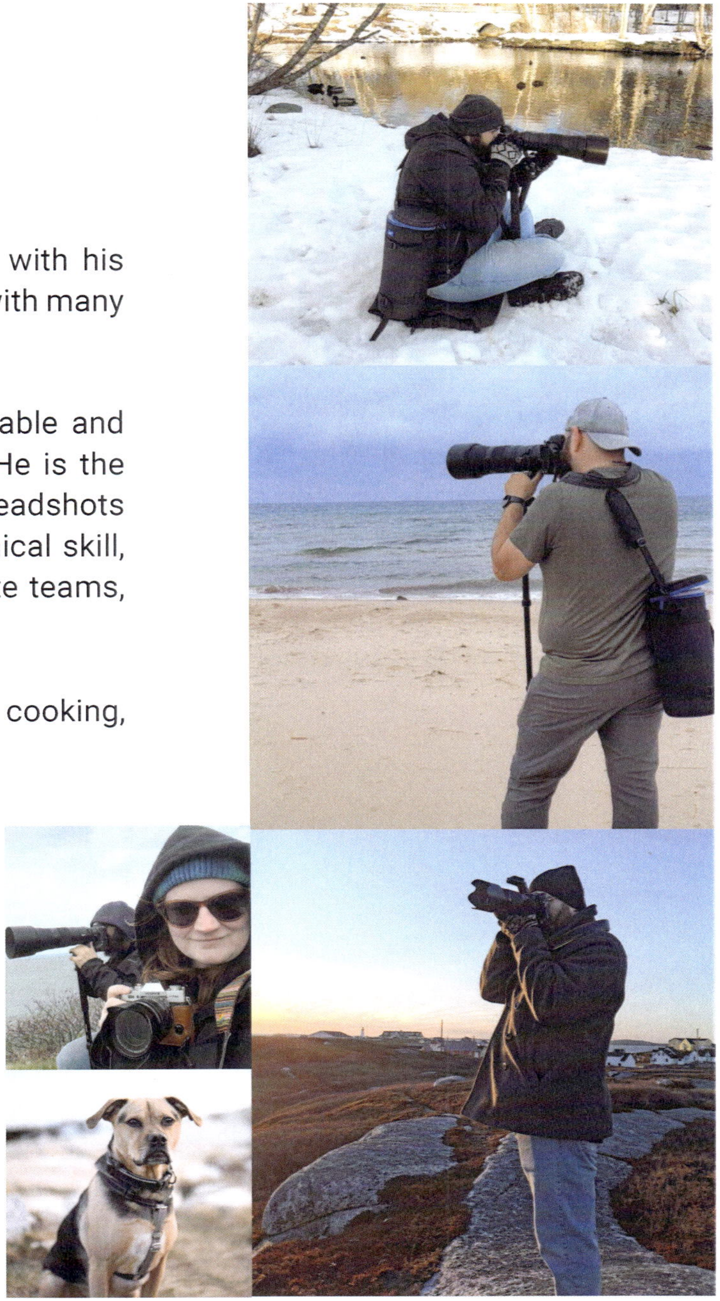

Author Photo Credit: Ashley Groves

Printed in the USA
CPSIA information can be obtained
at www.ICGtesting.com
JSRC071912061124
72975JS00005B/1